INTERNATIONAL GUIDE TO CURLING

Robin Welsh

PELHAM BOOKS
LONDON

First published in Great Britain by
Pelham Books Ltd
44 Bedford Square
London WC1B 3DP
1985

British Library Cataloguing in Publication Data

Welsh, Robin
  International guide to curling.
  1. Curling
  I. Title
  796.9′6   GV845

ISBN 0-7207-1573-3

Filmset, printed and bound in Great Britain by
Butler and Tanner Ltd, Frome and London

Contents

Photo credits

The author and publishers are grateful to the following for permission to reproduce copyright photographs in this book:
Associated Newspapers page 45; Aviemore Photographic page 170 (top); Ron Burgess (Scottish Daily Express) pages 70, 71; Michael Burns pages 78, 80, 81, 82, 84, 85, 86, 87, 89 (bottom), 90, 91, 93, 97, 99, 101, 105, 106, 121, 162, 185, 187, 191, 194, 198, 201, 202; Alex Cowper pages 33, 69 (top), 167, 168, 169; George Crawford page 217; Murray Donald pages 26, 115; Falkirk Herald page 163; Fife Herald page 234; Glasgow Herald page 69 (bottom); William Hill page 203; Lacash Photography page 170 (bottom); Joseph J. Lucas, Jr page 89 (top); William McCallum page 103; J. W. Macpherson page 13; Photo Illustrations pages 23, 111; Scotsman Publications page 46; Star Photo page 16; Svenskt Pressfoto page 96. In some cases it has not been possible to ascertain the copyright holder and it is hoped that any such omissions will be excused.

1

The History of the Game

CURLING IS CALLED the 'roarin' game', not because of the shouts of carefree curlers but because of the roar a curling stone makes as it travels, particularly on outside ice. Over two hundred years ago, a young Scot, James Graeme (1749–72), a native of Carnwath in Lanarkshire, wrote a poem, excerpts from which are still used on menus at curling suppers. Graeme provided the best onomatopoeic description of the 'roar' when he wrote of a stone gliding along, *hoarse murmuring*.

The noise of stones is heard to the best advantage on a hillside overlooking a bonspiel on a frozen Scottish loch. In the stillness of a clear frosty morning, the distinctive deep-throated boom reverberates through the valley and into the hills. The sound, like the ocean's roar, is the music of curling.

> '. . . the sweetest sound tae me
> Is music o' the channel-stane
> Gaun currin' tae the tee.'*

How far does the sound reach back in time? No one knows. The origin of curling is lost in the mists which also shroud the origin of golf, the other great game which Scotland has given to the world.

Recent research by Sheriff David B. Smith, in his *Curling: An Illustrated History* (1981), takes us back to the year 1540 when John McQuhin, a notary in Paisley, Renfrewshire, recorded in his protocol book a challenge between John Sclater, a monk in Paisley Abbey, and Gavin Hamilton, representative of the abbot, John Hamilton. The report, in Latin, indicates that Sclater threw a stone along the ice three times and asserted that he was ready for the agreed contest of throwing stones – and that Hamilton replied that he would go to the ice for the contest.

David Smith admits that, because the record is in Latin, there is doubt that it refers to a curling challenge, although this seems highly likely.

* H. Shanks, Bathgate, 1884.

The earliest written record in English of the game of curling and curling stones appeared in 1638 – in the poem, *The Muses Threnodie or Mirthfull Mournings on the Death of Mr Gall*, by Henry Adamson (see chapter on the Literature of the Game).

The first landmark used in most curling histories is the Stirling Stone, which has the date 1511 etched on one side. This famous old stone, which lies in the Stirling Smith Art Gallery and Museum, Stirling, is a 26-pound Kuting (or quoiting or coiting) stone, the earliest-known form of stone used for curling, which, in its infancy, must have been a form of quoiting on ice.

Stirling has an honoured place in Scottish and curling history. The Stirling Stone lies in the shade of the Wallace Monument, the towering memorial to the Scottish patriot. Nearby, the old Borestone Club, now the Borestone and Stirling Club, made a curling pond on the site of the Milton Bog where the Scots routed the English cavalry at Bannockburn in 1314. (The Borestone Club took its name from the 'Borestone', on which King Robert the Bruce placed his standard at the battle.)

On one side of the Stirling Stone is the inscription 'St. Js. B. STIR-LING 1511' – a reference, according to Captain Macnair in *The Channel Stane* (1883) either to St James, a popular saint in Stirling, 'B' possibly being a contraction for 'Bridge', or the St James Hospital which was known to have stood at the Bridge-end of Stirling before the Reformation. On the other side of the stone are the words, 'A GIFT'.

It is fair to state that experts believe these inscriptions to be of a later date, perhaps a much later date, than 1511. There is doubt, as in so many matters concerned with the early history of the game, but, without doubt, the Stirling Stone, made of the same blue whinstone as Stirling Rock, is very old.

Even older in appearance are two other stones which lie alongside it in the Gallery. Both are more irregular, more primitive – one, of rough triangular shape, weighing $15\frac{3}{4}$ lb (7·14 kg). The other, a longer stone broken at one end, weighs $20\frac{1}{2}$ lb (9·3 kg); a channel whinstone, its sides have been pared down by a mason to reduce its weight. It was found by Mr James Sword, Curator of the then Smith Institute, in 1890, in a dyke at a blacksmith's door in the hamlet of Chartershall – near the Whins of Milton village on the site of the Milton Bog. Almost certainly, the stone was reclaimed from the bog, which, having served Scotland so well at Bannockburn, was drained in 1840.

Kuting stones are also known as 'loofies', loof being the old Scots word for the palm of the hand – the earliest stones were shaped like a palm and had grooves for fingers and thumb.* Such stones were thrown through the air to the ice with a sideways action, like the reverse sweep of a scythe.

The controversy, whether curling started in Scotland or the Low Countries, still rages. Two landscapes by the great Flemish painter, Pieter Bruegel (1530–69) add fuel to fiery discussions. These works, *The Hunters in the Snow* and *Winter Landscape with Skaters and a Bird Trap*, show a game resembling curling being played on frozen ponds.

The man mainly responsible for the controversy was the Rev John Ramsay† (1777–1871) whose book, *An Account of the Game of Curling by a Member of the Duddingston Curling Society* (Edinburgh 1811) is the oldest historical record of the game.

Ramsay wrote: 'We have all the evidence which etymology can give in favour of curling's Continental origin. The terms, being all Dutch or German, point to the Low Countries as the place in which it most probably originated, or, at least, from whence it was conveyed to us. For if it was not introduced from the Continent, but was first invented in this country, it must have been at a time when the German and Low Dutch were the prevailing languages. Now, though the Saxon was once pretty general in this country, and there are still many Dutch words in our language, yet those German dialects were never so general as to make it credible that our countrymen, in any particular invention, would employ them alone as the appropriate terms. In the history of inventions such a phenomenon is not to be found. Had there been only one or two foreign terms, these would not have militated much against the domestic origin of the game but the whole of the terms being Continental compel us to ascribe to it a Continental origin.'

This dictatorial statement, which was blindly accepted and repeated by later historians, was challenged by the Rev John Kerr, whose *History of Curling* (Edinburgh 1890) remains the classic book on the history and growth of the game. Refuting Ramsay's theories, Kerr enlisted eminent professors of his day to clear the air and one of these, Professor Masson,‡

---

* Loof: the palm of the hand; plural looves. (Jamieson's Scottish Dictionary.)

† Ramsay, born at Carstairs, graduated at Edinburgh University, and edited *The Scots Magazine* for two years while studying Theology. He was Minister at Ormiston for twenty years and, for the last thirty-eight years of his life, at Gladsmuir, and it was said of him: 'of nothing was he prouder than of the share he had taken in introducing and popularising the game of Curling in the County of Haddington'.

‡ David Masson, Professor of English Literature at Edinburgh University, was the author of the well-known book, *Edinburgh Sketches and Memories*.

a famous personality of the time, took a firm stand against Ramsay's views:

'I see no proof in them (the terms) collectively that the game came from the Continent. Most of the terms are of Teutonic origin in a general way; some are of French origin; some might even be claimed as of Celtic origin; and a few seem recent inventions by the natural *nous* of players of the game within the last century or so, to define recurring circumstances and incidents of the game previously unnamed. I do not think much can be made for your question on either side by chasing up etymologies. The matter seems mainly a historical one.

'Wherever there was ice, there must have been, since man existed, games on the ice; and the question is whether the particular game of Curling can be proved to have been in use anywhere out of Scotland without clear derivation from Scotland. If it ever existed anywhere else, it ought to be found in that place now; for, the ice still remaining, the extinction of the game, if once in use, may be voted impossible. Curlers, therefore, ought to drive at this question: Is there any Curling now, or anything like Curling, anywhere in the world out of Scotland, except by obvious and probable derivation from Scotland?

'The terms of the game, on the supposition of its Scottish origin are easily accounted for. The original inventors of the game, or of the germ of the present game, would use the words of their composite Scoto-English vocabulary – mostly Teutonic but some French and some Celtic for the purposes and situations of the game, just as they would for any other business; and, as the game grew, other words would be added for new developments of it or new intricacies, some of these with no antique reference in them at all.'

To these findings, the Rev John Kerr added a letter from Amsterdam which quoted Mr H.C. Ragge, Keeper of Amsterdam University Library, as saying: 'I believe I may assume that curling or a game similar to it has never been in use in this country.' (It must be said that, if the two men knew of Bruegel, they apparently did not know the two landscapes concerned).

Two significant points emerge from Professor Masson's findings:
1. *'Wherever there was ice, there must have been, since man existed, games on the ice.'*
In the Ice Age, or, even more appropriately in the Stone Age, a hairy monster, draped in skins, hurled the first boulder down the ice, to be

followed by another monster, who tried to outhurl his opponent; and these two primitive men, eventually tiring of brute strength, set marks on the ice and the game of Curling was born.

The myth could be reality. It is as reasonable as any other conjecture on the birth of the game.

2. *'Is there any Curling now, or anything like Curling, anywhere in the world out of Scotland, except by obvious and probable derivation from Scotland?'*

To this pertinent question, we answer, firmly and confidently, 'No, there is not'.

What then, of Bruegel's paintings? In the first edition of Jamieson's Scottish Dictionary (1808), it was suggested: 'Can it be supposed that this West Country name (Kuting – the earliest form of curling) has been softened from Teut. Kluyten?' Ramsay writing three years later, quickly grasped the suggestion to support his theories. Kluyten, according to Kilian's *Etymologicon Teutonical Linguae* (1632), was a Dutch game played on the ice 'with lumps or balls frozen'; and, in Dutch, the word Klyten signifies 'a clod'.*

Substantial supporting evidence for the claim that curling originated in Scotland is provided by the wide variety of old stones which, over hundreds of years, have been salvaged from lochs and ponds and unearthed in old buildings and diggings throughout the country. The Rev John Kerr brought the full weight of his argument to bear. 'It is absurd,' he wrote, 'to suppose that, if the game were Flemish and carried with Flemings wherever they settled, it would only be in Scotland that the primitive stones would be found.'

The question, even more pertinent than Professor Masson's, is: If curling was once played in the Low Countries, or any other country, why are there no relics of stones in any country other than Scotland?

The reasonable answer is that Bruegel's game on the ice was played with frozen clods of earth which disintegrated when the thaw came – as the claims for overseas origin now disintegrate before our eyes. For a game on ice with clods of earth cannot reasonably be called curling.

We hope that further evidence of early curling, like David Smith's fascinating discovery, will be 'unearthed'. But it is likely that the pioneers

---

* The Game of Eisschiessen (Ice shooting), played on ice with a wooden 'stone' and long stick-like handle, is an ancient national game in Bavaria, was once played in the Netherlands and is played in Switzerland and elsewhere in Europe. The Icelandic 'Knattleir' was a game played with bowls on ice. Both games may be forty-second cousins of Curling; they cannot be said to have any closer relationship.

of the past will remain hidden in the mists of Scottish history. Only one thing is certain: whether the first curlers were Scots, Dutch or prehistoric men, it was the Scots who nurtured the game, regulated it and exported it to many lands. The curling chain, forged in Scotland, now spans the world with links in twenty-three countries, and, as new countries and new clubs join the chain, the bonds of curling fellowship grow ever stronger.

2

A Sermon on Stones

As we have seen, kuting stones or loofies are the oldest curling implements known to us. The maximum weight of the examples which have survived are around 25 lb (11·3 kg), the smallest weighing no more than 5 or 6 lb (2·3 or 2·7 kg).

The famous Stirling Stone, an early type of loofie, which lies in the Stirling Smith Art Gallery and Museum.

As we can suppose that these stones were thrown part of the way along the ice in a quoit-like game, it is not surprising that they were small and light, in some cases little more than large pebbles. What *is* surprising is the immense size of the boulders which appeared in the next stage of curling-stone development. The shift from one extreme to the other was caused by the insertion of a rough handle – a move so simple that curlers of the period, surveying the phenomenon, must have looked quizzically at each other and said: 'Now, why didn't I think of that?'

There is evidence that the quoiting stone and the handled stone were in use together for a period after the introduction of the handle more than three hundred years ago, and, indeed, there are stones with notches for fingers and thumb with an iron handle inserted alongside.

> Gae, get twa whinstanes, round and hard,
> Syne on their taps twa thorn-roots gird,
> Then soop the ice for mony a yard,
> And mak' baith tee and colly.*

Roughly speaking, handled stones made their appearance in the first half of the 17th century. The handles – iron, wood or 'crooked thorn' – were set in the stones by the curlers themselves or by the local blacksmith, who did a more workmanlike job.

* From an Old Song published in the *Scots Magazine*.

The stones came in all shapes – conical, oval, square, three-neukit, pudding, rectangular, hexagonal and shapes which defy description – and all sizes, from large to larger. It was the age of the 'channel stane', so called because the stones were taken from the channels of rivers and were thus worn smooth.

A solid handle with which to swing a stone offered a challenge, full of exciting new possibilities, to the curling community in Scotland. The challenge was taken up in the wrong way. Instead of striving for greater skill and finesse with a controlled swing, curlers hurled their rough boulders with all their power, vying with each other in trials of strength with bigger and ever bigger stones.

Legends of mighty deeds with giant-sized blocks have been passed down in parish histories. Lochmaben curlers were proud of their President, who, at the beginning of the 19th century, accepted a challenge thrown out by Laurie Young of Tinwald. The President took his stone and threw it with such power that it sped almost a mile across the Mill Loch and hit the bank at the far side, tumbling on the grass. 'Now', said the President to Laurie Young, 'go and throw it back again and we'll confess that you're too many for us!'

> ... Long swings the stone,
> Then with full force, careering furious on,
> Rattling, it strikes aside both friend and foe
> Maintains its course and takes the victor's place.*

We hear that, on the ice at Denny, William Gourlay's 72 lb (32·7 kg) stone struck a guard 'full' and then moved on, hitting half-a-dozen other stones before gaining the shot which was thought to be impossible. It is some of the old tales which are 'impossible', or, at least, they have gained in the telling over the 'Beef and Greens' at curlers' suppers!

This middle era of curling was the blood-and-thunder period of the game when strong-arm methods were needed to reach the tee which was hidden by a wall of formidable stones and when the hero was carried shoulder-high from the bonspiel for blasting his way to victory.

> An' many a broken channel-stane
> Lay scattered up an' down

wrote David Davidson, a Kirkcudbright poet, of a stirring battle in 1789.

* From *British Georgics* by James Grahame.

What a waste of stones, you might say. Not so. In these days, stones cost nothing, except the effort to lift them from rivers or dykes.

Another of the objects of a really big stone must have been to hurl it into the house, from which position it would not be easily dislodged. It was said of the huge Lochmaben 'Hen': 'When once she settled, there she clockit!' How frustrating it must have been to play a perfect strike and watch your stone – possibly in several pieces – bounce off the winner without moving it!

A further frustration in these olden days was caused by the system of play, eight men forming a side and playing one stone each – in games which lasted until one side scored 21, 31 or even 51 shots. When a modern curler misses with his first stone, he is all the more determined to atone with his second. The old-time curler did not have the consolation of a second chance and had to wait to try to redeem himself at the next end.

Because each curler had only one curling stone, the misshapen boulders became objects of special veneration and were affectionately christened by their owners. The Hen, The Horse, The Cockit-hat, The Bannock, Whirlie, The Grey Mare, The Bible, Black Meg, The Whaup, Buonaparte, The Prince, Wallace, Hughie and hundreds more created a saga of stones in the parish bonspiels which for centuries fostered the rivalry and fellowship which is the stuff of curling.

> Rivalry and good fellowship,
> The twin pillars of the Bonspiel.
> Old Toast.

The majority of these handled stones weighed between 35 and 75 lb (34 kg) but there were some massive blocks which could have been wielded only by men of unusual strength. The Egg (115 lb (52·2 kg)), belonging to the Blairgowrie and Delvine Clubs, The Saut Backet (116 lb (52·6 kg)) from Coupar Angus and the supreme example of strength for strength's sake, The Jubilee Stone* (117 lb (53·1 kg)) are monuments to the giants of the past.

---

* The Jubilee Stone, presented to the Royal Caledonian Curling Club by John Wilson, Chapelhill, Cockburnspath, was exhibited at the Jubilee Meeting of the Royal Club in 1888. It belonged to John Hood, who died at Townhead in 1888. He had seen his father curl with the stone and had used it himself. The Stone is now displayed with other Royal Club relics in the Royal Caledonian Curling Club headquarters and it is interesting to know that Thomas Hood, a descendant of John Hood, still farms Townhead and is a keen curler. He believes that the Jubilee Stone was taken from the sea at the Mouth of the Pease Burn at Cockburnspath and was then laid upside down at the entrance to stables for a season so that the running surface could be worn smooth by horses' hooves.

The way our ancestors threw these cumbersome masses is a source of wonder, especially to those who find it difficult enough to throw a modern stone into the rings on drug (dour) ice.

Old stones are preserved in many of the Local Clubs in Scotland, often being displayed at curling suppers or used at Curlers' Courts. Many have served as weights on hay ricks and to keep thatch on roofs. Others have become door stops. Some have been relegated to lowly positions as foot-scrapers at front doors and some have been incorporated in battlements and other buildings, like the small loofie embedded in a wall in Edinburgh's Royal Mile.

The relics, found in all parts of Scotland, constitute a massively eloquent 'sermon on stones', which is part of the nation's heritage.

But, however nostalgic we may feel about those older days, we are glad they have passed. Graded stones have raised the game to a fine art. Brain is now the victor over brawn.

The history of curling is the history of curling stones and a search among stones yields evidence of changes much more revolutionary in their nature than historical changes in golf, tennis, rugby, cricket or, indeed, any game of which we can think.

The transformation from quoiting on ice to curling is bewildering enough. But the far more radical change from the rough boulder to the rounded stone is easily the most important revolution in the history of curling.

Towards the end of the 18th century, some genius, or, more likely, an average curler with a degree of perception, noticed that stones more spherical than others gave a higher standard of performance. Perhaps, also, as in many inventions, the discovery was made in different places at the same time and slowly evolved in several areas – eventually to take the curling community by storm.

The rounding of the stone changed the whole aspect of play and brought uniformity and order to the game. The new stone not only ran consistently but rebounded consistently from other stones, making angled raises or wicks as predictably possible as billiard shots.

A premium on accuracy was immediately established and the game became a test of skill, not strength. In addition, a curler could now control the curved line taken by a round stone. By turning the handle of

OPPOSITE Ewen Cameron, well-known Scottish sportsman and Highland Games personality, delivers the Jubilee Stone (117 lb). The stone is on display, with other relics, in the Royal Club headquarters in Edinburgh.

a stone, thus applying 'in-hand' or 'out-hand' motion – like the bias in bowls – stones 'curled' in paths which could be predetermined.

As in the case of the handle, the rounding of the stone seemed a natural and obvious evolution. But how long it took curlers to grasp the obvious! Is it possible that another remarkable, and remarkably simple, advance in the evolution of our game will soon be made, and that, at any moment, some average curler, or group of curlers, will see the 'natural' and 'obvious' and spring the discovery on a startled world?

During the 19th century, circular stones from established areas were the vogue. The best-known types were Ailsas – Blue Hone, Red Hone or Common – quarried from the famous little island of Ailsa Craig in the Clyde which, for more than one hundred years, provided stones to the curlers of the world.* Other 19th century stones were Burnock Waters, Crawfordjohns, Blantyres, Tinkernhills, Carsphairns and Crieffs, so called because of the localities which supplied the stone. All had different properties. Curlers chose those which they thought best suited to the conditions on their local lochs or ponds.

In curling literature through the years, curling stones have been called 'granites' but the word is a misnomer, granite by itself being much too easily broken or chipped to be of any use in curling. The important thing about the stone used for modern curling is that it must have a consistent hardness and toughness as any soft materials among the harder ones will result in uneven wear. Careful selection is therefore imperative. The stone also has a homogeneous quality which binds it together and prevents flaking. A fine grain provides a strong interlocking structure and, in addition, a low water absorbency; when stones dry out, the fine crystals are not dislodged by the outflow of water as heavier crystals would be. This is why curling stones are not brittle, why they seldom chip and why a good pair of curling stones lasts a lifetime.†

When stones were rounded, their weight dropped to manageable proportions. Polishing and other refinements were added, like striking bands to preserve the stones and concave bases with running rims. Reversible

---

* Some years ago, the quarrying on Ailsa Craig was found to be uneconomic and stone-makers, forced to look elsewhere, turned to the Trefor quarry in North Wales. The world-famous Andrew Kay & Company of Mauchline in Ayrshire first used Trefor stone, in addition to Ailsa Craig stone, in 1946.

† In busy ice rinks, where matched sets of stones are used daily from morning to night, it is estimated that stones will last for perhaps ten years – five years' running on each side. Then they can be reground, to sharpen the running edges, with a loss of between 8 and 10 oz (227 and 284 g) per side (1 to $1\frac{1}{4}$ lb (454 to 567 g) per stone) each time the operation is carried out.

stones, with dull and keen sides, were introduced; these stones, cupped on one side only, are not now manufactured. On the flat, keen side, the stone travelled further on dull ice but it slithered along, often out of control, without drawing or 'taking the hand'.

Today, with the advent of indoor ice rinks and the high quality of ice-making in the countries not yet served by indoor rinks, curling stones have been standardised - or very nearly so.

In general, stones for indoor curling are now made with cups 5 in (127 mm) in diameter on top and bottom. For outdoor play in Switzerland, where big variations are caused by sunshine and shade, stones with $3\frac{1}{2}$-in (89 mm) and $4\frac{1}{2}$-in (114 mm) cups are used, and, in Sweden, the outside stones are cupped 4 in (102 mm) on one side and 5 in (127 mm) on the other.

The general rule is: cups of smaller diameter with a dulled running edge for outdoor play; and 5-in (127 mm) cups with a finer running edge for indoor play.

After learning the game in the big ice rinks, newcomers to curling in Scotland will be keen to participate in outdoor bonspiels and to share the exhilaration and companionship of a day spent under a wintry sky in cauld, cauld, frosty weather. Many Scottish clubs own their own outdoor stones, for use when the frost comes. If more pairs are needed - for large-scale bonspiels like the Grand Match of the Royal Caledonian Curling club,* for example - well-used indoor stones with dulled running edges are suitable on normal ice.

A modern curling stone is a thing of beauty, its smooth and polished surface made more beautiful by reflected shades of blue, red or grey. It is a pity that many ice rinks cover the tops of their matched sets of stones with coloured plastic caps. The object - to make the stones of the opposing sides more easily identifiable - is achieved but much of the intrinsic beauty of the stone and the skill of the stone-makers' art is lost to view.

Many ice rinks have also introduced plastic handles. Unattractive to look at, they adversely change the 'feel' of the grip and in many cases cause an unusual hollow thud when two stones meet - as if the stones were complaining about their 'handling'!

The provision of matched sets of stones in the Scottish ice rinks is a recent development which began only twenty-five years ago. Before that, each curler had his own pair of stones and ice rinks were lined with

* Hereafter called the 'Royal Club'.

serried rows of lockers, in which thousands of stones were housed. Great was the activity each day as the appropriate stones were lifted from lockers to the ice, to be returned after each session and replaced by other groups – and great was the wrath of the curler whose favourite stones had, for a variety of reasons, been forgotten. (It was no use putting the stones on the ice at the start of the game as stones require a three-hour period to cool before play.)

This was hard labour for ice rink staffs who heaved a huge sigh of relief when matched sets were introduced. These sets remain on the ice for all sessions and are used by all curlers who are not now permitted to play their own stones.

Under the Rules of Curling, formulated by the Royal Club, 'all curling stones shall be of a circular shape. No stone, including handle and bolt, shall be of greater weight than 44 lb (20 kg) or of greater circumference than 36 in (914 mm), or of less height than one-eighth part of its greatest circumference.' The stones in general use in Scottish ice rinks weigh 40 lb (18·1 kg) each. The addition of 1½ lb (·7 kg) for the handle and bolt make the total weight to be thrown 41½ lb (18·8 kg).

Many people who do not curl know that the average weight of a curling stone is 40 lb (18·1 kg) but few curlers know how a stone is made. The process, a traditional Scottish craft, is highly specialised and undertaken by highly skilled men. Stated very simply and by courtesy of Andrew Kay & Company, the stages are:

1   The rock is blasted. The pieces are carefully examined and only stone of good texture is selected. This is rough-hewn into fat, round blocks weighing roughly 100 lb (45·4 kg).

2   Each 100-lb (45·4 kg) block is levelled on both sides to the required thickness and a true perpendicular hole is drilled. At this stage the stone still weighs between 80 and 90 lb (36·3 and 40·8 kg).

3   The stone is then turned in a lathe 'between centres' and reduced by circular cutter to within 2 lb (·91 kg) of the final weight. Then follows the grinding process and formation of the cup and the rim. The rim, the running edge of the stone, is all-important and must be precisely positioned.

4   Now close to its final weight, the stone is placed on a vertical shaft and polished. It is at this stage that the running edge is carefully adjusted to suit ice requirements.

5   The stone, now smooth and glistening, is then given its striking band, or 'belt'.

6   The stones are then matched in colour and texture into pairs and sets of four pairs.

7   Finally, the holes, already drilled, are countersunk square to receive the bolts which take the handles. The bolts, originally made of iron, have progressed through various stages, from galvanised steel, then brass to aluminium bronze which is stronger than brass and which, unlike iron and steel, does not rust.

The stones are then ready to skim the ice of the world, for Scottish stones, which have qualities which cannot be matched elsewhere, are sent to every curling country.

3

The Paraphernalia of
the Game

HANDLES

We have seen that the first handles inserted in stones were made of iron, wood or thorn. When stones were rounded, towards the end of the 18th century, more sophisticated handles were introduced. Among the first of these were the 'Dalmellington hands', from Dalmellington in Ayrshire, which were set in holes cut between the centre and side of stones.

Handles became increasingly beautiful and ornate. The 19th century examples were made of wood, brass, gunmetal, bone, or a combination of these materials; they were nickel-plated or made of solid nickel or even solid silver. The handles were richly mounted in ebony, buffalo horn, vulcanite and ivory. They were items to be prized, and, indeed, were given as prizes or awarded to curlers for services to the game or the local club.

When ice began to still the waters on Scottish lochs, curlers would polish the handles of their stones . . .

> auld handles, wi' an age untold,
> are made to shine like minted gold.*

When the manufacture of stones became centralised in a few factories, and matched sets were produced, handles were standardised. Today, they are made of chromium-plated brass or bronze; and, in some cases, which we hope will diminish but fear will not, of plastic.

HACKS AND CRAMPITS

The equipment needed for curling is simple in design and straightforward in use; consider the 'Hack', the implement from which a curling stone is thrown.

In its simplest form, the hack is, as its name implies, not an implement

---

* James Hogg (the Ettrick Shepherd).

Famous Scottish skip Willie Young, who played from the crampit, illustrates the delivery action - 'wrong foot' forward - which he used to devastating effect in a long period of dominance in Scottish competitions.

at all but it is a hole in the ice. It began as a hole, and, after many vicissitudes through the ages, it is regarded as a hole again in many parts of the world.*

At outdoor bonspiels in Scotland today, the ice is still hacked by some curlers and the foot inserted in the hole as a purchase for throwing curling stones. It is the oldest 'foothold' in the game. The curlers of

* The Rev John Kerr, in his *History of Curling* 1890, stated that the hole in the ice was not the oldest form of foothold but a later development. It is one of the few findings in Kerr's great book with which we disagree.

Sanquhar, for many years a principal stronghold of the game, cut a notch in the ice, in which a curler placed the side of the foot, and this practice was followed in Lanarkshire and elsewhere.

It is also the most modern. In Canada and the United States, where curling is almost exclusively an indoor sport, the sunken hack, as it is called, is universal. The hole is lined with rubber to give stability and to prevent slipping.

This form of hack, which provides the most secure base for delivery, is not in general use in Scottish ice rinks because, on a sheet of ice which is also used for skating, it is not practical to fill the hack holes before skating and to cut new holes before the next curling session. In these circumstances, a raised hack, with prongs which fit into small holes bored in the ice, is used. It is lifted before the skaters take the ice and – a most important and too often neglected point – should also be lifted after each end of play in case a player, with his mind on other things, trips over it behind the rings at the next end. With the growth of international competitions and the provision of ice exclusively for curling, sunken hacks have now made their appearance in Scotland.

Many curlers believe that the crampit as we know it in Scotland is the oldest type of grip for delivering stones. This popular misconception is very wide of the mark. The crampit is, in fact, the modern form of the foot-iron introduced early in the 19th century by John Cairnie, first President of the Royal Club, the one-armed, single-minded naval surgeon whose name shines brightly in the annals of curling. Cairnie's foot-iron was a piece of sheet-iron 3 ft 9 in (1,143 mm) long by 9 in (228 mm) wide, punched or well frosted on both sides and turned up about an inch (25 mm) at the end to give purchase to the back foot.

By coincidence, however, the earliest contrivances used as holds for hurling curling stones were also called crampits (or cramps or tramps). But they were very different instruments, being iron or steel pads, with prongs underneath, which were attached to the feet by straps.

They were in use in Scotland until the middle of the 19th century and there was considerable controversy before Cairnie's foot-irons were generally adopted in place of the strapped-on crampits or tramps. Cairnie called these crampits 'almost barbarous' but, in 1830, Sir Richard Broun, in his *Memorabilia Curliana Mabenensia*, stated forcibly: 'It must ever be kept in view, however, that sweeping forms a most important item in the Curler's task. Nor can we see how this can properly be performed unless the player stands *sicker* upon the ice. The alert sweeper has little in common with the mincing steps of the slip-shod looker-on. He who cannot play a scientific game in tramps, will never play one out of them.'* So curlers did not merely throw their stones with tramps attached to their boots but also ran all over the ice on them; this is one rule which has changed with a vengeance, the present rule stipulating that 'no player shall use footwear or equipment that may damage the surface of the ice'.

Another problem with these strapped-on grips was that, if an opposing stone was guarded, it was simplicity itself to take a step or two to the right or left to make the shot easier – an advantage to the player but a disadvantage to the game. The first Rules of the Royal Club, published in 1839, came down hard on the practice in these words in Rule 6: 'A player stepping aside to take a brittle (or wick), or other shot, shall forfeit his stone for that end.'

Other old grips used in varying forms by the clubs of Scotland were the trickers (triggers, grippers or crisps). The remarkable feature of these is that they were made in sets, one to hold the heel of the right foot, the other for the toe of the left foot. The game of curling must have been a 'tricky' business in those days!

The modern form of crampit is still seen on Scottish lochs. Curlers who were *thirled* on it continue to use it on outside ice but, since that great player, Willie Young of Airth, stopped curling, the crampit has not been seen in Scottish ice rinks.

When the indoor ice rinks were established in Glasgow and Edinburgh in 1907 and 1912, the crampit was the vogue and curlers gazed in awe when Col. T.S.G.H. Robertson Aikman, President of the Royal Club in 1924-25, brought his own type of hack to the ice. His invention, made of wood, was a much bigger version of the hack now used but we believe that the Colonel, whose son, Bill Robertson Aikman, followed him as Royal Club President (1965 to 1967), was a prime mover in popularising the hack in modern Scottish curling. When the Colonel introduced his hack, which, as Captain of the Royal Club team, he took to Canada in 1912, several curlers from the West of Scotland used 'crisps' (metal hacks) in the Scottish Ice Rink in Glasgow.

THE DUSTER

The duster has suffered an even steeper decline than the crampit. Up to twenty years ago it was used by almost all Scottish skips. The duster,

---

* Condemning the practice, a Kilmarnock curler wrote, in 1830: 'We cannot conceive how a crampetted player can attend to the sweeping of stones without so mangling the ice as to make it unfit for use. Shoes, and a kind of boots, made of carpet, dreadnought, or felt, are in universal use. With felt shoes, a man may walk or run on the keenest ice.'

Bill Robertson Aikman of Hamilton and Thornyhill Club, a Past-President of the Royal Club, delivers a stone from the wooden hack made by his father. This forerunner of the modern hack has a semi-circular notch in the wood into which the foot is set at an angle.

often a yellow car cloth, sometimes a handkerchief or a bundle of coloured wool, was used as a marker to indicate where the stone should come to rest, or, when placed on top of a stone, the stone to be hit. The cry, 'you're on the duster', which rang through the Scottish ice rinks, is heard no more, the duster now being obsolete.

THE BOTTLE AND THE DOLLY

Equipment now also extinct in Scotland includes the tee-marker, a mis-shapen wooden skittle, which showed the position of the tee or centre of the circles. This all-important spot, which is the aim of all curlers, was originally indicated by a button (now the expression used for the tee in Canada and U.S.A.), a bawbee (a half-penny) or a pinch of snuff. Later, a special iron ring with a prong was pressed down on the ice. Later still, a wooden bottle* marked the spot; still used in Points Competitions (see Rules Section), it is never seen in normal games.

But its big sister, the Dolly, a squatter and fatter 'bottle', plays a role on the ice in many parts of Europe as a tee-marker, and has been hon-oured by Geneva curlers, whose 'Dolly Cup' is one of the most important Swiss competitions. The trouble with the Dolly is that it can obstruct stones, or even become checked between stones if the skip is not alert enough to lift it out of harm's way.

TASSELS, BASKETS

Tassels – little baubles of coloured wool attached to the handles of stones – have been superseded in Scotland by coloured plastic discs which cover the tops of stones for identification, each side playing with eight stones of one colour. But tassels are still used in Switzerland and other parts of the Continent and Scandinavia, and stones are transported there, as they once were in Scotland, in handsome baskets, now almost unknown here.

BESOMS, BROOMS AND BRUSHES

A cutting from the osier tree was the earliest curling besom we know of. The twigs of the osier, a species of willow, are used for basket-making, and cricket bats have been traditionally made from willow. Our curling ancestors found its slender, pliant branches ideal for sweeping snow from the ice and for encouraging laggard stones.

Brooms were made of twigs of broom bound together and old-time curlers did not call them besoms but kowes or cowes. Birch, blaeberry and other varieties of trees and plants were used for broom-making through the ages and kowes came to be recognised as the twigs of any plant or shrub tied together.

When the Royal Club rules were first published, in 1839, Rule 15

---

* 'The Delvine Bottle', used by the Delvine Club in Perthshire (instituted 1732), was a wooden replica of a quart whisky bottle complete with cork. 'Come to the bottle', 'guard the bottle' and 'smell the bottle' were well-known expressions on outdoor ice.

began: 'Every player to come provided with a besom.' From the earliest times, when a curler cut his besom from a tree, to the beautifully-fashioned, brightly-painted brooms of today, the value of a good broom has been recognised by curlers. Sweeping has always played a major part in the game. (See the Chapter on Sweeping.)

Last century, delicately-made brooms, with small tightly-bound sweeping areas and curved walking-stick handles, were much sought after. Silver bands were wrapped round the handles for inscriptions and the brooms were played for in club competitions in Scotland, the trophies being comparable to old-style putters, suitably engraved, which are competed for at golf.

Two main types of besom are used today – the brush in Scotland and Europe generally and the broom or whisk broom in Canada and the United States. The use of the two types is sharply divided by the Atlantic Ocean although the Canadian-type broom, once common on Scottish lochs and ponds, is still seen on outdoor ice in Scotland – and is now used by some top Swedish and Swiss teams; and the Scottish-type brush, increasingly being recognised as the more effective implement, is now widely used by competitive Canadian and U.S. curlers.

The corn broom, traditionally the sweeping instrument in Canada, tends to strew straws on the ice and it is now all too common for sweepers in major competitions to run up and down the ice to clean the surface before each stone is played – a precaution against stones being fouled but a practice which stops the flow of the game and adds to the already lengthy time taken to play ten ends.

Since Scots made the game international, it is appropriate that Scottish brushes, which vary in price according to the materials used, should be international in character, the best type of brush being made of hog-hair, imported from the cold areas of China. Horsehair is another good material and other types are Mexican fibre, a mixture of Mexican fibre and flagged polypropylene and pure flagged polypropylene. 'Flagged' means that the tips of the fibre have been broken up to give a softer effect. And 'polypropylene'? We are ninety-nine per cent certain that curlers have no idea that the tough man-made fibre with which they beat the ice is also used for making artificial heart valves. The game has come a long way since a curler selected a branch from a tree on his way to the bonspiel!

4

Outdoor Curling Through the Ages

The frost bade for abune sax ouks, till the hinner
end of Feberwar.
The ice of the loch was 23, of the Brigend-Dam
18 inches thick.

IN SCOTLAND, OUTDOOR curling has been superseded to a large extent by indoor play in the big artificial ice rinks. But a true curler longs for frost, and, when a cold 'snap' grips the country, a sense of urgency and suspense pervades the scene.

In frosty weather, the air is expectant and this atmosphere conveys itself to curlers who pace the ground in anxious agitation, their eyes raised to the sky.

In the country districts – where, by tradition, the game has been played in the 'interlude of rural life'* when the plough was frozen in the furrow – curlers inspect their local loch or pond, prepare their equipment, make sage weather forecasts – and hope. If the frost continues, meetings are hastily convened, a day is set for the bonspiel and word is quickly passed round the neighbourhood that the ice is bearing.

In the old days, it was common knowledge in the village that the tradesman or lawyer, a keen curler, would not be available for business when the temperature dropped below freezing point. Those not in the know who called would be given a cold reception.

> 'Is Mr Macgregor in?'
> 'I'm afraid not.'
> 'Well, when will he be back?'
> 'When the thaw comes!'

Such dereliction of duty, which is not unknown today, is forgivable. Consider the miserable lives led by old-time Scottish curlers. For years

---

* Farmers have always formed a major section of the Scottish curling population. In the twenty-strong Scottish team which made the first official tour to U.S.A. in 1955, only two were not connected with the farming industry.

on end, those men, hoping and fearing, laid plans for parish bonspiels, to be thwarted by thaws. In bad years, their stones would languish in the stone house, or the attic. The frustrations caused by the vagaries of Jack Frost must have been almost too much to bear.

'Alas,' groaned a keen curler in 1883, 'the good old times seem to have passed away, when for weeks on end

> O'er burn and loch the warlock Frost
> A crystal brig would lay.*

and good ice might be confidently counted on for a long time.'

In such conditions, every advantage was taken of the opportunities for a game, and, after a spell of barren winters, curlers would often play all day and well into the night in case the dreaded thaw came the following morning.

The 19th century opened promisingly with a series of hard winters between 1800 and 1838. But the early 1840s were disappointing years and an *Annual* of the Royal Club of the period complained of 'the privations to which the fickle state of the thermometer has subjected us, one day raising our spirits by letting down its own to the neighbourhood of zero and the next laying prostrate all our hopes by mounting above the freezing point'.

In 1846, however, the frost returned and a song was written to celebrate the occasion:

> Johnny Frost is back again,
> The queer auld body's back again,
> Tell the news to Curling men,
> Johnny Frost is back again;
> Johnny thocht he was to blame
> For staying a' last year at hame,
> Quo' he I'll just draw on my breeks
> An' I'll gie them twa or three Curling weeks.

Many and various were the methods employed by curlers to gauge the conditions of frost prior to a bonspiel. A wet handkerchief, placed on the garden hedge, would be brought in at regular intervals to test its stiffness.

---

*From *The Music of the Year is Hushed*, by the Rev Henry Duncan, Ruthwell (1774–1846), the Scot who founded the Savings Bank movement.

A ringing earth, a ringing air and a multitude of stars shining clear in a cloudless sky were favourable symptoms while bad signs were clouds in the west, a southerly wind, shooting stars, a tremulous movement of the stars and a suspicious *sough* of the wind through doorways.

James Brown, Secretary of the Sanquhar Curling Society, reported that, if a cat passed her forepaw over her ear while washing, it was a sure sign of approaching thaw. Brown also told of the dedicated curler who deliberately broke a weather glass he had recently purchased with the words: 'I'm glad to have it oot o' the hoose for there has been nae gude weather since ever I bought it!'

The winters of 1795 and 1895 shine brightly in the record books. A well-satisfied curler wrote that 'the winter of 1795 was such an one as rejoices the hearts of a' keen curlers – frosts lay lang, snaws were deep'. A Kilconquhar report of that year tells of the man who curled all day and every day for six weeks, at the end of which 'his hand actually kept the position of a person's hand holding a stone and that it kept the *crook* for a considerable time afterwards'!

David Hutchison, Royal Club President in 1951–52, started his curling career, aged fifteen, in 1895, on Loch Leven which was frozen from early January until the end of March. He recalled that, in addition to numerous bonspiels, a wide variety of spectacular events was staged. There were skating carnivals at night to the music of pipes, melodeons and fiddles. Carriages and pairs were driven on the loch and horse-drawn sleighs were hired to drive round the historic castle in the middle of the loch where Mary Queen of Scots was imprisoned. Visitors came in special trains from all over Scotland to participate in these ice frolics, surely the gayest events of the gay nineties in Kinross-shire.

In 1956, the 80-year-old Willie Brown, well-known personality in the Royal Montreal Club, advised us that he remembered curling being played for fourteen weeks on the lochs at Sanquhar in 1895, shortly before he emigrated to Canada.

We have no record of curling during three famous winters in history – 1684, when English oaks were split by the frost and the ice on the Thames was eleven inches deep; 1691, when hungry wolves entered Vienna, attacking cattle and even men; or, the most famous of all, 1709, known as the 'cold winter', when the seas round Britain were frozen up to several miles from the shore and the frost penetrated three yards into the ground.

We know, however, that the great frost of 1746 was too much of a good thing for curlers. Church-goers on the south side of Lochwinnoch walked over the ice to the kirk on thirteen successive Sundays. Wells, fountains and burns were frozen. The ice on the loch was bent and bowed down to the bottom and curling was stopped because of the curve on the ice.

But this was an exceptional year. Complaints of too little rather than too much ice is the continuing thread in the story of Scottish curling and it is a tribute to the patient and long-suffering nature of the Scots that the game survived through so many *thin* periods.

In recent years, as in the past, outdoor curlers in Scotland have had their ups and down, the frustrations of mild seasons being forgotten in the excitement and bonhomie of hard winters, particularly 1958-59, 1962-63, 1967-68 and 1978-79, when joy was unconfined for weeks on end in many parts of the country. In 1963, our good friend Dr Alex Dimtza reported that two rinks had been marked and curling enjoyed on the Lake of Zurich, the first time the Lake had been frozen since 1929, and, before that, 1891.

The conditions at the 1979 Grand Match at the Lake of Menteith (see chapter on the Grand Match) were perfect – bright sunshine and curling in shirt sleeves – and not typical of outdoor curling through the ages which was often played in snow and wind which froze the breath. But the curling fraternity, a hardy breed, shrugged off petty ailments when the bonspiel was called. In the early part of the 19th century, the Rev Norman Macleod captured this sturdy spirit in comic verse:

> A' nicht it was freezin', a' nicht I was sneezin',
> 'Tak care', quo' the wife, 'gudeman, o' yer cough'.
> A fig for the sneezin', hurrah for the freezin',
> For the day we're to play the bonspiel on the loch.

In addition, curling is just the game for world-weary cynics, tired businessmen and worriers of all types:

> Hae ye trouble? Hae ye sorrow?
> Are ye pinched wi' warldly care?
> Redd the roaring rink tomorrow,
> Peuch! they'll fash ye never mair.

Scottish schools have now included curling in their curricula (see chapter on Youth and Age). But it must be stressed that the game can be started at any age, the term 'a young curler' meaning a curler young in curling experience.

Some Scots throw their first stones at the age of eight or nine. Some are pressed into service in their 'teens when their fathers are a man short. The majority start between the ages of twenty and fifty and a minority first take the ice when they retire from business and enjoy games which are not too serious in club or veterans' leagues.

Those who claim they are too old to start a new sport, and those who, feeling old, huddle round the fireside in the winter of their lives, should

Droukit! While playing on the Comrie pond in his estate in Perthshire in 1965, Sir Robert Dundas and his fellow curlers fell through the ice and were helped to the bank. The photographer, Mr Cowper, also went through the ice while making a television film which ended dramatically with a view of trees and sky as the camera fell with the cameraman!

be reminded of curling's powers of rejuvenation, so aptly summed up by James Grahame in *British Georgics* (1809):

> ... Aged men,
> Smit with the eagerness of youth, are there,
> While love of conquest lights their beamless eyes,
> New-nerves their arms and makes them young once more.

Curling lifts the spirit and captivates the mind. The fascination of the game itself and its aspects of teamwork and friendship are the factors which make curling the ideal form of relaxation.

The traditions of the game have been built on the rigours and uncertainties of outdoor play and it is obviously desirable to continue to nurture the old outdoor connection in Scotland while the majority of the curling population plays indoors.

There is a place for both forms in modern curling. Indeed, after regular play in the big indoor ice rinks, curlers keenly anticipate a chance to participate in outdoor bonspiels. In addition to enjoying the thrill of a day out of doors, they can take a step into the game's history.

On occasion, outdoor ice is smooth and true – sheer perfection for curling. It can be rough, heavily biased by ridges and runs, wet, unplayable. In general, outdoor play is more chancy, less artistic, far less precise than indoor curling. But it has an invigoration all its own, the scenery, the bracing air, the bustling activity, the stops for sustenance and a drop of the 'auld kirk', the roar of stones and the fellowship under a wintry sun combining to provide an exhilaration unique in sport.

5

The Birth of the Birl

THE ROUNDING OF the stone brought many refinements to curling but easily the most important was the introduction of the 'in-hand' and 'out-hand' which controlled the curved path of a stone.

This rotary movement of the handle, the 'birl', was reputedly first used to advantage by Fenwick curlers and was first known as the Fenwick Twist or the Kilmarnock Twist. A song in John Cairnie's *Essay on Curling and Artificial Pond Making* (1833) contains this verse:

> Six stones within the circle stand,
> And every port is blocked,
> But Tam Pate he did turn the hand,
> And soon the port unlocked.*

The reference illustrates the most spectacular advance gained by the turning of the hand – to draw round guards – but the new method was an advantage in all types of shot. The Twist not only turned the stone but turned upside down all previous conceptions about delivering a stone. The Curler's 'Word' in the old initiation ceremony runs:

> If you'd be a curler keen,
> Look at the mark with all your een,
> Foot sure, *shoot straight* and soop clean.

To shoot straight meant to deliver a stone without any 'handle' or 'birl' and to aim directly at the mark – a difficult operation since a stone which, on delivery, starts with no handle, will almost always begin to rotate one way or the other while travelling. But, in old-style curling, an in-hand or out-hand shot was considered to be a bad shot and players continued to try to shoot straight until the birth of the birl – and, in the case of many diehards, for some time after.

---

* Tam Pate, a cadger (pedlar) from Kirk o' Shotts, played last stone in the Duke of Hamilton's rink in many famous games, particularly at Lochwinnoch in 1784. It was written: 'Tam never missed a single aim and the spectators dubbed him for a warlock.'

When twisting started to spread, at the beginning of the 19th century, it was violently opposed in conservative quarters. A curler, wryly calling himself Timothy Twist, wrote: 'There are few players who can avoid twisting their stones and this almost universal fault is the great cause of the ill success which attends their play. I have seen large parties of curlers twisting their stones and complaining with one voice of the heavy bias on the ice when the ice was perfectly level and the disappointment of the players was to be ascribed solely to the rotary motion of their stones. To guard against the habit of twisting is the first lesson to be learned by the young aspirant and he who has learned to play a straight stone has already overcome one of the greatest difficulties of the art, for, in ordinary circumstances, this is the style of play which will tell most on the success of the game.'

A Fenwick curler, John Fulton, rushed into print, in his *Account of the Scientific Movement*, to defend the revolutionary new theory:

'If I recollect aright, and I am pretty certain on that point, the first year of the century (1800) was the year of its birth. That year was memorable for the length and severity of its winter. It is told that day after day, for a period of over six weeks, a few Fenwick curlers were never absent from a small loch in this parish, on the farm of Meikle-wood, then in possession of a Mr William Carse, who, being also a keen curler, was always one of the party. Here they played every imaginable shot, or 'points' as they are now termed.

'While thus engaged, they observed the effect of the rotatory motion a stone naturally takes on the ice and saw that the stone always twisted from the straight line in obedience to that motion. They felt assured that a discovery of importance to the game had been made, and that they had hit on a right principle, so they patiently set themselves to make it of practical value to curlers, and from that time to the present all young curlers in Fenwick are taught the power of twisting as an element of first-rate value, and are so taught the use of it that they know at once from the skip's broom what twist is to be used.

'We think it a scientific style of play, requiring more skill than brute force, depending much more upon intelligent calculating judgment for success than on the strong arm. With good level ice and good curlers, masters of the twist, it is very interesting and beautiful, and to a stranger, wonderful to see how the stone twists into the desired place, ignoring guards as of no consequence. But to see the twist at its best, it must be seen at Craufurdland Loch, which is perhaps the best-conditioned curling pond in Scotland, and where the ice is always the best to be found anywhere.

'There was also another circumstance which helped to make the twist a success, which was this. At the time the twist was discovered, there were living in the village of Fenwick a number of as capable young men as could be found anywhere. Intelligent and moral, active and lithe of body and limb, full of spirit for sports of all kinds, they entered with zest into the new style of curling.

'They formed themselves into four rinks, in which they played always together, and thus acquired an *esprit de corps*, a confidence in each other which made them very formidable antagonists to all comers. They were known as the Fenwick "sixteen", and, like Wellington's invincibles, could have gone anywhere.'

But many other curlers bewailed that 'the good old maxim shoot straight' was being discarded. The controversy, which continued for many years, is remarkable to a modern curler. Indeed, the fanatical attempt to preserve a policy which maintained that the in-hand and out-hand was bad curling is probably the most fantastic single feature in a history which often soars into the realms of fantasy.

Eventually, good sense prevailed and we now play accurate shots – or it is our fault if we do not – by turning the handles of our stones.

6

The Royal Caledonian Curling Club and the Rules of the Game

EDINBURGH'S CONTRIBUTION TO curling has been on the grand scale. Ramsay wrote the first account of the game (1811) anonymously as 'A Member of the Duddingston Curling Society'. Curling enjoyed such a vogue in Edinburgh at the beginning of the eighteenth century that the Magistrates of the City, in ceremonial robes, paraded, in step with curling marches specially composed for the occasion, to open the season on the Nor' Loch (which, when drained, became Princes Street Gardens).

Canonmills and Duddingston Loch were famous curling settings and the old Duddingston Society is the best-known local club in the annals of the game. In 1802, the club instituted a silver medal, probably the first badge ever worn by curlers,* 'to distinguish the members from other gentlemen,' and, in 1809, originated the Points Competition – with three Points, Drawing, Striking and Inwicking – which the Currie Club enlarged to the system now in general use. The club also went further than any other club in collecting historical data and curling songs and verses.

But easily the greatest curling contribution made by the Duddingston Society was the framing of rules which earned for Duddingston the proud title of 'the most influential local club in curling history'.

With the growth of clubs in the 18th and early 19th centuries, it became clear that districts, towns and villages could not continue to play the game in haphazard fashion under local or club rules and that there was a need for national regulations.

Duddingston led the way towards this goal with a remarkable document, framed in the Curlers' Hall, Duddingston, 'upon the 6th January, 1804'. It was called 'Rules in Curling' and here it is in full:

I. The usual length of a rink is from thirty-six to forty-four yards inclusive; but this will be regulated by circumstances and the agreement

---

* Clubs all over the world now have their own club badges, or 'pins' as they are called in Canada and the United States. Badges are exchanged during overseas tours, and on many other occasions, and curlers display their collections in show cases and under glass table tops. Fanatical collectors boast of a store of well over 1,000 badges. The old and rare 'pins' are the most sought after.

of parties. When a game is begun the rink is not to be changed or altered, unless by the consent of the majority of players; nor is it to be shortened, unless it clearly appears that the majority are unable to make up.

II. The hog score to be one-sixth part of the length of the rink distant from the tee, and every stone to be deemed a hog the sole of which does not clear the score.

III. Each player to foot in such a manner that, in delivering his stone, he brings it over the tee.

IV. The order of playing adopted at the beginning must be observed during the whole course of a game.

V. All curling-stones to be of a circular shape. No stone is to be changed throughout a game, unless it happens to be broken; and the largest fragment of such stone to count, without any necessity of playing with it more. If a stone rolls or is upset, it must be placed upon its sole where it stops. Should a handle quit a stone in the delivery, the player must keep hold of it, otherwise he will not be entitled to replay the shot.

VI. A player may sweep his own stone the whole length of the rink; his party not to sweep until it has passed the hog score at the farther end, and his adversaries not to sweep until it has passed the tee. The sweeping to be always to a side.

VII. None of the players, upon any occasion, to cross or go upon the middle of the rink.

VIII. If in sweeping or otherwise a running stone is marred by any of the party to which it belongs, it must be put off the ice; if by any of the adverse party, it must be placed agreeable to the direction which was given to the player; and if it is marred by any other means, the player may take his shot again. Should a stone at rest be accidentally displaced, it must be put as nearly as possible to its former situation.

IX. Every player to be ready when his turn comes, and to take no more than a reasonable time to play his shot. Should he, by mistake, play with a wrong stone, it must be replaced where it stops by the one with which he ought to have played.

X. A doubtful shot is to be measured by some neutral person whose determination shall be final.

XI. Before beginning to play, each party must name one of their number for directing their game. The players of his party may give their advice to the one so named, but they cannot control his direction, nor are they to address themselves to the person who is about to play. Each director, when it is his turn to play, to name one of his party to take the charge for him. Every player to follow the direction given to him.

XII. Should any question arise the determination of which may not be provided for by the words and spirit of the rules now established, each party to choose one of their number in order to determine it. If the two so chosen differ in opinion, they are to name an umpire, whose decision shall be final.

These early rules are remarkable not only for their solid commonsense but also because they bear a striking resemblance to the rules in use today, particularly in the following sections: 'The order of playing adopted at the beginning must be observed during the whole course of a game.' 'No stone is to be changed throughout a game, unless it happens to be broken; and the largest fragment of such stone to count, without any necessity of playing with it more. Should the handle quit a stone in the delivery, the player must keep hold of it, otherwise he will not be entitled to replay the shot.' 'If, in sweeping or otherwise, a running stone is marred by any of the party to which it belongs, it must be put off the ice; if by any of the adverse party, it must be placed agreeable to the direction which was given to the player.' 'Every player to be ready to play when his turn comes and to take no more than a reasonable time to play his shot.'

When the Grand Caledonian Curling Club, later to become the Royal Caledonian Curling Club, was formed in 1838, the new club paid Duddingston the sincerest form of flattery by basing their Code of Rules on the Edinburgh Club's rules. The fact that these rules have stood the test of time for over 180 years is a tribute to the good sense and sagacity of the administrators whose Rules received 'the approbation and sanction of a general meeting of the Duddingston Curling Society' in 1804.

All curlers owe a debt to the Duddingston Curling Society and to administrators down the years from 1838 for retaining the basic rules, for constantly striving for simplicity – the keynote of legislation – and for refusing to be steam-rollered into widespread and needless rule changes.

When dealing with rules, time for thought, and plenty of it, is the first priority. The ramifications of change are far-reaching. The alteration of one sentence, even one word, in a rule almost always affects another rule or other rules. At rules meetings outwith Scotland in recent years, rash and over-hasty changes have been made and later found to be ill-advised, requiring further change or a reversion to the original rule. It should always be borne in mind that prolonged thought and discussion are needed before changes are proposed. Time for thought is of the essence in rule-making.

Legislators should also remember that, however many new rules are introduced and however carefully they are worded, there will always be loopholes or situations which are not covered. The highly complex rules of golf, and the book of interpretations which goes with them, do not cover all eventualities, and never will. Commonsense, therefore, must point to short and simple rules and a sensible interpretation of the rules by the curlers themselves – and by umpires, where necessary. We are pleased, therefore, to use so little space at the end of this chapter with the playing rules of the Royal Club, which cover only eight small pages of the rules booklet.

We do not know them but there may be a few, very few, 'curlers' who try to take an unfair advantage of rules which are intentionally short and some administrators argue that this proves the need for more comprehensive rules. The answer to that argument is that, whatever rules are made, it will be possible to break them. In other words, rule-makers cannot legislate for that type of 'curler'.

Prior to the formation of the 'Grand Caledonian' in 1838, the organisation of big bonspiels had become increasingly difficult. At the matches between Midlothian and Peebles (1823) and Midlothian and Lanarkshire (1831), the sides could not agree about the rules, the size of stones and the composition of rinks. It was reported: 'there was a want of co-operation between the players'. In 1834, an attempt to form an Amateur Curling Club of Scotland – with, among other distinguished office-bearers, James Hogg, the Ettrick Shepherd, as one of its Secretaries – proved abortive. The curlers of Scotland were slow to act, and, ironically, when a meeting was finally called, it very nearly broke up in disorder.

Despite claims from various parts of the country to the contrary, it is still uncertain who placed this advertisement in the North British Advertiser of 26 May 1838:*

'To Curlers. – In consequence of what is suggested at p. 11 of the '*Laws in Curling*' (a pamphlet just published by Maclachlan & Stewart, Edinburgh), it is hoped that the Initiated Curling Clubs in Scotland will depute one of the Brethren of their Court to meet in the Waterloo Hotel, Edinburgh, on Wednes-

---

*In his book, *Curling, The Ancient Scottish Game* (1884), the Rev James Taylor wrote: 'There can be little or no doubt that Mr Cairnie was the author of the anonymous advertisement and that the lateness of his appearance at the Meeting was owing to the tediousness of a journey across the country from Largs.' This seemed eminently logical but Cairnie later stated that he was not the author (Royal Club *Annual*, 1844).

day, the 20th June next, at 11 o'clock a.m., for the purpose of making the mysteries more uniform in future, and, if requisite, to form a Grand Court, to which all provincial ones shall be subject, and to elect a Grand President, with other Office-bearers. It is hoped that all Brethren who see this notice will direct the attention of their President or Secretary to it without delay. – 16th May 1838.'

A dozen curlers assembled at the Waterloo Hotel. It quickly became evident that the author of the advertisement was not present and the company split into uncertain little groups. Without a lead, without an agenda, no one knew where to start and the meeting seemed about to disintegrate. At this psychological moment, a dapper one-armed figure entered, presented his card and announced himself, 'in a blunt, off-hand but frank and genial manner', as Mr Cairnie of Curling Hall.

He brought books which he had written on pond-making and other aspects of curling. The magnetism of his personality so impressed the meeting that, although no one knew him personally, he was unanimously elected Chairman.

John Cairnie, first President of the Grand Caledonian Curling Club in 1838, standing on the foot-iron which he invented. The Grand Club became the Royal Club when Queen Victoria granted Royal patronage after a visit to Scone Palace in 1842, when the Earl of Mansfield demonstrated the game on the floor of the Palace ballroom.

John Cairnie, born in Denny about 1769, inventor of artificial pond-making and of the foot-iron, which lasted for 100 years in Scottish curling, was a 'bonnie little man', a first-class curler, a benefactor to needy causes and a general favourite. He lost his left arm in a gunpowder explosion but this scarcely restricted his activities in his yacht or on the curling rink. After service as a surgeon in the East India Company and at sea, he settled in Largs, Ayrshire, in 1813, and built Curling Hall* where he hoisted a banner on a high flagpole when curling was possible on his pond. He died in 1842 and his friend, Captain Paterson, wrote an elegy in his memory:

> 'Why droops the banner half-mast high,
> And curlers heave the bitter sigh?
> Why throughout Largs the tearful eye,
>   So blear'd and red?
> Oh! listen to the poor man's cry!
> John Cairnie's dead!
>
> 'While winter's breath as waters freeze,
> Lays waste the fields and bares the trees,
> Or well-rigged yachts in joyous breeze
>   For prizes ply,
> Cairnie! thy name by land or seas
>   Shall never die.'

Cairnie's dramatic intervention saved the day and he guided the first perilous steps of the new national body. The meeting came to order and resolved to issue another advertisement, under Cairnie's name, in three editions of the same newspaper, reporting the findings of the members at the meeting and adding: 'But, anxious for a fuller representation of the different clubs throughout the country, in order to perpetuate and connect more closely the brotherhood in this ancient national game, they adjourned to Wednesday, 25th of July next, at twelve o'clock in the Waterloo Hotel, when they hope the different Clubs of Scotland will make a point of sending deputations.'

This second meeting, attended by representatives of 36 clubs, was a complete success. Dr Renton of Penicuik proposed that the Grand

---

* The mansion later became the Marine & Curlinghall Hotel, the entire contents of which, including a set of five carved stone heads 'of John Cairnie and his curling cronies', were sold by public auction in November, 1983.

Caledonian Curling Club, to be composed of the initiated Scottish clubs, be instituted. This was agreed and Cairnie was unanimously elected President and James Skelton, W.S., of the Kinross Club, Secretary. A Committee was formed to consider regulations, mysteries and ceremonies and to prepare a mode of initiation and a set of Rules and Regulations.

The representatives met as strangers in the morning. Later in the day, a Curlers' Court was constituted by John Wright Williamson, Kinross, with the ancient ceremony for which he and the Kinross Club are famous. At a dinner in the evening, the members greeted each other as brothers and were loath to part. It was the perfect example of the fellowship of curling and augured well for the future of the game's first national association.

The Club was soon to become international, but, first, it was to be honoured by Royal patronage – christened, as it were, by The Queen, and properly launched to serve not only on Scottish waters but in many parts of the world.

In 1842, the Earl of Mansfield, then President, entertained Queen Victoria and the Prince Consort at Scone Palace and presented to Prince Albert a pair of curling stones 'made of the finest Ailsa Craig granite, most beautifully finished and ornamented', with silver handles.* The Prince immediately accepted an invitation to become the first Patron of the Club.

After the presentation, Queen Victoria asked the Earl of Mansfield for details of curling and the Earl gave a demonstration of the game on the oak floor of the Palace ballroom, stones being thrown along the polished surface. The Queen herself threw a stone, understandably 'hogged' it and expressed surprise when told the length of a normal rink.

In the following year, 1843, the 'Grand Caledonian' became the 'Royal Grand Caledonian'. Permission was quickly granted to refine the title and the Royal Caledonian Curling Club was established.

Today, in a bookcase in the office of the Secretary of the Royal Club, a complete library of *Annuals* (Year Books) from the year 1839 forms an impressive record of the Club's meteoric rise from an association of 28

---

* We recall three other important presentations of curling stones. In 1863, a pair of green Serpentine stones from Crieff were presented by the Royal Club to the Prince of Wales. In 1867, a pair of stones, of fine Peebles porphyry, were sent by William Chambers, the Lord Provost of Edinburgh, to the Paris International Exhibition, and, at the end of the Exhibition, were presented to Emperor Napoleon III; and, in 1964, the Council of the Royal Club presented a beautiful pair of Red Hone Ailsas, suitably inscribed, to the Duke of Edinburgh, after the Duke's installation as President of the Royal Club.

Major Allan Cameron, 1963-64 President, pins the badge of office on the Duke of Edinburgh when the Duke was elected Royal Club President in 1964 – with Willie Wilson, Gilbert McClung and Robin Welsh alongside. The Royal Club flag hangs behind.

local clubs to the world-wide organisation now called the 'Mother Club of Curling'.

In 1833, John Cairnie expressed the wish that all Scottish clubs should correspond 'and give in a list of their office-bearers, the number of curlers, matches played and any matter connected with the game that was interesting'. This is, basically, what the *Annual* is. In addition, the book now contains details of all overseas associations and clubs affiliated to the Royal Club and a section composed of reports from all curling countries. The *Annual* has been called 'the curler's Bible' and it is certainly required reading for all curlers and for those keen to start the game. The book

OPPOSITE The Duke of Edinburgh shares a joke with Major Allan Cameron and other office bearers after his election as Royal Club President at Falkirk in 1964.

also contains a verbatim report of the Annual Meeting of the Club, a spread of photographs and ... Buy a copy and read it for yourself!

Once started, the Royal Club took firm root. The number of affiliated Scottish clubs almost doubled in two years, more than trebled in three years and quadrupled to 116 clubs in five years. The first edition of the *Annual* – containing a recommendation to use Cairnie's foot-iron, a plea to equalise the weights and sizes of curling stones and a request to clubs 'to contribute such funds as they may think proper' in the first year of management – ran to only 300 copies.

Now, in addition to the 650 Scottish clubs affiliated to the Royal Club, many thousands of overseas clubs are affiliated through their national associations; and the *Annual* is circulated to each Scottish club, to the English and Welsh Curling Associations and to all overseas countries.

A member of the Royal Family was Patron of the Royal Club each year from the date of its inception until 1900. When Edward VII succeeded to the throne, he became the first King to be Patron, and, since then, the Patron has been The King or The Queen.

The Prince of Wales was elected President in 1925, the Duke of Edinburgh in 1964, and, through the years, distinguished Presidents, famous in many walks of Scottish life, have served the Royal Club. The post has become much more onerous in recent years, entailing a busy round of meetings, functions of all types and tours overseas. The reason is simple: the Royal Club has kept abreast with the tremendous upsurge in curling interest since the Second World War and, indeed, has led the way in many of the exciting moves brought about by the curling boom throughout the world.

Similarly, the members of the Royal Club Council give, willingly and at their own expense, more and more of their time and energy for love of the game and the fellowship it engenders. The wide, and ever-widening, range of curling activities demands additional sub-committees,* thought, imagination and hard work each year.

In 1966, the Royal Club purchased premises at 2, Coates Crescent, Edinburgh, and thus became the owners of headquarters for the first time. In his Presidential year (1981–82), Jim Whiteford initiated plans

* The Royal Club committees are: Finance, 'Annual', Grand Match, Competitions, Ice Rinks Liaison, Scottish Young Curlers, Coaching, Fabric, Historical, Tours and additional Tours committees are created to deal with specific tours.

for the reorganisation and redecoration of the headquarters. His successor, Sam McColm, held further meetings with planning authorities and Ian Turnbull, the 1983–84 President, supervised the final renovations – with Kenneth Gumley, Chairman of Gogar Park Curling Club and Estate Agent. Ian Turnbull selected the furniture and furnishings and celebrated the completion of the job with a drinks party for the Council. Meetings and receptions can now be held in a luxurious first-floor boardroom with the Royal Club's large Grand Match oil paintings on the walls and old stones and other relics in a corner alcove.

With the men properly accommodated, it was time to think of the ladies. For eleven years, Anna Smith had given outstanding service as Ladies Branch Secretary from her office in Falkirk and she gave notice of her retirement. In 1981, the President and President-Elect of the Ladies Branch had been added to the Royal Club Council – a large contingent of ladies turning up at the Royal Club Annual Meeting to ensure that the required motion was passed! Everything pointed to a closer relationship with the ladies!

Working offices on the ground floor had been provided with the headquarters reorganisation, and, after meetings with the Ladies Branch, it was agreed that Royal Club and Ladies Branch business would be coordinated under the same roof at 2, Coates Crescent. The progressive move coincided with the retiral of Royal Club Secretary Robin Welsh and Ladies Branch Secretary Anna Smith.

All Royal Club Secretaries have been based in Edinburgh and it is interesting to note that the present Secretary, Jim Aitken, is only the ninth man to hold the post since 1838 – a remarkable record when you consider that the first Secretary, James Skelton, held the position for two years and the second, George Ritchie, just one year more.*

---

*Three Secretaries served the Royal Club for a span of exactly 100 years – Alex. Cassels, W.S. (33 years from 1843 to 1876), A. Davidson Smith, C.A. (40 years from 1880 to 1920) and Andrew H. Hamilton, S.S.C. (27 years from 1920 to 1947). He was succeeded by his son, James, Secretary from 1947 to 1958 and Jim Aitken's predecessor, Robin Welsh, was Secretary from 1958 to 1984.

ROYAL CLUB RULES

Grateful acknowledgement is made to the Royal Caledonian Curling Club for permission to reprint the Rules of Curling.

SECTION A – THE RINK

1   The length of the playing area shall be 42·06 m. (46 yards). It is recommended that the width of the playing area shall be a minimum of 4·75 m. (5·20 yards) and that, where possible, the ice be continued a further 1·22 m. (4 feet) or more behind each Foot Line.

2   The length of the Rink from the Foot Line to the Tee shall, subject to the provisions of Rules 5 (Section A) and 1 and 2 (Section H) be 38·40 m. (42 yards).

3   The Tees shall be 34·75 m. (38 yards) apart and – with the Tees as centres – Circles having radii of 1·22 m. (4 feet) and 1·83 m. (6 feet) shall be drawn.

4   Additional inner Circles may also be drawn. Dividing lines may also be drawn or barriers placed between adjoining Rinks.

5   In alignment with the Tees, lines, to be called Centre Lines, may be drawn from the Tees to points 3·66 m. (4 yards) behind each Tee; at these points Foot Lines 45·72 cm. (18 inches) in length, shall be drawn at right angles, on which, at 7·62 cm. (3 inches) from the Centre Line, the inside edge of the Hack shall be placed. When Hack and Crampit are both being used in the same Rink, the Crampit shall be placed immediately behind the Hack except on outdoor ice when the heel of the Crampit will be placed on the Foot Line and the Hack, if used, placed immediately in front of the Crampit.

6   Other lines shall be drawn across the Rink at right angles to the Centre Lines as in the diagram, viz:—
   (a) A 'Hog Line', distant from each Tee, one-sixth part of the distance between the 'Foot Line' and the further Tee.
   (b) A 'Tee Line', across each outer Circle and through each Tee.

(c) A 'Back Line', behind and just touching the outside of each outer Circle.

7   All lines shall be as in the accompanying diagram which shall form part of these Rules subject to Rules 1 and 2 (Section H).

Diagram to be drawn on the Ice and referred to throughout the Rules as
'THE RINK'

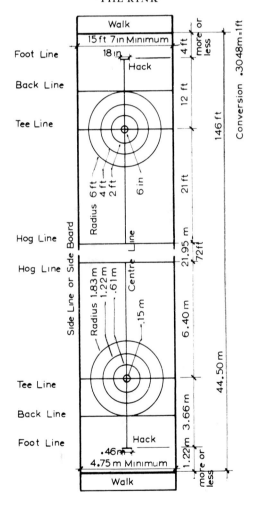

DIRECTIONS

1 The Tees shall be 34·75 m. (38 yards) apart.

2 Around each Tee draw circles having radii of 1·22 m. (4 feet) and 1·83 m. (6 feet).

3 In alignment with the Tees, centre lines may be drawn to points 3·66 m. (4 yards) behind each Tee.

4 Draw lines across the Rink at right angles to the central line, viz:—

   (a) The *Foot Line* – 45·72 cm. (18 inches) in length, 3·66 m. (4 yards) behind each Tee.

   (b) The *Back Line* – behind and just touching the outside of each outer circle.

   (c) The *Sweeping Line* – across each outer circle and through each Tee.

   (d) The *Hog Line* – distant from the Tee one-sixth part of the distance between the Foot Line and the farther Tee.

SECTION B – THE CURLING STONE

Shape, Weight and Dimensions of Stone

1 (a) Curling Stones shall be of a circular shape.

   (b) No Stone, including handle and bolt, shall be of greater weight than 19·96 kgs. (44 lbs.), or of greater circumference than 91·44 cms. (36 inches), or of less height than 11·43 cms. (4·5 inches).

Substitution, Reversing and Breaking of Stone

2 (a) No Stone shall be substituted for another except under Rules 2c (Section B) or 5 (Section C) after a game has started.

   (b) During a game, the sole of a Stone may be reversed, provided the player be ready to play when his turn comes.

   (c) Should a Stone be broken, the largest fragment shall be counted for that End, the player using another Stone, or another pair, thereafter.

Stone Rolling Over, Handle Quitting

3 (*a*) Any Stone which rolls over in its course, or comes to rest on its side or top, shall be removed from play immediately.

  (*b*) Should the handle quit the Stone in delivery, the player is entitled to replay the shot.

SECTION C – DELIVERY OF STONE

1 Left-handed players shall play from the Hack or Crampit placed on the right-hand side of the Centre Line and right-handed players shall play from the Hack or Crampit placed on the left-hand side of the Centre Line.

Delivery from Wrong Hack or Crampit

2 (*a*) A Stone delivered from the wrong Hack or Crampit should, if possible, be stopped in its progress and removed from the ice.

  (*b*) However, if the Stone so played has come to rest or struck another Stone, the played Stone shall be removed from play and the displaced Stone or Stones be placed as nearly as possible where they originally were, to the satisfaction of the opposing Skip; both Skips should agree upon the position, but failing agreement, the Umpire shall decide.

Release of Stone

3 (*a*) In the delivery of the Stone, the Stone shall be released from the hand before the Stone reaches the nearer Hog Line.

  (*b*) If the player fails to so release the Stone, it shall be removed from play immediately by the playing Rink. If the Stone has struck another Stone, the played Stone shall be removed from play by the playing Rink and any displaced Stone shall be placed as nearly as possible where it originally lay to the satisfaction of the opposing Skip.

Holding Stone, Returning for Another Delivery

4 No player may hold his Stone and return to the Hack or Crampit for another delivery if the Stone has reached the

nearer Tee Line, in which event the Stone shall be removed from play by the playing side.

Playing Wrong Stone
5   Should a player play a wrong Stone, a Stone belonging to his rink shall be put in its place.

Playing Out of Turn
6   (*a*) If a player should play out of turn in his Rink, the Stone so played should, if possible, be stopped in its progress and returned to the player.
   (*b*) Should the mistake not be discovered until after the Stone has come to rest or has struck another Stone, the End shall be continued, as if it had been played properly from the beginning, but the missed Stone shall be played by the player missing his turn as the last Stone for his side for that End.
   (*c*) Where the Skips agree that a Stone has been missed but are unable to agree as to which player missed his turn, the lead of the Rink which made the mistake, shall play the last Stone for his Rink at that End.
   (*d*) Where two Stones of a Rink are delivered in succession at the same End, the opposing Skip shall remove the Stone played by mistake, replace to his satisfaction any Stone displaced by the Stone played by mistake and continue the End as if the mistake had not occurred, and the player who delivered the Stone played by mistake shall redeliver it as the last Stone for his Rink at that End.
   (*e*) Where a player delivers three Stones at one End, the End shall be continued as if the mistake had not occurred and the fourth player of his Rink shall deliver one Stone only at that End.

SECTION D – THE GAME

1   All games shall be:
   (*a*) of a certain number of Ends; or
   (*b*) by time

as may be agreed on, or as fixed by the Umpire at the outset (see Section 1).

Composition of Rink, Order of Play, Disqualification, Accident

2 (*a*) Every Rink of players shall be composed of four-a-side, each player using two Stones, and playing each Stone alternately with his opponent.

    (*b*) Any Rink not having its full complement of four players shall be disqualified except in the case of illness or accident during the game, in which case the first and second players shall play three Stones each.

    (*c*) When, in a competition, owing to illness, accident or any other valid reason, a player is unable to play in any round, he may be replaced by another player as substitute, provided this substitute has not already taken part in that competition in any other Rink. A substitute may play in any position in any round but not higher than the position of the curler he is replacing. The Skip shall declare any substitute in the first round of a competition or the Rink in the first round will be understood to be the entered Rink. No Rink shall take into play more than two substitutes, in any game, match or competition. All substitutes must be eligible in terms of the rules of the competition.

    (*d*) The Rinks opposing each other shall settle by lot which side shall lead at the first End, after which the winners of the preceding End shall lead, and shall continue to do so if any extra Ends be played.

    (*e*) The rotation of play observed during the first End of a game shall not be changed.

    (*f*) The Royal Club may modify the above rules to meet with requirements of a specific competition.

Finishing of Games Played by Time

3 (*a*) When a game is being played by time, no End shall be started after the finishing time signal has been given, except where extra Ends are required.

    (*b*) If the time signal has not been given when the last Stone of the last played End has come to rest, then another End shall be played. (*Note:* the intention of this rule is that another End will not be started if, when the time signal is given, the last Stone or any Stone in play is still in motion.)

Stone Not Clearing Hog Line

4   A Stone which does not clear the farther Hog Line shall be a Hog and shall be removed from play immediately except where it has struck another Stone lying in play.

Stone Crossing Back Line

5   A Stone having crossed the Back Line, and lying clear of it, shall be removed from play immediately.

Stone Touching Sides of Rink

6   Any Stone which in its progress touches swept snow on either side of the Rink, or raised sides and divisions of Indoor Rinks, shall be removed from play. But, if a Stone crosses a dividing line drawn on the ice between Rinks or sheets and returns to finish within the Rink clear of the dividing line, it remains in play, provided it has not touched any object in the adjoining Rink. (See 10b.)

Running Stone Touched

7   (*a*) If, in sweeping or otherwise, a running Stone be touched by any of the side to which it belongs, or by their equipment, it shall be removed from play, but if by any of the opposing side it shall be placed where the Skip of the side to which it belongs shall direct, in a position as nearly as possible where he estimates it would have come to rest.

   (*b*) Should the position of any Stone be altered by such affected Stone, the Skip opposed to the side at fault shall have the right to replace it in a position as nearly as possible where he estimates it rested before its position was altered.

Displaced Stones

8   (*a*) If a Stone which would have affected the course of a running Stone is displaced by the playing team, the running Stone shall be removed from play and any affected Stone

shall be placed as nearly as possible where the opposing Skip considers it originally lay.

(b) If a Stone which would have affected the course of a running Stone is displaced by the opposing team, the Skip of the playing team shall replace any affected Stone as nearly as possible where he considers it originally lay or would have come to rest.

(c) If displaced in a way other than stated in (a) and (b) of this rule, both skips should agree on the positions to which the Stones are to be returned.

Measuring of Shots

9 (a) Skips may call for shots to be measured but not before the last Stone of the End being played has come to rest.

(b) Measurements shall be taken from the Tee to the nearest part of the Stone.

(c) If two or more Stones are so close to the Tee that it is impossible to use a measuring device to determine the scoring Stone, the End shall be scored as a blank End.

Scoring

10 (a) Games shall be decided by a majority of shots. A Rink shall score one shot for every Stone which is nearer the Tee than any Stone of the opposing Rink.

(b) Every Stone which is not clearly outside the Outer Circle shall be eligible to count, even if touching a dividing line.

(c) In the event of the scores being equal, play may be continued for one or more Ends, as may be agreed on, or as provided for by the conditions of the Game or Match, or as may be fixed by the Umpire.

(d) An End is decided when the Skips (or Acting Skips) in charge of the House at the time agree upon the score for that End.

SECTION E – THE SKIP: HIS AUTHORITY, PRIVILEGES, AND RESPONSIBILITIES

1 (a) The Skip has the exclusive direction of the game for his Rink.

(b) Subject to Rule 2 (e) Section D, he may play in any position in the game he pleases.

(c) When his turn to play comes, he shall select one of his players as Acting Skip.

(d) He may, however, return to the House for brief consultation.

(e) The Skip of the playing side has the choice of place, and he shall not be obstructed by the other Skip.

(f) Only Skips (or Acting Skips) are entitled to stand within or behind the Circle.

SECTION F – THE PLAYERS: THEIR DUTIES AND RESPONSIBILITIES

1　(a) Players, during the course of each End, shall be arranged along the sides, but well off the centre of the Rink.

(b) No player, except when sweeping according to Rule, shall go upon the centre of the Rink.

(c) No player shall cross the Rink when:
   (a) a player is about to play; or
   (b) in front of a Stone which is in motion.

(d) No player, other than the Skips and Acting Skips, shall stand within or behind the Circle while play is proceeding.

(e) Each player shall be ready to play immediately when his turn comes.

(f) A player shall not take more than a reasonable time to play.

(g) Where the Chief Umpire considers that play is unnecessarily slow, he shall notify the Skip of the team at fault that if their next stone is not delivered within 30 seconds from the time he gives a signal, he will order the stone to be removed from play immediately.

(h) No player shall use footwear or equipment which may damage the surface of the ice.

SECTION G – SWEEPING

1　The sweeping shall be under the direction of the Skips.

Method of Sweeping

2   The sweeping motion shall be from side to side across the entire running surface in front of the Stone and clearly finish to either side of the Stone.

Limitations of Sweeping

3   (a) The player's side may sweep the ice from Tee Line to Tee Line but any Stone set in motion by a played Stone may only be swept by the side to which it belongs, except behind the Tee Line, where both Skips have an equal right to sweep.

    (b) Only Skips (or Acting Skips) shall be allowed to sweep behind the Tee Line and shall not start to sweep an opposing Stone until the Stone reaches this Line.

SECTION H – ABNORMAL CONDITIONS

Shortening or Changing rink

1   (a) If from any change of weather after a game has begun, or from any other reasonable cause, one side should desire to shorten the Rink, or to change to another, and if the two Skips cannot agree, the Umpire shall, after seeing one End played, determine whether and by how much the Rink shall be shortened, or whether it shall be changed, and his decision shall be final.

    (b) In no case, however, shall the Rink be shortened to less than 29·26 m. (32 yards) from the Foot Line to the Tee.

    (c) Should there be no Umpire, or should he be otherwise engaged, the two Skips may call in any neutral curler to decide, and his powers shall be equal with those of an Umpire.

Stopping, Postponing a Game

2   (a) Should the Skips not agree, the Umpire shall, in the event of the ice appearing to him to be dangerous, stop the game.

    (b) He shall postpone the game, even if begun, when the state of the ice is, in his opinion, not fitted for testing the curling skill of the players.

(c) Except in very special circumstances, of which the Umpire shall be judge, the game or match shall not proceed, or be continued:

  (i) when a thaw has fairly set in;

  (ii) when snow is falling and likely to continue during the game or match; or

  (iii) if darkness comes on to prevent the played Stones being well seen by players at the other end of the Rink.

(d) In every case of such postponement to another day the game or match, when renewed, must be begun anew.

Cleaning Rink

3 (a) At the completion of any End, either of the Skips may call upon all the players to clean and sweep the entire Rink.

  (b) If objected to, this shall be subject to the approval of the Umpire.

Sweeping

4 When snow is falling or drifting, both Skips have equal right to clean and sweep the ice behind the Tee Line, except while a player is being directed by his Skip.

SECTION I – THE UMPIRE

1 An Umpire may be appointed in any game, match or competition. He shall be a member of the Royal Club and shall be acquainted with these Rules.

2 The duties and powers of an Umpire shall be the general superintendence of a game, match or competition, the power of settling disputed shots, enforcing these Rules and other questions that may arise in course of play.

3 He shall satisfy himself that all the players are duly qualified.

4 He may depute a neutral curler who is a member of the Royal Club and acquainted with the rules to act in his stead.

5 His decision in respect of all questions affecting the game, match or competition shall be final.

SECTION J – THE CHIEF UMPIRE

1   The Chief Umpire shall hear and determine any appeals from a decision of an Umpire and his decision is final.

2   Where the Royal Club has authorised the Chief Umpire to do so he may intervene in any game at any time and give such directions concerning the conduct of the game as he considers proper.

NOTE: The rules of the International Curling Federation, which are based on the Royal Club rules, varying only to cover international competitions, are listed in the chapter on the Federation.

The rules most commonly broken, through ignorance, are:
Section E. 1 (f): 'Only Skips (or Acting Skips) are entitled to stand within or behind the Circle'. Keep your place on the ice!
Section F. 1 (e): 'Each player shall be ready to play immediately when his turn comes'. Be prepared and don't waste time!
Section G. 3 (b): 'Only Skips (or Acting Skips) shall be allowed to sweep behind the Tee Line ...'. A skip often directs a player to strike a stone at the back of the house; when the shot is narrow, his sweepers frequently continue sweeping past the Tee Line to the back stone. This is wrong; the sweepers should stop sweeping at the Tee Line when the Skip takes over.

Curlers should also ensure that the hack is in the right position before delivery, expecially if a left-hander is on the rink.*

THE POINTS GAME

The Game of Points, the individual curling game at which the curler scores for himself alone, is viewed from different angles by curlers. Some say it is a poor game compared with the real thing and will have nothing to do with it. Further criticisms are that team spirit is lost, that it is wrong for curlers to play without a broom to aim at and that it can be a boring business to wait in a queue to play.

---

* 'In 1820, a left-handed player was admitted a Member of the Club, and although an excellent curler, a condition was made that he should forfeit one gill of the best whisky every time he forgot to shift the board.' From the Minutes of the Largs Curling Club. (Today, it is encumbent on the player about to play to shift the hack.)

But, viewed in its proper perspective as a form of practice, 'Points' can give valuable basic training to beginners. A well-known American curler, J. Nelson Brown of Detroit, added another dimension to the game when he wrote: 'The Points Game is the best tonic for the curler who has gotten too big for his britches and has the ill-conceived notion that he is far and above his fellow curlers.'

The argument that first-class curlers are not good at Points does not bear scrutiny. James Sellar, thought by many to have been, at his best, the top curler in Scotland, was also a master at Points. He compiled many scores in the forties and held the Merchiston Club's Points title from 1927 to 1955, a phenomenal run of 28 years.

In the 1960s, 50 became the target and James Scott (Falkirk), Jack Lamb (Lesmahagow), Tom McGregor (Lesmahagow), Willie McIntosh (Findo Gask), Robin Welsh (Watsonian) and Jimmy Stewart (Colmonell) broke that barrier, Jimmy Stewart's 57 at Ayr ice rink beating the previous 53 by James Scott. In 1984, Andrew McQuistin and Norman Brown of Stranraer, former world junior titleholders, gave notice that a new target of 60 points was within reach, Andrew scoring a 59 and Norman a 58.* (Some high scores quoted in record books are 'eclectic' scores, compiled by adding together the best scores at various points in more than one attempt in the Competition. These should be disregarded.)

The ladies, who have humbled their menfolk on many occasions in Scottish competitions, have also shown their prowess at Points. Betty Law, Abdie Ladies, for many years in the top rank of lady curlers in the country, has a 47 to her credit and there may be higher scores by ladies.

A normal procedure at presentation ceremonies in Scottish ice rinks is to ask the winning skip to tell the assembled company how he did it – and his normal reply is that he was clever enough to place three better players than himself in his rink! But it is every man for himself, and every woman for herself, at Points.

---

* James Sellar, the Manager, who was connected with Edinburgh ice rink for 47 years until 1966, recalled that from 1912 to 1936 no one scored 40 at Points. Then, as in the four-minute mile, the barrier was frequently broken once the elusive figure had been achieved.

7

The Grand Match

EASILY THE MOST spectacular Royal Club event – if it comes off – is the Grand Match between the North and South of Scotland on outside ice. The 'Nation's Bonspiel' is a magnificent sight with six hundred rinks of Scots curlers fighting it out in friendly rivalry on a major Scottish loch. The Match, the biggest bonspiel in the world, receives the privilege of precedence in the Constitution of the Royal Club: 'All matches should give place to the Grand Match'.

But 7 in (135 mm) of good black ice are needed for the Match and too often the planning undertaken by the dedicated members of the Grand Match Committee is in vain. Each year, the Match is planned, down to the last detail, by fifty keen curlers. It is a labour of love. Four venues are possible – Loch Leven in Kinross, the Lake of Menteith near Stirling, Lindores Loch near Newburgh in Fife and Stormont Loch at Blairgowrie – and the one which offers the best conditions under hard frost is chosen.

There have been three Grand Matches since the Second World War. The first two of these, on Loch Leven in 1959 and the Lake of Menteith in 1963, were organised with skill and his own brand of native wit by William Murray of Glenfarg,* who was Convener of the Grand Match Committee for seventeen years. Willie refused to listen to the post-war prophets of gloom who proclaimed that the Grand Match was a thing of the past – and his re-establishment of Grand Matches was his greatest curling achievement.

James Hamilton of Milnathort, an outstanding curler who represented Scotland in the Scotch Cup, became Convener when Willie died in 1973. Having been second-in-command for many years, he already knew every aspect of the big operation and all curlers who have enjoyed a Grand Match or who are looking forward to one are indebted to him. Each year he presides, with efficiency and humour and without fuss, at two official

---

* When a group of Scots travelled to Montreal in March 1968 to attend the World Championship for the Air Canada Silver Broom, they flew over Greenland. Looking down at the superb view of ice fields and glaciers, Royal Club President Lord Bruce, now the Earl of Elgin, remarked: 'What a paradise for Willie Murray!'

meetings – first to make the draw for the March, from entries which pour in from clubs in the early summer. At this meeting, a demarcation line dividing North and South is cunningly drawn; this 'sliding line' varies with the mass of entries each year but a happy compromise is always reached and three hundred teams are placed on the North side and three hundred on the South.

The second meeting is in November when James Hamilton presides over a full-scale meeting of the Grand Match Committee, at which all aspects of preparation are delegated to sub-committees which deal with ice marking, car parking, loudspeakers, safety arrangements, pipe bands, flagpoles, latrines and other items, including the provision of a helicopter to bring the Royal Club President to the Match in style and to take Press photographers for aerial pictures.

The organisation is in the nature of a military operation, in which a highly-proficient corps of men, led by James Hamilton, prepare for the final command from General Jack Frost. The 'Match-on' signal, relayed by the B.B.C. the night before the big day, is the climax to months of preparation. Only those involved in the preliminary work can fully appreciate the build-up necessary for the greatest bonspiel in the world.

> They come frae glens at John o'Groats,
> And south frae Gallowa',
> And eastward frae the Neuk o'Fife
> And west frae dark Loch Awe.
>
> The day has dawned, the tees are marked,
> The crampits pointed fairly,
> The cannon booms, the besoms wave,
> The combat opens rarely.
>
> Jas. Christie, Dollar, 1867.

A cannon is fired to start the Match* and 2,400 curlers from all parts of Scotland engage in a three-hour battle on rinks feverishly marked out by the Ice Committee on the previous two days. The marking is carried out by skilled men who use 'tee-ringers' – boards with nails inserted – and iron pencils to scrape circles and lines on the ice. These specialists must accomplish their task, to mark three hundred sheets of ice for play,

---

* A six-pounder gun, captured at the siege of Acre in 1779 and gifted to the Royal Club by Sir John Ogilvy in 1853, was used to start Grand Matches. Unfortunately, this gun has been lost. A cannon is now provided – and fired – by the Earl of Elgin.

in two days; if they take longer, a thaw may come and the chance of holding the Match could well be lost. For this reason, the annual entry of well over seven hundred rinks is reduced, as fairly as possible, to six hundred rinks.

There are various types of ice. Only two concern us – transparent or black ice; white, opaque or snow ice. Black ice, the type needed for a Grand Match, is the result of frost on a sheet of still water. Although actually colourless and transparent, it appears to be black or dark-green. This is by far the safest type of ice.

White ice is produced when snow is partially melted and then congealed on the ice or when snow falls while the first frost crystals are formed on the water. Being full of air bubbles, white ice is dangerous and not to be trusted.

The first Grand Match was held at Penicuik, a few miles from Edinburgh, on 15 January 1847. The Match, twelve-rinks-a-side, was played in the grounds of Sir George Clerk, Bt., who, in 1839, had become the second Royal Club President, and the painting of the occasion is owned by the present Baronet, Sir John Clerk of Penicuik House. A spectator in 1847 reported that 'the day throughout was one of unmingled pleasure, and, saving the absence of a barrel of exhilarating ale, which was unfortunately omitted among the items of preparation, there was nothing but universal satisfaction felt and expressed'.

The second Grand Match, on Linlithgow Loch in 1848, attracted a bigger entry – two hundred and eighty curlers competing compared with ninety-six at Penicuik the year before. The increase was moderate, predictable. But the Match at Linlithgow, the subject of a well-known painting by Charles Lees, R.S.A., had far-reaching consequences.

More than six thousand people came to watch and many of them congregated in large groups round the play. Among others, Sir John Ogilvy, later to become President of the Royal Club, left the Loch contemplating the dangers of similar support at future Grand Matches. Sir John's fears prompted him to propose, at the Royal Club Meeting in 1851, 'that the Royal Club should have a piece of ground which could be flooded for the purpose of affording a safe sheet of ice for the Grand Matches'.

Mrs Home Drummond Stirling Moray of Abercairney granted permission to use her land at Carsebreck – between Greenloaning and Blackford, near Gleneagles in Perthshire – at a rent of £15 for 63 acres from November to February each season. A plan was prepared by Alex Drummond, a Perth surveyor and engineer, and the construction work was

Watercolour sketch by Jemimah Wedderburn of the first Grand Match of the Royal Club, held at Penicuik House, Midlothian, on 15 January 1847. (The original painting is owned by Sir John Clerk, Bart.)

supervised by Sir James Falshaw. The area was flooded, and, from 1853 to 1935, twenty-five Grand Matches were played at Carsebreck. To begin with, the deepest point was 5 ft 9 in but, before the Second World War, the level of water had risen to 7 or 8 ft, and, because the pond was solid with weeds, it was described as a 'white elephant'.

The last Match there, on 24 December 1935 (on 5 in of ice, the safety minimum at that time) was the biggest ever held – 2,576 curlers enjoying the experience despite the fact that a sudden thaw ruined the final hour, rain started to fall and the players finished 'up to the fetlocks in water'!

One of the rinks of the winning club in 1935, Monzievaird and

(OVERLEAF) 'Grand Match on Linlithgow Loch' (1848) by Charles Lees, R.S.A. This massive oil painting of the second Grand Match, which contains portraits of well-known figures of the period, hangs in the Royal Club offices in Edinburgh.

Strowan, won by 46 shots to 2. Other runaway victories were 44–5, 39–10, 36–6, 34–3 and 30–2. One rink, which shall remain nameless, was 'soutered' – the name taken from an invincible team of Lochmaben shoe-makers, or souters, at the end of the eighteenth century – 23–0. On the same ice, there were two drawn games, 21–21 and 6–6.

Such wide scoring variations are common at Grand Matches which have also produced the three most sensational results in the long history of the game. Donald Fisher, Dunkeld, in 1855, and John Laurie, Bute, in 1867, scored only one shot each but won their games; and, in 1853, Alexander Cunningham of the Currie Club recorded a 71–1 victory. The remarks of his wretched opponents are not recorded!

The only other outdoor venue was Lochwinnoch (1850 and 1864), and, in all, thirty-eight Grand Matches have been played since 1847, thirty-three of them on outside ice, of which one was played in November, nine were played in December, sixteen in January and seven in February. The other five Matches were held indoors in the Edinburgh and Glasgow Ice Rinks, in order to defeat the vagaries of Jack Frost, and there have been recent suggestions to repeat the experiment. However well intentioned, such proposals miss the whole point of the operation and we hope they will not be pursued. A Grand Match in an ice rink is, surely, a contra-diction in terms.

The winter of 1978–79 was one of the most severe in recent times, to be compared with the winters of 1946–47, 1958–59 and 1962–63, and hopes were high that the Grand Match would be held in January, 1979. The required ice thickness was achieved but heavy snow rutted the ice surfaces and it seemed that the Match, last held sixteen years before, would again be deferred. But a short thaw followed by prolonged frost galvanised James Hamilton and his Committee into action. James tele-phoned the Royal Club and threw the staff in Edinburgh into confusion.

(OPPOSITE, ABOVE) Some of the equipment used in preparing for a Grand Match. On right, Willie Murray, former Convener of the Grand Match Committee, holds an axe for breaking the ice and a stick for measuring the ice thickness. Beside him, Tom Stark, who supervised the ice marking for many years, holds a tee-ringer for cutting circles. Snow scrapers are also shown. The present Grand Match Convener, James Hamilton, a well-known curler and personality, presides over a fifty-strong Committee which makes arrangements at four possible sites.

(BELOW) At the Lake of Menteith in 1979, the Earl of Elgin prepares to fire the cannon which signals the start and finish of the Grand Match.

(OVERLEAF) This aerial photograph shows about two-thirds of the 2,500 curlers engaged in the Grand Match at the Lake of Menteith on 7 February 1979 – with the old kirk and headquarters hotel in the foreground.

Normal business was stopped as the B.B.C., the Police, the Royal Automobile Club, the Press and the insurance company were contacted, late printing organised and warning postcards sent to all competing skips. A telegram was sent to Her Majesty The Queen, Patron of the Royal Club. The office telephone rang continuously for three days.

The Match was called for 7 February. Bill Meyer, Secretary of the 1979 Canadian touring team who had been visiting relatives in England after the tour, travelled north for the occasion and joined Captain Jack Anderson, Royal Club President, and Secretary Robin Welsh at the Lake Hotel, Port of Menteith. Between radio interviews and frequent telephone interruptions, the three men completed the numbering of cards – for showing rink numbers on wooden blocks on the ice. (Bill Meyer won his game on Rink 80 the following day, playing with Ronald Grant, Sandy Smith – and Don Cowen and Bob Woodhouse from Wales, who alternated while Don made a film of the Match.)

Jack Anderson, Bill Meyer and the Secretary stayed the night at Coldon, home of Sandy and Mona Callander, long-time supporters of the Match, and, at 7.30 the next morning, the view over the Lake from the bedroom window swept away the frustrations of the previous sixteen years. As the sun rose in a clear blue sky, the Lake of Menteith shone brightly in a ringing frost. All was right with the world.

Under James Hamilton's guidance, every possible chance of holding the Match is explored – to make the possibility, under continuing frost, a probability, eventually a reality. The Convener's diary of 'Operation Grand Match 1979' proves the point:

January 28:	Lake of Menteith – 5 in of ice and surface good. Other venues – depth good, surface rough.
January 29:	4 in of snow at Lake. 5 in Stormont Loch and Lindores Loch and 2 in Loch Leven.
January 31:	Rain – melted all snow – followed by hard frost at Lake.
February 1:	Top layer frozen at Lake but not fused with ice below.
February 2:	Continuing frost. Top layer now fused with bottom layer. Asked Secretary to issue warning postcards. Match provisionally planned for 7th. $6\frac{1}{4}$ in of good ice. Forecast from Pitreavie 'frost continuing'. Arranged police coverage, car parking, medical attendance.
February 4:	Took marking equipment from Loch Leven to Lake of Menteith.
February 5:	Commenced marking with two squads (25 in each) led

by Willie Wilson and Dave Arnott. Sent each squad in opposite directions from front of hotel.

February 6: Examined rinks already marked out and decided to cut out 21 because of condition of ice. Continued marking to a total of 330 rinks. 'Match on' signal given on B.B.C. radio. A busy day for Jack Paterson, Convener of parking and toilets.

February 7: Arrived at Lake 9 a.m. Official measurement – $8\frac{1}{4}$ in of ice. Loudspeaker equipment, safety equipment, ropes, ladders and life-belts put out. Maps showing layout of rinks placed at entry points. Numbered cards placed on blocks. Flags raised and final arrangements for opening ceremony made.

Competitors started arriving at 10 a.m. and parking arrangements went smoothly, also the checking in of the rinks. At 11 a.m. the helicopter carrying the President arrived and toured the Lake – he had to repeat this tour for the benefit of the media!

The opening ceremony began with speeches, the Queen's telegram, and music from six pipers from the Queen Victoria School, Dunblane, ending with the Earl of Elgin firing the cannon to signal the commencement of the Grand Match.

It was a perfect day, the sun shining from start to finish and the curling interrupted only by an occasional very low flight by the helicopter and breaks for refreshments. Someone tried to work out the weight carried by the ice on the great day but the exercise failed because no-one could measure the weight of the provisions. The number of sheets of ice used – 308.

The cannon signalled the end of the Match and the curlers gathered to share final drinks and to chat with all around them and slowly, very slowly, the ice cleared and in orderly fashion the crowds wended their way home. The end of a memorable occasion.

The day after: Willie Wilson, in charge of tidying up the Lake, reports that four men collected two whisky bottles, one broken glass and two sacks of rubbish. He considers that curlers should be congratulated on their tidiness. The car park was in a similar tidy condition.

RESULTS

North beat South by 3,942 shots to 3,143.

Challenge Trophy (club on the winning side with highest average majority of shots per rink): Edzell Club. Four badges (highest-up rink) to Dave Hood's rink.

Second Trophy: Hercules Club. Four badges (highest-up rink) to Mike Thomson's rink.

Medal (second highest club on losing side): Lundin and Montrave Club.

First English Province Irving Cup (highest-up ladies' rink): Abdie Ladies (who scored one more end than Orwell Ladies).

Strathcona Medal (rinks skipped by President and President-Elect): Shared by Jack Anderson and Tom Dickson who finished 'peels'.

All Scots curlers should play in a Grand Match and more should respond to James Hamilton's call to come in something tartan, if only a ribbon round the balmoral. In *The Complete Curler* (1914), Gordon Grant says of the Match: 'there is nothing to equal it in the wide world'. It is played for three hours, exactly as at Penicuik in 1847. An essentially Scottish experience, the Grand Match is a national institution.

8

Curling in Canada

FAMOUS AS OVERSEAS settlers, Scotsmen have made 'their ain game' everybody's game and their missionary activities in many lands have built curling into an international sport. The seeds sown by Scots have taken firm root and we devote two chapters to 'potted' histories of curling around the world.

The game was introduced in Canada by early Scottish fur traders and by soldiers in Fraser's Highlanders after the Siege of Quebec in the latter part of the 18th century. Wearying for their national game, and finding ideal conditions in the hard Canadian winters, the soldiers melted down cannon balls and curled on the St Lawrence River.

Because of a shortage of suitable stones – the local granite proved to be too brittle, causing endless breakage on the rink – the curlers in Quebec resorted to cast-iron stones, with iron or brass handles, weighing between 46 lb and 65 lb and these 'irons' became the vogue in Eastern Canada and passed from the competitive scene only thirty years ago.*

The Royal Montreal Curling Club, not only the first curling club in Canada but the first sporting club of any kind on the North American Continent, was founded in 1807 'by natives of Scotland who wished to introduce their favourite game to the St Lawrence'. Membership was confined to twenty 'sporting merchants' and one of the original rules was that, after play on Wednesday every fortnight, 'the Club shall meet at Gillis's at four o'clock and dine on salt beef and greens. The losing party of the day shall pay for a bowl of whisky toddy, to be placed in the middle of the table for those who may chuse it'.†

The booklet, *One Hundred and Fifty Years of the Fergus Curling Club* (1984) gives an indication of the primitive nature of early curling stones

---

* Irons were originally developed because of the difficulties and delays in procuring stones from Scotland in the days of sailing ships. Iron players concentrated on the drawing game.

† The Royal Montreal Club's 150th celebrations in 1957 were attended by 700 curlers, including Royal Club President Sir John Gilmour. The guest of honour was the Governor-General of Canada, the Rt Hon Vincent Massey. The Duke of Edinburgh is a life member and the winners of the Invitation Competition received commemorative Duke of Edinburgh badges.

The only four-time winners of the World Championship – and the Canadian Champion-ship – the famous Richardson rink from Saskatchewan, pictured at the start of their glittering career. From *left to right*, Wes, Sam, Arnold and Ernie Richardson (skip). Mel Perry took the place of Wes in the rink's last triumph.

in Ontario. Blacksmiths cut blocks from the maple tree, turned them on lathes and girded them with bands of iron before inserting rough handles. Curling was entirely localised in the early settlements. There were no railways, the roads were rough trails. Travel by sleigh or wagon through snow, mud and rivers was a hazardous adventure.

In 1835, the first match between clubs in different parts of the country was played between Quebec and Montreal at Three Rivers. Quebec won 31-23 and the losers paid for the dinner, after which the Montreal Secre-tary reported: 'As this is the first, so I hope it will be the last time that ever we shall hear of champagne being exhibited at a bonspiel dinner'. Colonel Dyde answered diplomatically that there was no good, not even tolerable, whisky to be had in Three Rivers!

The Canadian Branch of the Royal Caledonian Curling Club was founded on 27 March 1852, with headquarters in Montreal, with the object of 'promoting the game of curling in Canada and fraternising with neighbouring curling associations loyal to the Royal Caledonian Curling Club'. The Branch made rules about the weight of irons – setting a maximum of 70 lb (31·8 kg) in 1888, and, in 1893, a maximum of 64 lb (29 kg) and a minimum of 56 lb (25·4 kg) – and about the number of ends to be played in important matches – twenty-four, reduced to twenty in 1893 and twelve in 1950. The famous Gordon Medal, presented by Robert Gordon, Patron of the Grand National Curling Club of America for play between the Branch and U.S. rinks, was started in 1884 and the centenary was celebrated in style last year with a match of thirty rinks a side. In 1873, the membership of the Branch was thirty-nine clubs of which six were iron-playing in the Province of Quebec and the Ottawa Valley in Ontario while the remainder were stone-playing clubs in Ontario.*

With the growth of curling in Ontario and because of the distance from Montreal, it was natural that the majority should wish for more control of their own affairs. In 1874, a Committee framed a petition for the establishment of the Ontario Branch of the Royal Club. The petition was granted in Edinburgh in November, and, on 22 December 1874, the new Ontario Branch was ratified.† In 1892, the title was changed to the Ontario Curling Association.

In the latter part of the 19th century, curling spread rapidly in the Western Provinces and Winnipeg became a major centre of Canadian curling. In 1876, Winnipeg curlers subscribed to build their own ice rink – after the opening game, the losers gave a barrel of oatmeal to the local hospital – and in the 1880s the creation of other clubs encouraged the launching of the first Manitoba Bonspiel (1884). The Manitoba Branch of the Royal Club was formed in 1888 and this became the Manitoba Curling Association in 1908.

The first curling club in Alberta was founded in Edmonton in 1888 and affiliated to the Manitoba Branch but curlers in Alberta sought

---

*W.E. Findlay, the Branch Secretary, reported in 1913 that, during the Canadian season (15 December to 15 March), stones were used in Nova Scotia and New Brunswick, in Central and Western Ontario and in the Western Provinces – and that, in Quebec and Eastern Ontario, irons weighing between 58 lb (26·3 kg) and 61 lb (27·7 kg) were used. The ladies played with smaller irons, weighing 30 lb (13·6 kg).

†Bill Meyer, famous Canadian tourist who has many friends in Scotland, was President of the Ontario Curling Association in its centenary year (1974).

independence in 1904 and withdrew from the Manitoba authority to form the Alberta Branch of the Royal Club in Calgary.

In 1851, the Royal Club had granted the status of a Branch to the Halifax Club (instituted in 1824) and the Nova Scotia Branch, with three member clubs, was established in 1852. The Branch fell into abeyance in the 1860s and was re-established in 1904. Nova Scotia has provided three outstanding names connected with Scottish-Canadian Tours – Lieutenant Governor Duncan Cameron Fraser and Judge George Patterson, who captained the first two Canadian teams in Scotland (1909 and 1921), and Charlie Clarke, long-time Secretary of the Branch, who captained the 1979 team in Scotland and organised the 1983 Scottish Tour in Canada.

Curling began in Prince Edward Island in 1887, and, in 1889, the New Caledonian Club of Pictou, Nova Scotia, came to Charlottetown – on the ice-breaker *S.S. Stanley* – to play a friendly match. This was the first visit by an outside club to the Province. A Curling Club House was opened in Charlottetown in 1913 and this was superseded by a new well-appointed ice rink in 1938. The Prince Edward Island Curling Association was formed in 1934.

Stones from Winnipeg were sent to British Columbia in 1895 and the

Hec Gervais (*left*), for long a formidable force and personality at the top level of the game, with his winning Alberta rink in the 1961 Scotch Cup – Ray Werner, Vic Raymer and Wally Ursuliak.

Kaslo Club was started with sixteen members. The club joined other new clubs in Nelson, Sandon and Golden to form the Kootenay Curling Association in Rossland in 1898, the inaugural meeting being called during the first bonspiel held in British Columbia. At the 1906 Annual Meeting, the name was changed to the British Columbia Curling Association of the R.C.C.C. The first club in Vancouver was formed in 1912. The Selkirk Curling Association, including clubs in Eastern British Columbia, was instituted in 1925.

The Quebec Curlers' Bonspiel was first organised in 1902 to coincide with the visit of curlers from the Thistle Club, St John, New Brunswick. At that time there were two curling clubs in Quebec City with five sheets of ice. The St John curlers brought stones with them as only irons were available in Quebec. The 1920 Bonspiel was significant because the organisers decided to include granite, in addition to iron, events in honour of an entry from the Brae Burn Club of Boston. In 1921, the Quebec Club, one of the oldest curling clubs in Canada, celebrated its centenary at the Bonspiel which was attended by many new clubs, including an entry from Detroit. This established the Quebec Bonspiel as a major competition, attracting champion rinks from Western Canada. The event became known as the Quebec International Bonspiel and, with the demise of iron play, Quebec became the principal curling centre in Eastern Canada. The Quebec Curlers Bonspiel Association became the Province of Quebec Association.

Organised curling in Saskatchewan, the most curling-conscious of Canadian Provinces, began with the Assiniboia Branch of the R.C.C.C. in 1904, the title changing to Saskatchewan Curling Association in 1905. Prior to establishing their own authority, Saskatchewan curlers had been under the jurisdiction of the Manitoba and North West Territories Branch of the R.C.C.C. It is believed that, in the latter part of the 19th century, members of the North West Mounted Police spread the game in the far-flung areas of Saskatchewan. In the fiftieth year of the Association (1954), 511 clubs were affiliated, representing 19,000 curlers.

Regina, where a bonspiel was held in 1889 and where the meeting to form an Association was held, is internationally famous in modern curling as the site of two World Championships, in 1973 and 1983. At both highly-successful events, Laurie Artiss, a Canadian representative to the International Curling Federation, was the Organising Chairman. He reported that there had been eight hundred visitors in 1973 and over three thousand in 1983 – spectacular proof of the growth of the Air Canada Silver Broom.

Lyall Dagg's World Championship-winning team which beat Scotland's Alex Torrance at an extra end in the Scotch Cup final in Calgary in 1964 – from *left to right*, Barry Naimark, Fred Britton, Leo Hebert and Lyall Dagg.

Ron Northcott's rink receives the Scotch Cup from Sir Ronald Cumming, Chairman, The Scotch Whisky Association, at Vancouver in 1966 – from *left to right*, Ron Northcott, George Fink, Bernie Sparkes and Fred Storey.

The small Crow's Nest Pass Curling Association, composed of clubs ranging from Alberta to British Columbia, was founded in 1912. In Eastern Canada in the same year, the tour by Scottish curlers acted as a catalyst in the spread of the game. A member of the Scottish team, Andrew Blair, offered to donate a silver trophy if the New Brunswick curlers formed a Branch. Expatriate Scots in the membership acted swiftly and within a year the New Brunswick Branch of the Royal Club was instituted and the trophy accepted! Appropriately, curlers from New Brunswick have been prominent members of Canadian touring teams in Scotland.

The title, Northern Ontario Curling Association, succeeded the Northern Ontario International Curling Association which had been formed in 1905 for the purpose of staging bonspiels which included American rinks. Some curlers from the northern Temiskaming district also competed but many found the distances to be travelled too great and this led to the formation of the Temiskaming and Northern Ontario Curling Association after a successful bonspiel in a steel-framed six-sheet ice rink at New

Liskeard in 1931. The large Province of Ontario was further divided administratively with the creation of the Northwestern Ontario Association in 1949.

As with the early growth of the game is Scotland, when clubs, areas and associations outgrew the excitement of establishment and felt the need for national cohesion and guidance, so the same feeling grew in Canada. The difference was geographical. In Scotland, representative meetings could be arranged with relative ease but in the vast areas of Canada contact was difficult and progress slow. There was correspondence between curlers in Toronto and the Eastern Provinces in 1883 but responses were 'neither numerous nor encouraging'. In 1890, the Canadian Branch of the Royal Club initiated moves to consider a nation-wide organisation but no firm proposals were made.

The first positive step towards the establishment of a national Association was taken by the New Brunswick Branch of the Royal Club in 1927 when the Branch sent a letter to the other Canadian Associations suggesting the formation of a Dominion Curling Association. The next significant move was made by Ontario Curling Association office-bearers who called a meeting in the Granite Club, Toronto, in 1933 when it was agreed to send proposals to the various Associations and Branches with

The Don Duguid rink, twice World champions (1970 and 1971) – *left to right*, Bryan Wood, Rod Hunter, Don Duguid and Jim Pettapiece.

a request that the proposals be discussed at annual meetings and delegates appointed to attend a meeting in Toronto the following year.

At the 1934 meeting, a Committee composed of John T. Haig (representing the Western Associations), E.P. Mackay (the Maritime Associations), P.H. Walker (the Canadian Branch) and E.P. Atkinson (Ontario) was elected with E.P. Atkinson as Chairman and it was agreed that the Committee would present a draft constitution at the same venue a year later.

At the final meeting in the Granite Club, Toronto, on 6 March 1935, E.P. Atkinson read the Committee's report which contained the plea: 'It is not fair to ask any one Association to make a decision of national importance and we submit, having made a general and careful survey, that the curlers throughout this country will welcome an organisation which has authority to deal with curling questions of importance to the whole Dominion.' The recommendations were adopted and John T. Haig, K.C. (Winnipeg), was appointed first President of the Dominion Curling Association with E.P. Atkinson (Toronto) as Honorary Secretary-Treasurer.

The following Branches and Associations were founder members of the national body: Alberta Branch, R.C.C.C.; Alberta Curling Association; Crow's Nest Pass Curling Association; Manitoba Curling Association; New Brunswick Branch, R.C.C.C.; Northern Ontario Curling Association; Ontario Curling Association; Saskatchewan Curling Association; Temiskaming and Northern Ontario Curling Association. Other Associations joined later – Prince Edward Island and British Columbia (1936), Selkirk (1939), Quebec Bonspiel (1943) and Nova Scotia Branch, R.C.C.C. (1944).

When the national Association was formed in 1935, eight hundred clubs were affiliated. Twenty-one years later, the number of clubs had doubled and the number of affiliated curlers had increased five-fold. The Dominion Curling Association became the Canadian Curling Association in 1967.

The growth of the game and the rearrangement of boundaries and responsibilities after the Second World War caused further Provincial changes. The Canadian Curling Association records show that the Northwestern Quebec Association was affiliated in 1947; that the Newfoundland and Northwest Territories Associations were affiliated in 1948; that the Crow's Nest Pass Association joined with the Peace River District and British Columbia Block Associations in 1950, becoming the Peace Association; that the Selkirk Association disappeared in 1955; that the

The 1972 Canadian and World champions with Yves Pratte, Chief Executive Officer, Air Canada, at Garmisch-Partenkirchen - *left to right*, Pat Hailley, John Hanesiak, Dave Romano and Orest Meleschuk (skip). The Canadians won after a controversial last end at which the U.S. skip, Bob LaBonte, who thought he had won, jumped and fell on the ice, moving a Canadian stone. The eventual measure forced an extra end and Meleschuk played a winning draw round guards.

Yukon Association joined in 1958; that, after the formation of the Pacific Coast Association in 1961, the British Columbia Association became the British Columbia Interior Association in 1979; that, later in the 'sixties, Northern and Southern Alberta Associations replaced the Alberta Branch, R.C.C.C., and the Alberta Association.

Eighteen Provincial Associations are affiliated to the Canadian Curling Association. The other two members, the Canadian Branch and Nova Scotia, have retained their titles as Branches of the Royal Club.

In every Canadian Province, curling is a main topic of sporting conversation. The fanatical interest in the game was perfectly illustrated at the 1978 World Championship for the Air Canada Silver Broom in Winnipeg, with an attendance of over 102,000 spectators over the week. A play-off game, Norway *v* Scotland, was needed to determine the last semi-final place, and, despite the fact that a Canadian rink was not involved, over 7,000 supporters turned up for the extra game.

The Canadian Branch of the Royal Club launched organised Canadian curling in 1852 but Western Canada, with its highly-competitive urge, has contributed most to the Canadian curling boom of the last fifty years. In the old days it was said that, when a Canadian outpost was established, the top building priorities were a church and a curling rink. It is estimated that there are now one million curlers in Canada which is easily the biggest curling country.

The Canadian Championship for the Macdonald Brier Tankard, sponsored by the Macdonald Tobacco Company, was started in 1927. It did not create large spectator interest until the mid 'thirties but since then the event has become one of the wonders of the curling world. The event is now the Labatt Brier, Labatt Breweries having assumed sponsorship in 1980. Apart from its excitement as a spectacle and its promotional value, the 'Brier' brought a new look to Canadian curling. The game suddenly became a spectator sport in colourful arenas with amenities for supporters. In addition, the new concept inspired curlers to go home and rebuild or upgrade their own ice rinks and provide better facilities, lighting and colour.*

* The Macdonald Tobacco Company, which withdrew from the Canadian Championship sponsorship after fifty years of service – the last Macdonald Brier being held in the national capital, Ottawa, in 1979 – chartered a train exclusively for curlers in Montreal in 1952. On the journey to the 'Brier', pullman carriages were added at various centres. The curlers were entertained to a complimentary dinner and retired to luxurious sleeping cars – to awake the next morning in Winnipeg.

The World champions at Moncton in 1980. From *left to right*, Ron Mills, Rick Folk (skip), Claude Taylor (President, Air Canada), Tom Wilson and Jim Wilson.

Al Hackner, winning World Championship skip at Garmisch-Partenkirchen in 1982, exhorts his sweepers – Bob Nicol, Bruce Kennedy and Rick Lang – to greater efforts.

In addition to the 'Brier', the Canadian Curling Association runs three other national championships – the Men's Junior (started in 1950), the Mixed (in 1964) and the Men's Senior (in 1965). The Canadian Ladies' Curling Association runs the national Ladies' Championship and national junior and senior competitions.

In 1968, when the Dominion Curling Association became the Canadian Curling Association, Canada's *Financial Post* reported that the sale of curling equipment, including stones, brooms, shoes, sweaters, trophies and even ice scrapers, yielded an annual total of six million dollars. The importance of curling in Canada has been acknowledged by the issue of curling postage stamps.

It was natural that Canada, with its curling population and fierce competitive play, should dominate early world championship play and it remains true that for every top-class team provided by other curling countries Canada could provide half a dozen teams of equal quality.

Canada's strength-in-depth is the dominant force in world curling. But, having stressed this dominance, it is clear that, while the Canadian game still reigns supreme, it is now being challenged by European countries. The 1984 Norway *v* Switzerland World Championship final is a case in point.

The modern curling boom is now in Europe where the Norwegians, Swedes and Swiss in particular, having adopted the Canadian game, are employing it with devastating effect; where Scotland has emerged as victor and major contender in the Uniroyal World Junior Championship; and where new countries like Finland and Luxembourg are joining the curling colours. In this context it must be said that Canadian instructional clinics have contributed largely to the new-found confidence in Scandinavia and Continental Europe.

We end with one criticism of the greatest curling country on earth. We know that the vast Canadian continent with its widely-spread communities presents special rules problems but we wish that the Canadian rule-makers would try to bring their rules more into line with those of the International Curling Federation, of which Canada is a founder member, the Constitution of which lists as one of its Objects: 'To work towards agreement upon universally recognised rules of the game of curling.'

Claude Taylor presents the Silver Broom to the 1983 World champions in Regina - *left to right*, Neil Harrison, John Kawaja, Paul Savage and Ed Werenich (skip).

9

Curling Around the World

UNITED STATES OF AMERICA

AT THE END of the 18th century, many Scottish artisans settled in the United States and, during hard winters, introduced curling in widely-spread areas. In the wilds of Michigan, eight hardy Scots formed the Orchard Lake Club in 1832, the first recorded curling club in America. As they had no curling stones, they started with hickory blocks. The New England Club of Boston began before 1839 and other pioneering clubs were Milwaukee (1845), Portage (1850) and New York Caledonian (1854).

An advertisement in the *Scottish American Journal* called a meeting of delegates from United States clubs - in the Caledonian Club rooms in Sullivan Street, New York - on 26 June 1867, and the Grand National Curling Club of America was established. David Bell of Buffalo, originally a Scot from Dumfries, was elected President and presented the first trophy, the Bell Silver Quoit Medal - a novel choice because the medal was for a game of quoits 'played exclusively on the natural sod'.

The first curling medal was presented by the first Patron, Robert Gordon of New York City, who also hailed from Dumfries. A business-man of repute, he was benefactor as well as Patron from 1867 to 1884, when another Scot, Alexander Mitchell from Aberdeenshire, succeeded him. As President of the Chicago, Milwaukee and St Paul Railway, Alex Mitchell provided a special train for delegates at the nineteenth Annual Meeting of the Grand National in Milwaukee in 1885 for an excursion 'to the dells of the Wisconsin River'.

Robert Gordon's final act as Patron in 1884 was to donate the famous Gordon International Medal for competition between the United States and Canada. The first match was played with two rinks a side in 1884 - in flour sheds in Montreal. (See Section on Canada.)

All early bonspiels and matches were played on ponds or in open sheds. The Boston Club made arrangements with the Boston Arena, a skating rink, around 1910 for three sheets of ice for curling and this is thought to have been the first indoor curling in America, though exhibition games were played in covered rinks in Brooklyn, New York, before

Hughston McBain of McBain presents the U.S. National Championship trophy to the first winners in Chicago in 1957 – Harold Lauber (skip), Matt Brklich, Louis Lauber and Pete Beasy from Hibbing, Minnesota.

Bud Somerville and his team scored America's first World Championship victory at Perth in 1965. The rink receives the Scotch Cup from Sir Ronald Cumming – *left to right*, Bill Strum, Bud Somerville, Al Gagne and Tom Wright. Bud also won the world title in Berne in 1974.

Bud Somerville, America's best-known curler.

the turn of the century. The Country Club, Brookline, built a four-sheet indoor rink in old racing stables in their club grounds; it was opened in December, 1920, and this was the first ice rink in America used solely for curling.

The Grand National Curling Club celebrated its centenary in 1967 under the Presidency of Edward Childs, a far-travelled and popular figure, and published a commemorative booklet containing a fascinating account of the history of American curling. The Grand National is 118 years old and still going strong; President Kenneth Cooper and his office-bearers were in great heart when we met them during the 1984 Air Canada Silver Broom in Duluth.

In March, 1957, the first United States National Men's Curling Championship was held in the Chicago Stadium. The event was sponsored by Marshall Field and Company, the Chairman of which, Hughston McBain of McBain, threw the first stone. The competition was televised and a huge American audience saw the game for the first time. Harold Lauber and his rink from the Hibbing Club, Minnesota, became the first national champions.

The Championship Chairman was Walter Rhodes of Madison, Wisconsin, a Past-President of the Midwest Curling Association which served the midwest of America from 1945 to 1964 – the Association in co-operation with the Grand National Curling of America laid plans for the first official tour by a Scottish team in 1955. But, after the Second World War, increasing demands for national guidance led to the establishment of the United States Men's Curling Association in 1958 with Walter Selck as President and Walter Rhodes as Vice-President. In the 1962–63 season, Ray Meddaugh, Convener of the *Annual* Committee, prepared the first Association *Annual*, in which President Ralph Trieschmann re-

Bruce Roberts (top left) and his U.S. rink – Joe Roberts, Gary Kleffman and Jerry Scott – after winning the 1976 world title in Duluth. In front are the Scottish runners-up, Bill Muirhead (skip), Derek Scott, Len Dudman and Roy Sinclair.

ported that the membership had grown to over one hundred clubs. During his Presidential years (1964 to 1966), Ray Meddaugh masterminded the production of a film, *The Sport of Curling*, and the publication of a book, *How to start a Curling Club*. A further crucial factor in the spread of the game in America was the dramatic victory by Bud Somerville and his team – Bill Strum, Al Gagne and Tom Wright – in the 1965 Scotch Cup in Perth.*

The 1967–68 President, Joseph LeVine, reported: 'The steady growth of curling in the United States continues. Every State on the northern border of our country now has curling, from Maine to Washington (3987 miles). Add 500 miles to Alaska – we're really spread out! Of course, we have curling in the Central States too, Nebraska, Colorado, California, Illinois, for instance. With our National Championship Playdown limited to twelve rinks, it is obvious that we must have area playdowns among our twenty-three curling States. Bonspiel activity is tremendous. If you are an ardent Spieler, you can compete in a different one every week-end, and mixed bonspiels are increasing fast.'

Glenn Harris, who, as editor of *The North American Curling News*, was an important contributor to the growth of the game in the United States, wrote in 1960: 'Vast changes have come. Prior to the birth of the *News* in 1944–45, refrigeration for curling ice was practically unknown. Matched stones had hardly been thought of. In a great section of the country, curling clubs but a short distance apart were not aware that others existed'. Glenn Harris retired in 1960 and another active and articulate curler, L.T. 'Tink' Kreutzig, occupied the editorial chair until 1979 when Mr and Mrs Frank Rhyme of Portage took over as editors and publishers.

Tink Kreutzig, President of the National Association in 1976 and Vice-President of the International Curling Federation from 1979 to 1981, had been associated with international curling since the early days of the Scotch Cup and was a member of the Advisory Committee of the Uniroyal World Junior Championship. In recognition of his services to international junior curling, he received the 1983 Claude Allard Award from Uniroyal. A carefree and wayward golfer, Tink caused a stir on one memorable occasion when, with his opening drive, he brought down two pantiles on the clubhouse roof at a prestigious Scottish golf club – in full view of the Secretary!

---

* After their victory, the team were introduced to the U.S. Congress in Washington and received a standing ovation – and they were welcomed to their home town as conquering heroes by two thousand well-wishers.

Claude Taylor, President of Air Canada, presents the Air Canada Silver Broom to the winning U.S. rink in Winnipeg in 1978 - from *left to right*, Bob Nichols (skip), Bill Strum, Tom Locken and Bob Christman.

The U.S. Women's Curling Association was instituted in 1947 and became directly affiliated to the Royal Club in 1968. The Association, which runs its own affairs, held the first national Senior Ladies Bonspiel in 1983. There are over ninety clubs in the Women's Association with a total membership in excess of five thousand curlers.

In 1984-85, the American representatives on the International Curling Federation were Art Cobb, Don McKay and Don Barcome. Art Cobb, who has served as President and Secretary of the U.S. Curling Association, accepted another important post in 1984 when he was elected Treasurer of the International Federation.

The member Associations of the U.S. Curling Associations are: Alaska (2 clubs), California-Oregon (3 clubs), Colorado State (2 clubs), Grand National Curling Club of America (37 clubs), Illinois (8 clubs), Indiana (1 club), Michigan (3 clubs), Minnesota (20 clubs), Nebraska (1 club), North Dakota (17 clubs), Ohio (3 clubs), Washington State (3 clubs) and Wisconsin State (30 clubs).

Curling in the United States continues to grow, surely but slowly. An exciting new idea, outlined by Lt-Col Roy Fisk at breakfast during the

1984 World Championship in Duluth, Minnesota, could accelerate the growth of the American game. Roy Fisk, keen curler, traveller and supporter of international curling, has prepared a fascinating programme for the expansion of ice rink building in Alaska, where he lived for seventeen years, serving three terms as President of the Anchorage Curling Club.

The proposed programme, to be placed before the State Legislature, lists the many advantages of building ice rinks in Alaska, a natural centre for winter sports. The establishment of rinks and community centres would initially provide jobs in construction and allied industries, followed by a continuing spread of services, transport and tourism. In addition, the expansion of recreational facilities, so vital for the long Alaskan winters, would lead to the setting up of curling clubs which in turn would foster local loyalty and feelings of friendly rivalry with other curling areas.

The ambitious promotional programme calls for the establishment of about twenty strategically placed locations, to be selected by the Legislature. The imaginative scheme, which includes guidelines for forming and running curling clubs with specifications, plans and estimated costs, deserves to succeed.

SWEDEN

William Andrew Macfie, of the Macfie Sugar Refining Company of Greenock, who was born in Scotland in 1807, introduced curling to Sweden in 1846 at Uddevalla on the west coast. He formed the first curling club, the Bohuslanska Curling Klubben, on 5 March 1852, and, in the 1860s, Oscar, the Crown Prince of Sweden, who was a curler, became Patron of the Club.

Curling was played primarily by the nobility in Sweden in those early days but the game became more widespread when the first club in Stockholm, the Amatorerna Club, was instituted in 1901. A Scottish group visited Stockholm in 1913 and a new club was instituted under the patronage of the Crown Prince. A year later, curling started at Are, a famous sports resort, which, in the years when all competitive curling in Sweden was outdoors, attracted the best Swedish curlers – and a number of Scottish rinks.

The Swedish Curling Association was instituted in 1916 and the first national Championship was held in 1917. In 1923, a Swedish team made the first official tour in Scotland. The same year, team member Erik Akerlund – father of 'Totte' Akerlund, who reached the Scotch Cup final in 1967 – presented the Swedish Cup which became an international event. While President of the Royal Club in 1965, Major Allan Cameron

The 1963 Swedish touring team in Scotland. *From left to right*, Gunnar Eriksson, Rune Jonsson, Hakan Berga, Per Odlund (captain), Herbert Kastengren, Bill Piper (Scottish courier) and Harry Wickstrom. *Back, left to right*, Ture Leijonclou, Ove Ingels, Bertil Svanfeldt, Sven Palmquist, Tore Rydman, Helmer Reveman, Gosta Jonsson, Erik Norell, Bengt Wallerstedt and Arne Johansson.

won the competition with Willie McIntosh, Tom Pendreigh and Ken MacLennan.

In 1954, there was no indoor ice in Sweden and the curling membership was nine hundred. The following year, 1955, was a red-letter year in Swedish curling; the national Association was accepted as a member of the Swedish Sports Federation and this ensured that curling would receive annual Government subsidies.

In the period of transition between outdoor and competitive play, Per Odlund, President of the Swedish Curling Association, captained the 1963 Swedish team in Scotland and travelled widely on behalf of Swedish curling. In 1957, he made the first tour by Swedish curlers to Canada and U.S.A. in company with Erling Bennetter, a famous Swedish name in the 'fifties and 'sixties, Bertil Reibo and Ake Soderstrom. It was fitting that the climax of Per Odlund's many years of devoted service as national President should be his Chairmanship of an international gathering of six hundred curlers at the Jubilee Dinner of the Association in the Stockholm Town Hall in 1966. Per's term as President acted as a springboard to competitive curling in Sweden.

Competition is fierce in Sweden because the Swedes are competitive curlers and they have proved their worth at world level. Sweden entered the Scotch Cup, joining Scotland, Canada and U.S.A., in 1962 with a rink skipped by Rolf Arfwidsson. In 1967, the Swedish team skipped by Canadian Bob Woods reached the Scotch Cup final, losing to Scotland's Chuck Hay. In this period, Swedish competitive curling started to move indoors, modern ice rinks being built in Orebro, Nassjo and Karlstad.

H.R.H. Prince Bertil, President of the Swedish Sports Federation, congratulates the 1973 world champions - *left to right*, Boa Carlman, Tom Schaeffer, Bengt Oscarius and Kjell Oscarius (skip).

Don McLeod of Air Canada presents the Silver Broom to the Swedish world champions in Karlstad in 1977 – *left to right*, Ragnar Kamp (skip), Hakan Rudstrom, Bjorn Rudstrom and Christer Martensson.

Curlers in Stockholm played on eight sheets of ice in a huge tent-like structure – a reinforced plastic covering weighing three tons being kept in position by warm air fans.

The new facilities gave Swedish curlers the impetus they needed. After a disastrous Air Canada Silver Broom in 1972 in Garmisch-Partenkirchen, where they lost all their games, the young team from the Djursholm Club outside Stockholm skipped by Kjell Oscarius bounced back brilliantly to win the world title by beating Harvey Mazinke's home rink at Regina the following year. In 1977, an even younger team skipped by Ragnar Kamp won the second World Championship for Sweden with a final victory on their home ice at Karlstad over Jim Ursel, Canada. The same Kamp rink won the European title in Oslo the same year.

The spectacular successes by the Oscarius and Kamp rinks attracted the youth of Sweden to the game and Swedish juniors scored two victories in the Uniroyal World Junior Championship – in the inaugural event in 1975 (Jan Ullsten) and in 1982 (Soren Grahn).

Some comparisons are odious but this one certainly is not. The successes of the Swedish men have been matched, even surpassed, by the ladies and in particular by the Elisabeth Hogstrom rink. When Elisabeth, Katarina Hultling, Birgitta Sewik and Karin Sjogren won the European title in Vasteras in December 1983, the rink was generally acknowledged to be the top ladies team in the world. Carina Olsson played in place of Katarina Hultling in Sweden's world victory in 1981 and, at the end of the 1983–84 season, the record of the five ladies was: Carina Olsson (World 1981, European 1980), Birgitta Sewik and Karin Sjogren (World 1981, European 1980, 1982, 1983), Katarina Hultling (European 1982, 1983) and the superlative skip Elisabeth Hogström (World 1981, European 1976, 1980, 1982, 1983). Earlier Swedish victories in the European Ladies Championship were scored by skips Elisabeth Branas (1976, 1977) and Inga Arfwidsson (1978).

Sweden scored another international success in 1984 when Katarina Hjorth skipped the winning team in the Bank of Scotland European Junior Ladies Championship at Gogar Park, Edinburgh. In March 1985 Jonkoping will be the first Swedish venue for the Ladies World Championship and will be sponsored by Hennes and Mauritz.

Axel Kamp, father of world victor Ragnar and a fine curler in his own right, is the current President of the Swedish Curling Association and one of the Swedish representatives on the International Curling Federation. The other is Hakan Sundstrom who reported in 1984 that there were five thousand curlers in Sweden with capacity for another two thousand in the ice rinks. In 1982–83, Hakan took over as Secretary of the Swedish Curling Association on the retiral of the internationally-famous Sven Eklund, President of the International Curling Federation from 1979 to 1982 (see chapter on the Federation).

SWITZERLAND

In 1879, a Scot sent four pairs of curling stones and the *Annual* of the Royal Club, containing the rules of the game, to Johannes Badrutt, proprietor of the St Moritz Kulm Hotel, who had four more pairs made from local stone. On 22 December 1880, the first curling game in Switzerland was played at the St Moritz Curling Club. Other early Swiss clubs were Davos (1888), Grindelwald (1898), Arosa (1900), Celerina (1909), Villars (1910), Murren and Wengen (1911). In 1914, there were twenty-four

Otto Danieli in action in Perth in 1975 when he skipped the rink which won the first World Championship for Switzerland. Otto's rink was Ronald Schneider, Rolf Gautschi and Ueli Mulli.

curling centres in Switzerland. The Bernese Oberland Curling Association was formed in 1935 and the Swiss Curling Association was instituted in 1942 with twenty-two clubs and four hundred members. Today, there are two hundred and ten clubs and over eight thousand three hundred curlers in the Eastern, Central and Western regions of Switzerland.

In the first seventy years of Swiss curling history, the game was conducted exclusively on outside ice, play being concentrated in the spectacular Alpine resorts. The first indoor competition, the Zurich Cup, was organised by the Zurich Curling Club - founded by Dr Alex Dimtza, famous surgeon and later President of the Swiss Association - in 1951 in the Hallenstadion, a large arena in Zurich. The event, which attracted curlers from all over, continued in the same format until the modern four-sheet ice rink at Wallisellen, just north of Zurich, was opened in 1968.

The first Swiss indoor ice rink providing ice solely for curling was built in 1964 in Berne, next to the Allmend stadium, site of the 1974 and 1979 World Championships. Ten years later, Switzerland had forty curling ice rinks with 126 sheets of ice. The remarkable transformation was caused by the change from flat ice to pebbled ice. Scots rinks, led by Bill Piper, 1960–61 Royal Club President, made many trips to the Zurich Cup and made pleas for the change when they competed on the flat, swinging ice in the Hallenstadion – we remember Bill Piper holding his broom over the barrier on the end sheet to give directions.

Another contributory factor in the shift of curling opinion occurred in 1957 when a group of American curlers came to Switzerland to play in the Swissair Cup, the brainchild of Ernst Scherz, Gstaad, Past-President of the Swiss Association and a well-known hotelier. The visit was returned and the Swiss tourists lost heavily and thought deeply on prepared American ice.

In conjunction with the change of ice surface, the modern attacking game was introduced and adopted and for this two men deserve special credit – Roberto Carugati of Geneva and Walter Albiez of Wallisellen. Apostles of the wide-open Canadian game, they studied the new techniques, held seminars and published instructional guides.

The first major competition on pebbled ice was held at the new Wallisellen ice rink in 1969. Shortly thereafter, the progressive Zurich Crystal Club launched the International Crystal Trophy at Wallisellen. 'Sliding' instructional booklets were published in 1970. Canadian techniques were adopted with alacrity and the modern competitive game swept like wildfire through Switzerland.

The first fruits of the Swiss revolution were gathered in Perth in 1975 when Otto Danieli and his Zurich Crystal team scored a dramatic victory in the Air Canada Silver Broom. We remember the double celebration, organised by Jean Schild, President of the Swiss Curling Association, on his fiftieth birthday. Jean prepared and served the Aberdeen-Angus beef himself at a memorable party.

The second Swiss world success was in London, Ontario, in 1981, when Jurg Tanner and his rink beat Canada in the semi-final and U.S.A. in the final. Nor should we forget the superlative performances of the Peter Attinger rink on three particular world occasions – in Berne in 1974 when the Swiss team went through the round-robin undefeated only to lose at the second extra end to Bud Somerville, U.S.A., in the semi-final; in Berne again in 1979 when Peter's last stone for final victory over Norway's Kristian Soerum slid through the house; and in Duluth in 1984 when Eigil Ramsfjell's Norwegian team beat the Swiss in a high-quality final.

The ladies of Switzerland have also reached the peaks of world curling, scoring World Championship victories in the first Royal Bank Ladies World event in Perth in 1979 (Gaby Casanova) and the Pioneer World Championship in Moose Jaw in 1983 (Erika Mueller). Organised Swiss ladies' curling dates back to 1952 when the Grindelwald Ladies Club, with Heidi Dimtza as the driving force, was formed with thirty members. Zurich (1954), Berne (1955) and Basle (1959) followed this lead and the Swiss Ladies Championship was started in 1964. The Swiss Junior Championship was launched in 1972 and the Junior Ladies Championship in 1983.

The Swiss have amassed an impressive array of European titles – the men's event in Berlin in 1976 and Morzine in 1984 (Peter Attinger), in Aviemore in 1978 and Grindelwald in 1981 (Jurg Tanner) and in Vasteras in 1983 (Amédée Biner); and the ladies' event in Varese in 1979 (Gaby Casanova) and in Grindelwald in 1981 (Susanne Schlappbach). Only the Swedish ladies have a better European record.

In 1961, Swiss Association delegates turned down, by forty votes to

The Swiss world champions with Air Canada's Claude Taylor after their triumph in London, Ontario, in 1981 – from *left to right*, Jurg Tanner (skip), Jurg Hornisberger, Patrick Loertscher and Franz Tanner.

thirty-four, an invitation to play in the World Championship for the Scotch Cup – because they were against international matches being sponsored by Scottish distillers! In 1963, a Swiss team made the first official tour in Scotland, the start of exchange tours which continue on a regular basis, and, presumably, the sampling of the distillers' products softened the Swiss attitude because Switzerland joined the Scotch Cup the following year – in Calgary, where Alex Torrance's Scots team went down fighting at the extra end of the final to Canada's Lyall Dagg.

Erwin A. Sautter, who founded the Swiss magazine, *Curling*, in 1959 and edited it for many years, gave drive and direction at a critical stage to Swiss curling. A man steeped in the lore of the game and an international figure of repute – he attended meetings during the Scotch Cup in Vancouver in 1966 which led to the formation of the International Curling Federation – Erwin was the ideal choice as President of the recently-formed European Curling Media Association.

Switzerland has been called the curlers' paradise because the sun so often shines from a blue sky in perfect settings in the mountain resorts with comfortable hotels only a step away from the ice rink. Erwin Sautter reports that, consistent with the meteoric rise of the Swiss competitive game, there has been a strong resurgence of interest in outdoor play. This is splended news; the excitement of competitive curling in the ice rinks and the exhilaration of playing in the Swiss Alps are separate but perfectly complementary features of the Swiss success story.

NORWAY

The Elverhae Club, which was admitted to membership of the Royal Club in 1880, had strong connections with the Scottish Club, Evenie Water, members of each club being honorary members of the other. The Hon Mrs Arbuthnott was Patroness of the Elverhae Club. This is the first record of curling in Norway.

Norwegian curling began in earnest in 1954, when, accepting an invitation from the Norwegian Travel Association, four Scots curlers visited Oppdal. The Scots – Bill Piper, Gilbert McClung, Balfour Kerr and 'Bunty' McWhirter – were welcomed by Erik Schonheyder, who formed the Oppdal Curling Club. The visit also inspired the formation of a new club in Oslo, Rolf Christensen being elected Chairman in 1955.

In 1955, another Scottish visit was made by John Monteith, 'Bunty' McWhirter, Rab Mitchell and Courtenay Morrison to Geilo and the Geilo Club was founded. In the 1979–80 season, three sheets of natural but covered ice were opened at Geilo.

The first Norwegian touring team in Scotland in 1965. *Left to right*, Kjell Lefstäd, Ottar Holm, Ola Leftstad, Harald Oekelsrud, Christian Walter (vice-captain), Odd Loen, Per Forsberg, Per Holaker, Gerd Mortensen, Lars Tveter (secretary), Per Falster, Per Finn Hansen, Arvid Melum Hansen, Josef Bjaanaes, Eivind Kirkeby, Ulf Engh, Birger Mortensen (captain) and Rolf Carlem. Erik Gyllenhammar joined the team later.

Rolf Christensen, who was educated at Glasgow High School, was elected first President of the Norwegian Curling Association in 1956, and, in 1958, he made a short but rewarding tour to Scotland with Erik Schonheyder (Vice-President of the Association), Christian Walter and Finn Hegle.

John Monteith, who presented curling stones to Norway, returned to Geilo in 1958 and played a match against and made a broadcast with Rolf Christensen. Later that year, John Solheim, the conscientious Secretary of the Norwegian Association for ten formative years, reported increasing activity and the launching of the Nordic Bonspiel, to be played alternately in Norway and Sweden. There were fifteen Norwegian clubs in 1961.

In answer to a Norwegian invitation, Major Allan Cameron led two Scots rinks on a short tour to Oslo, Lillehammer and Trondheim in 1964. The visit coincided with the tenth anniversary of the Oslo Club, founded after the Oppdal games in 1954. Enjoyable matches were played at

Bygdoy ice rink against rinks from Oslo, Frogner, Bygdoy and Stabekk Clubs. The tour ended with warm hospitality at Trondheim. One of the main events of the 1967–68 season was the tenth anniversary bonspiel of the Frogner Club.

Rolf Christensen retired from the Presidency of the Norwegian Curling Association after nine years' service and was succeeded by Birger Mortensen, who captained the team, with Christian Walter as Vice-Captain, which made the first large-scale tour (eighteen men) in Scotland in 1965. During the tour, we heard that the Norwegians played principally on natural outdoor ice from December to March, that there was only one artificial ice rink where curling was played at limited periods and that there were fewer than five hundred curlers in Norway.

Birger Mortensen's wife, Gerd, started curling, quickly spread the good news to her friends and the Oslo Ladies Curling Club was founded in 1967–68. Ladies' curling spread and the first official ladies' championship was held in 1979. Bente Hoel, a splendid curler who has represented her country in world events, is Norway's representative on the Ladies Committee of the International Curling Federation.

Birger and Gerd Mortensen travelled extensively on behalf of Norwegian curling and Birger became an international administrator. He was the Norwegian representative on the International Federation from 1966 to 1971 and 1979 to 1982, and, in 1979, was elected President of the European Curling Council and served for four years, his direct Norwegian approach and zest for curling being admired by all. He received a standing ovation after demitting office at the closing dinner of the 1983 European Championships in Vasteras in Sweden.

Birger, who served two terms as President of the Norwegian Curling Association (1965–69 and 1977–81), and his successors, Erik Schonheyder (1969–73) and Georg von Krogh (1973–77), presided over the eventful transition period when Norway moved from irregular competitive play, much of it on natural ice, into the international arena.

Norway entered the Scotch Cup World Championship in Calgary in 1964. The first major international success for Norway was achieved by Knut Bjaanaes, who skipped the winning rink in the first European Championship in Megeve in December, 1975, beating Sweden's Kjell Oscarius at an extra end in the final. In 1977, Norway staged its first big international event, the third European Championships, in Oslo.

Norwegian curlers were delighted when the Askerhallen, near Oslo, became the principal curling ice rink in Norway in 1969 – and were shocked when the arena was burned down in May, 1972. The lack of indoor curling ice has been the continuing story in Norway and the Norwegian victories in the World Championships of 1979 (when there were five hundred curlers in Norway) and 1984 (when there were twelve hundred) represent the most remarkable achievements in international curling. The Silver Broom victories of the teams skipped by Kristian Soerum and Eigil Ramsfjell have made the history of the ice facilities – or lack of them – in Norway into a saga; and, like their Viking ancestors, the modern Norwegians have triumphed over adversity to conquer the world and have proved that, with the right spirit, anything is possible.

Strenuous efforts by an enthusiastic group of Norwegians led to the building of a new indoor ice rink in Snaroen, outside Oslo (opened in 1978), and, in 1984, when there were twenty-four clubs in Norway, Stanley Flostrand, the knowledgeable Secretary of the Norwegian Curling Association, reported: 'We are well under way with a new ice rink in Brumunddal, where Kristian Soerum was born, and are also working on introducing curling in the western part of Norway.' There are also two sheets of ice used exclusively for curling at Bygdoy.

Well-organised Norwegian coaching programmes have proved their

Air Canada's Michel Fournier presents the Silver Broom to the Norwegian rink after the 1979 World Championship in Berne – from *left to right*, Eigil Ramsfjell, Morten Soerum, Kristian Soerum (skip) and Gunnar Meland.

The Norwegian team with Claude Taylor, President of Air Canada, after their triumph in the 1984 World Championship in Duluth - from *left to right*, Eigil Ramsfjell (skip), Sjur Loen, Gunnar Meland and Bo Bakke.

value and the introduction of a national curling week in Norway has attracted new curlers to the game.

Peter Lange, President of the Norwegian Curling Association since 1981, is a dedicated worker for curling, an able administrator and delightful colleague. His country's representative on the International Curling Federation from 1977 to 1979 and since 1982, Peter also serves as the Scandinavian representative on the Federation's Executive Committee. He was a happy man when Eigil Ramsfjell's rink won the 1984 World Championship in Duluth - and immediately threw an international champagne party which ended when the victorious Norwegian team were thrown into the adjoining swimming pool by the Swedish rink.

NEW ZEALAND
The New Zealand Province of the Royal Club was formed with seven clubs in 1886 and Thomas Callander, a curler from the West of Scotland, was elected the first President. He was the driving force behind the early spread of curling in New Zealand and his efforts led to the founding of

a club at Dunedin in 1873. Five years later, a club was formed at the gold-mining town of Naseby, where the prospects for curling were better at 2,000 feet, and the Mt Ida Club was founded.* Palmerston curlers travelled fifty miles to play the first bonspiel in New Zealand against Naseby in 1879. Other clubs quickly followed as the miners, their claims and water supplies frozen, turned to curling.

Gerald Dowling, Ranfurly, keen curler and faithful correspondent, paints a picture of curling, played mainly in July and August, at the other side of the world:

'Most of the clubs are bounded by the mountainous country of Central Otago, from Ranfurly west to Alexandra, and including our two main curling centres, Naseby and Oturehua. As you can imagine, playing outdoors, the ice deteriorates about mid-day on the warmer days and requires a good swing on the keen side. Later in the day, you will be taking the weight off on the drug side as the ice tightens. Of course, we always use a crampit, and are not able to add the finesse to our shots possible on indoor ice of consistent quality. Being outdoors in the colder atmosphere, we always shout our orders to team members. We also include the bottle of Scotch among our ice necessities'.

As long ago as 1896, New Zealanders bemoaned the brevity of the curling season and considered the need for 'a Glaciarium'. But there is no indoor curling ice and the game is played in rugged conditions on frozen dams.

When conditions are right, excitement rises as curlers from far-flung areas foregather on the ice. New Zealand curlers are strong traditionalists. There are twenty-eight clubs in the Province and they have their own colours. The Hamilton Club, formed in 1965, adopted the Hamilton tartan. After bonspiels, they enjoy 'Beef and Greens' and initiate their young curlers at well-organised Curlers' Courts. Beef and Greens and Courts were started when the game started in New Zealand and have been maintained ever since. It is recorded that, in 1881, the Dunedin Club held its annual, convivial meeting in Wains Hotel where members 'partook of beef and greens and the white wines of Scotland!'

In the early 1970s, the whole course of curling in New Zealand changed. In 1970, to celebrate the visit of the Duke of Edinburgh,

---

*When Junior President-Elect of the Royal Club in 1978, Philip Dawson attended the centenary celebrations of the Mt Ida Club and the 75th anniversary dinner of the Naseby Club. He reported on wonderful hospitality and a game of curling on the Styx, a small loch, where only crampits were used and twenty-one ends were played between 9 a.m. and 4.30 p.m.

In 1973 the first official New Zealand team toured Scotland. *In front*, Jim Becker (organiser), Maisey Griffiths (President, New Zealand Province, R.C.C.C.) and Terry McKnight (Secretary, New Zealand Province). *At back*, Charlie Brown, Doug Francis, Scobie Harley, Bob Laurenson, Merv Jamieson, Viv Cross, Bill McConnochie, Kitch Thurlow, Maurice Mee, Harry McNally and Bill Dowling.

Honorary Member of the Royal Club, and members of the Royal Family, the enterprising New Zealand curlers rigged up sheets of black polythene to simulate a rink and laid out crampits and stones at Queenstown.

In 1971, Royal Club President Willie Wilson led a Scottish party – Gilbert McClung, David and Janette Duncan, Bob and Chris Gardner – and Willie threw the first stone ever played from a hack (made by Gerald Dowling to the Scots' specification) on New Zealand ice.

David Duncan reported that they visited the Mt Ida dam and saw the curling hut erected for £10 in 1905. The Scots showed films in Naseby town hall and attended a special Curlers' Court in Oturehua where the two ladies made history – Chris as the first lady to attend as an initiated curler and Janette as only the second lady to be 'made', the first being Mrs Moffat-Pender in 1934 (see section on Australia). The ladies carved another slice of history by being the first ladies to skip on New Zealand ice. On this occasion, in David Duncan's words, 'the ice began to crack as the last stone was played and there was a shout to save the stones – never mind the curlers!'

The 1971 visit led to the first tour by New Zealand curlers to Scotland in 1973. Maisey Griffiths, President of the New Zealand Province, brought a team of fourteen curlers, with seven wives. Jim Becker was the tour organiser and the Secretary was Province Secretary Terry McKnight. The three-week tour of twelve ice rinks, planned by David Duncan, was full of fun and fellowship.

Neil McKnight, Oturehua, a keen curler with family roots in the game, is the present Province Secretary. In 1983, the Upper Manuherikia and Otago Central Clubs celebrated their centenaries and the Ranfurly Club commemorated fifty years. In the same year, Wilson Mawhinney captained a New Zealand party which toured Scotland, a highlight being participation in the Weatherseal Highland Week of International Curling at Aviemore – and Wilson returned home determined to encourage New Zealand curlers to reach out from their curling outpost to create stronger links with other curling nations.

The exciting news for the future is that the Royal Club has invited New Zealand to make an official tour in Scotland in February/March, 1986, the centenary year of the New Zealand Province.

FRANCE

French curling began in isolated groups early this century. But the French influence on Scottish curling was strong over one hundred and fifty years ago for we read, in John Cairnie's *Essay* (1833), that among his favourite stones were Napoleon, Belle Poulle, La Liberté, La Forte and La Fidelle!

Twenty years ago, Marc Maisonny, Honorary President of the French Federation of Ice Sports (instituted in 1941) and President of the Sporting Club of Megeve, the first French club affiliated to the Royal Club (in 1959), reported that modern curling started in France in 1920 when he and Dr Agnel of Chamonix organised clubs and inter-club play.

The Winter Olympic Games at Chamonix in 1924 – when curling was included as a medal-winning sport for the first and only time – gathered the tributaries of curling in the Haute Savoie area into a main stream and this concentration of effort led to the French Curling Championship which began then and has been held ever since.

For many years from 1925, the contestants in the national Championship were two teams from Chamonix and two teams from Megeve, which became the centre of French curling. The event was held annually at

Megeve where the Sports Club and the Sporting Club of Megeve had a curling rink reserved beside an outdoor skating rink. In 1955 an artificial ice-making plant was installed.

From that time, curling spread to other districts in the Mont Blanc area of the French Alps as refrigerated ice rinks were constructed in Chamonix, Megeve and Saint-Gervais, the ice rink in Megeve being exclusively a curling rink. Another reason given by Marc Maisonny for the spread of the game was the fact that excellent bowlers in the area quickly became good curlers. The two clubs in Chamonix – Club des Sports and the Hockey Club – and four clubs in Megeve – Sporting Club, Curling Club, Curling Club d'Arbois and Club des Sports – were joined by the Curling Club and Jet Club, Saint-Gervais, the Curling Club Alpe d'Huez, the Curling Club Chamrousse and the Curling Club Voiron.

In 1966, a French team made its World Championship debut in the Scotch Cup in Vancouver. Understandably, the rink failed to win a game but the French skip, Jean Albert Sulpice, was undoubtedly the popular hero. A cheerful extrovert, he captivated the crowds with his smile and happy gestures and was even applauded as he walked down the ice *before* playing his shots!

Dr Albert Mure, President of the Curling Section of the French Ice Sports Federation, was another Frenchman with a twinkle in his eye. His sense of humour made him the ideal captain of the first French team to make an official tour in Scotland, which further strengthened the Auld Alliance, in 1968, the year pebbled ice was used for the first time in France. A highly-successful tour started with a cocktail party at Broom-hall, home of Royal Club President Lord Bruce (now the Earl of Elgin) and ended with a Curlers' Court, with Tom Stewart and David Kinnaird officiating, at which the tourists became the first initiated curlers of France.

The crowd-pleasing performance by Jean Albert Sulpice in 1966 was duplicated at the 1978 Air Canada Silver Broom in Winnipeg where two records were created – an audience of over 102,000 in the week and the eighth World Championship appearance of Pierre Boan, the French skip. Pierre caught the imagination of the huge crowds with a series of spectacular last draws and ended a remarkable performance with outstanding closing victories over Scotland and Norway, during which shouts of 'Come on Pierre' and 'We want Pierre' echoed round the arena.

Pierre Catella, popular Secretary of the Curling Committee of the French Ice Sports Federation and the French representative to the In-

The first French team to tour in Scotland - in 1968. *In front*, Solange Quaglia, Dr Albert Mure (Captain), Evelyne Juilliard and Claudine Pantalacci. *At back*, Pierre Dore, Jean Pantalacci, Raymond Brondex, Philippe Chambat, Jacques Juilliard, Ami Quaglia and Francois Monthyon.

ternational Curling Federation for many years, unfortunately suffered ill-health and was forced to retire. The new Federation representative is Gerard Alazet.

The stronghold of curling in France is still the Haute Savoie area; the European Championships and the Silver Broom and Uniroyal World Junior Championships have been staged at 4,000 feet in Megeve. In addition, competitions in Paris and Lyon have attracted curlers from many countries and have publicised the game in France. The attractions of a curling event in Paris, with a visit to the chateau at Versailles followed by cocktails in the Champs Elysées, are obvious. It is easy to imagine that a week-end bonspiel in Paris will be heavily over-subscribed!

ITALY

There are twenty curling clubs in Italy, including clubs in the Province of Trento, but the main centre of Italian curling is Cortina d'Ampezzo in its magnificent setting at 5,000 feet in the Dolomites.

Cortina has always been the curling capital of Italy. An advertisement in Bertram Smith's *The Shilling Curler* (1912) proclaimed the area as 'the Garden of the Gods' and invited British enthusiasts to curl on a skating rink of 25,000 square feet with excellent Scottish curling stones.

In *The Complete Curler* (1914), J. Gordon Grant wrote of Cortina: 'The village with the surrounding cottages contains 3,000 inhabitants of a hard-working, simple-hearted, honest race. It has a post and telegraph office, library, doctor, chemist, excellent guides and English Divine Service during the season. Special attention is drawn to a Vienna Cafe where drinks, harmless or inebriating, are served at all hours of the day and night. About the prices, travellers can come to an understanding with the hotel proprietor! The management and service are first-rate and entirely done by nice bright girls in Tyrolese costumes.'

Curling was revived in Cortina in 1953 by Leo Menardi, sporting personality and proprietor of the Cristallo Palace Hotel, who constructed two rinks at the hotel and became President of the Cristallo Club. The Miramonti Club, with Federico Manaigo as President, followed in 1955 and the Cortina Club in 1957.

In 1956, the Winter Olympic Games in Cortina provided a springboard for curling development and Cortina curlers seized the opportunity by launching a summer Bonspiel on the Olympic ice. The imaginative idea caught the interest of the European curling community. James Fleming, a keen Edinburgh curler and outstanding organiser who was on the planning committee and acted as umpire, described the event, which included five main competitions in a week, as 'a curler's dream come true'. An outdoor bonspiel in June was something new under the sun!

The event brought curlers in large numbers from many countries to Cortina. At the second bonspiel in 1959, sixty rinks participated, including twenty-two curlers from Scotland and ten from Sweden. There were seventy rinks in 1960 and the big summer tournament is now a major European event, attracting teams from all over the Continent in addition to overseas visitors.

We first heard of Ivo Lorenzi, internationally-popular Italian personality, in 1966 when the early Cristallo and Miramonti clubs were amalgamated to form the Dolomiti Club and Ivo was elected President. In the 1970-71 season, the Italian Curling Association was established with Ivo Lorenzi as the first national President. The following year, Italy joined the International Curling Federation and Ivo has been the Italian representative since that time.

The holding of the 1979 European Championships in Varese, where the Italian men's team was in contention throughout the week, eventually taking third place, gave a further boost to Italian curling and Ivo Lorenzi reported that the success of the event had been acknowledged by national sports officials, including the Minister of Tourism in Rome and members of the Italian Olympic Committee.

Italy joined the Air Canada Silver Broom line-up in 1973 and the Italians, with Andrea Pavani playing a series of spectacular last stones, gave their best-ever Silver Broom performance in the 1982 World Championship at Garmisch-Partenkirchen. They beat Canada (the winners), Scotland and Switzerland in a great run before losing in a controversial play-off for a semi-final place. The Italian ladies' team, skipped by Maria Grazia Constantini, reached the final of the European Championship in Kirkcaldy in 1982.

The Italian Curling Association runs men's, ladies', junior and mixed Championships at Cortina and the game is well organised nationally. But Italian administrators are far from satisfied. They have one overriding ambition – to have a covered ice rink in Cortina. If they succeed, the superb setting in the Dolomites could quickly become a scenic centre for major international competitions.

GERMANY

In 1984, Ulf von Malberg, who was writing a book on German curling, reported that curling had been played in Germany for fifty years. The first stone was thrown at Oberhof, Thuringen, where the World Championships of a number of winter sports was held. To enlarge the winter sports atmosphere, the Duke of Sachsen-Gotha invited a group of Scots to demonstrate curling on natural ice and brought an ice-master from Grindelwald in Switzerland to prepare the ice, on which the veteran German curler, David Lampl, who skipped the first German team in the Scotch Cup in Perth in 1967, began his curling career. Three rinks were prepared for curling, but, as the ice melted a few days after the demonstration, it was concluded that Oberhof was not cold enough for curling.

In the 1950s, German winter sports enthusiasts learned to curl in Swiss resorts and the game was introduced to Oberstdorf and Garmisch-Partenkirchen. In 1959, through the initiative of Carry Gross and Fritz Geiger, the first German club, the International Curling Club of Oberstdorf, was founded. Two years later, the C.C. Deutschland 61, Dusseldorf, was instituted with Erich Lindstedt as President.

Rolf Klug, lead player in David Lampl's rink at Perth in 1967, recalls that Roman Roussell, a German who had started curling in Switzerland, had met the Scottish curling organiser, James Fleming, in Kitzbühel in

Austria and persuaded him to help with the organisation of the first curling competition at Garmisch-Partenkirchen in 1961. Ice hockey players from Munich who had curled at Kitzbühel spread news of the game and Franz Eggenhofer made attempts to start the game in Munich. Following a match on the frozen Nymphenburger Canal, David Lampl and other keen curlers formed the Curling Section of the Munich Skating Club; and Werner Fischer-Weppler, a towering figure in the growth of German curling, was a driving force behind the formation of other clubs in Munich and curling sections at Bad Tölz and Landshut.

A chance get-together during meetings of the German Ice Sports Federation in 1965 led to discussions about the formation of a national curling body, and, in 1966, the German Curling Association was founded. The first President was Carry Gross who had helped to found the first club seven years before.

In 1967, David Lampl, Gunther Hummelt, Ottmar Paebst and Rolf Klug won the first German Championship and represented Germany in the Scotch Cup World Championship. In 1968, there were two hundred and fifty curlers in Germany, fifteen per cent of whom were ladies. The number rose to five hundred in 1972, when the ebullient Hans Thaut was Organising Chairman at the World Championship for the Air Canada Silver Broom at Garmisch-Partenkirchen, an outstanding event for Germany for three principal reasons – the sun shone brightly every day, Manfred Raederer and his German team reached the semi-final and the German media and television gave curling a massive boost. Hans Thaut was again Chairman of the world event when it returned to Garmisch-Partenkirchen in 1982.

In 1969, Werner Fischer-Weppler became the national President and he supported a proposal to hold the German Championship at the Canadian Air Force base at Lahr in 1970. The Canadians were splendid hosts and also taught the Germans the modern Canadian game. In 1971, a German junior team played in the international Junior Championship in East York, Toronto – the forerunner of the Uniroyal World Junior event. The first official German Junior Championship was held in 1977.

Ernst Johann Horn served as President of the German Curling Association in 1973–74 but Werner Fischer-Weppler returned as President after a year and he initiated training courses and brought Canadian instructors to Germany. The present German national coach is Otto Danieli, the Swiss skip who won the World Championship in 1975.

The European Championships were held in Berlin in 1976 under the direction of Peter Fischer-Weppler and Hermann Binder, and the ice-

The first official German team to tour in Scotland - in 1972. *Front, left to right*, Rolf Klug, Ernstjohann Horn, Werner Fisher-Weppler (Captain), Rolf Mittag, Eckhard Jahan, Siegfried Heinle. At back, Alan Johnston (Scottish Courier), Peter Fisher-Weppler, Karl Bischoff, Pepi Gasteiger, Adalbert Mayer, Ricky Mittag, Mike Mittag, Dieter Grasekamp and Gunter Olschewski.

maker was Keith Wendorf whose curling skill changed the course of German curling at international level. A Canadian from Toronto, Keith had been in Germany as a boy, his father being in the Canadian Forces. He revisited Germany as a student – and stayed to become manager of the Golf and Curling Club, Lahr.

Peter Fischer-Weppler introduced Keith to the Munich team in 1977, and, in 1978 and 1979, he skipped the winning national Championship and started a distinguished career in World Championships in which he reached the semi-final twice and the final once, at Regina in 1983, in his fifth Silver Broom appearance. He also reached the final of the 1982 European Championship at Kirkcaldy.

At the 1981 annual meeting of the German Curling Association, Werner Fischer-Weppler was appointed Honorary President and the reigning President is Charles Heckmann, well-known businessman and speaker who has a wide grasp of European and world affairs. His Vice-President is the genial Theo Hornung.

DENMARK

The Copenhagen Curling Club, the first club in Denmark, was formed twenty years ago. The Secretary, John Christiansen, reported that 'the Club enjoyed a nice accession after a great deal of publicity in the Press and Television'. The club hired an ice rink with space for five sheets for curling.

John Christiansen appealed to the Royal Club for curling stones, and, after a visit to Copenhagen in 1966 by Bill Robertson Aikman, President, and Robin Welsh, Secretary of the Royal Club, a supply of stones, some gifted by John Monteith of Dalkeith, was shipped to Denmark. Erik Mangor, leading spirit in the Copenhagen Club, was instrumental in arranging this and in the affiliation to the Royal Club in 1967.

The Danes also asked for general information on curling because 'we have been plunged headlong into battles against neighbouring towns without knowing the most elementary rules'.

Early in 1968, the Copenhagen Club held its first international bonspiel, for the Mermaid Cup, the entry including Swedish, Norwegian, Swiss and Danish rinks, and one Scots rink – Alan Johnston, James Hamilton, Jim Morrison and Sandy Aitken. Erik Mangor, the Club Treasurer, reported that there were forty-five members who toured extensively and played a series of competitions in Copenhagen.

It is clear that Danish curling started absolutely from scratch but the last paragraph of John Christiansen's historic letter showed the Danish resolve: 'As you can see, the material side of the matter does not promise well but the will and spirits are 100 per cent in order'.

Much hard work and dedicated planning transformed the early enthusiasm into the establishment of the Danish Curling Association on 6 November 1970 and there are now six hundred curlers in sixteen clubs. Erik Kelnaes, Vice-President of the Association, pays tribute to Kjell Oscarius and Boa Carlman of the 1973 Swedish World Champion rink, Kristian Soerum, 1979 World Champion and Dagfinn Loen from Norway and Ray Turnbull from Canada who have given valuable instruction in Denmark.

Denmark joined the Silver Broom in Regina in 1973 and also competed in the Uniroyal World Junior Championship and the Ladies World event which the Danish rink – Marianne Joergensen, Helena Blach, Astrid Birnbaum and Jette Olsen – won in 1982. The Danish men's and ladies' teams won bronze medals in the 1981 European Championships in Grindelwald and the junior men won bronze medals in the Uniroyal Junior event at Aviemore in 1976.

The youth of Denmark was given a boost when Helena Blach, Jette Olsen, Malene Krause and Lone Kristoffersen won the inaugural European Junior Ladies Championship in Helsingborg, Sweden, in 1983, beating Isobel Torrance's Scots rink in the final.

The 1980 European Championships in 'wonderful, wonderful' Copenhagen were outstandingly successful and Denmark has applied to hold the Championships again in 1986. At the Annual Meeting of the Danish Curling Association in 1984, representatives gave the go-ahead for plans to build a four-sheet ice rink exclusively for curling in the Copenhagen area.

Gunnar Stenholm, who died in 1984, aged 75, was the only Honorary Member of the Association and the founding father of Danish curling. He was elected first President of the Danish Curling Association and held the post for twelve years, guiding the Association through its formative stage to its present position as an established force in world curling.

Gunnar also served as Danish representative on the International Curling Federation, which Denmark joined in 1971. The present representative, Sten Willer-Andersen, and his twin brother, Per, are Danish ambassadors at many international events. Delightful characters and identical twins, they cause endless bewilderment and humour at social functions, taking advantage of mistaken identity and each quick to blame the other for any mild misdemeanour!

AUSTRIA

Curling was played at Kitzbühel before the First World War – a brochure of the time proclaimed that an artificial rink of 35,000 square feet was kept in excellent condition for skating and curling – but the game did not take firm root in Austria until 1955 when the Kitzbühel Curling Club was founded. The previous year, Baron Carl Menshengen was a leading figure in moves which led to the provision of three sheets of curling ice alongside the skating rink.

Twenty-four pairs of Ailsa stones were imported from Scotland and the Edinburgh organiser, James Fleming, also came from Scotland each year until his death in 1962 to organise the curling events.

Curling was also started at St Anton in 1959 and at St Johan, eight miles from Kitzbühel, in 1960. In 1964, the Winter Olympic Games at Innsbruck added another dimension to Austrian curling; the 1983 national championships were held at the Olympic ice stadium.

Kitzbühel, famous ski-ing resort in the Tyrol, remains the principal curling centre in Austria, with two active clubs. In 1984, there were also clubs in Kirchberg, Aurach, Sillian, Innsbruck, Salzburg, Graz and Vienna and there were moves to establish clubs in Linz, Bregenz, Mödling and Eisenstadt.

One of the main aims of the Austrian Curling Association, instituted in 1980, is to build an arena exclusively for curling in western Austria, probably in Kitzbühel or Innsbruck. Another priority is the encouragement of young players – curlers of world standing, Jurg Tanner, Otto Danieli and Keith Wendorf, have been engaged for training programmes.

Austria joined the International Curling Federation in 1982 and immediately challenged to compete in the 1983 World Championship – and, in separate matches, beat England and France to qualify for the Air Canada Silver Broom in Regina. The same year, the Austrian ladies also entered world competition when they participated in the Pioneer World Ladies Championship at Moose Jaw.

Gunther Hummelt, the personable President of the Austrian Curling Association, created history in 1984 when he became the first curler to play for two countries in World Championships. In the Scotch Whisky Cup in 1967, he played in David Lampl's German team when Germany made their debut at world level, and, in 1984, he played as a substitute for Austria when the Austrian skip was taken ill during the Air Canada Silver Broom at Duluth.

Gunther is the Austrian representative on the International Curling Federation and his wife, Lilly, represents Austria on the Ladies Committee of the Federation.

THE NETHERLANDS

In 1961, a group of enthusiastic Dutch curlers founded the Amsterdam Curling Club, the first curling club in Holland. Games were played on a new outside artifical ice stadium, specially built for speed skating, one of the most popular winter sports in Holland. The cost for play in this rink was considerable and the humidity of winters in Amsterdam posed additional problems. But the hard core of enthusiasts persevered, meeting twice a week for play. Winter holidays in Swiss resorts and curling in Scotland, at Edinburgh and Dundee-Angus ice rinks, maintained the interest of members.

In 1966, S. Waterman, Secretary of the club, wrote that, to improve their play, members had examined ways and means of building an indoor rink but that the cost of such a venture was too much for the forty members to bear. In 1970, Hans Engelhard and Eric Harmsen established the Utrecht Curling Club. Shortly thereafter, clubs in Den Haag, Rotterdam and Leiden – the University club 'All the Way' – were founded. The Netherlands Curling Association was instituted in 1974 and admitted to the Royal Club in 1975.

In 1984, there were approximately two hundred and fifty regular curlers in Holland but there is still no true curling ice and junior curling is difficult to promote because of the cost of ice charges which is reflected in the annual subscriptions. Many Dutch curlers form touring teams and enjoy bonspiels in other countries.

The standard of play has improved greatly and men's and ladies' teams regularly participate in the European Championships, usually finishing in the upper region of the final scoresheet. At world level, the Dutch ladies have played in the Ladies World Championship and the men's team, with Wim Neeleman skipping and Robert van der Cammen playing fourth, failed narrowly in their bid to compete in the 1984 World Championship, losing to Italy having beaten Wales and England in initial challenge matches.

Holland stages one international bonspiel, the Windmill Cup, which celebrated its tenth anniversary in 1984. The famous early-season event is organised by a highly efficient Committee and attracts entries from all over Europe.

A founder member of the first Dutch club, the Amsterdam Curling Club, in 1961, Eric Harmsen served as Secretary and is now President of the Netherlands Curling Association. A brilliant linguist and able businessman, he represents the Netherlands on the International Curling Federation and was a natural successor to Birger Mortensen when Birger retired as President of the European Curling Federation in 1983. On assuming office, Eric immediately appointed an Executive Committee and held meetings to up-date the Federation constitution and lay plans for the European Championships in Morzine in the French Alps in 1984.

A delightful Dutch lady is Secretary of the European Federation – Annemie de Jongh, the efficient Netherlands representative on the Ladies Committee of the International Curling Federation.

FINLAND

Our first curling contact with Finland was in December 1960, when Jim Draper, Secretary of John Haig & Co. Curling Club, reported that John Imrie, a colleague in the Haig whisky firm and a keen amateur radio operator, had been asked by a Finnish operator for information on curling. We sent literature in the hope that the game would spread to another country.

Organised curling started in Finland in 1971. In 1973, Isto Kolehmainen, member of the Curling Board in Hyvinkaa, wrote: 'We are a beginner group, having played for two years. There are only a few active teams in Finland and we are anxious to develop in the game. We have excellent conditions for outside curling'.

After correspondence, and with support and encouragement from Swedish curlers, the Finns spread the game, and, in 1978, Captain Jack Anderson, Royal Club President-Elect, took a rink to Hyvinkaa to take part in the celebrations to mark the institution of the Finnish Curling Association (affiliated to the Royal Club in the same year) and the official opening of the first artificial ice rink in Finland – two refrigerated sheets of outdoor ice.

Osmo Anttila, President of the Association since its inception, is also Mayor of Hyvinkaa, fifty kilometres north of Helsinki. The inaugural ceremony was attended by the Governor of the Province, Mr Pitsinki, who, with Osmo, welcomed the Scottish and Swedish visitors. Curling was followed by lunch which started at 1 p.m. and finished at 6.30 p.m. There were one hundred Finnish curlers in 1978 and Jack Anderson reported that they were 'keen and most sportsman-like'.

In his first Presidential year, Osmo, a big, jovial man, full of enthusiasm, brought his wife, Henny, to Scotland to attend the 1978 Royal Club Annual Meeting, at which he brought greetings from Finland. The Vice-President of the Association is Eero Vilevaara, a splendid English speaker.

The Finns held their first international competition in March 1979, with Jack Anderson and his team again representing the Royal Club. In 1983, Leif Gronlund, Secretary of the Finnish Association, reported that the principal curling centre was Hyvinkaa; that curling had been started in Joensuu, 450 kilometres from Helsinki, where sixteen teams were playing in a league; that forty rinks played in three divisions of the Hyvinkaa league from December to March; and that schoolboys had started curling and a team called 'Four boys' was showing distinct promise.

The Finnish Association joined the European Curling Federation in 1980 and participated for the first time in the European Championships (at Grindelwald in 1981) when Osmo Anttila provided Finnish vodka with orange. Finland joined the International Curling Federation in 1983.

LUXEMBOURG

Luxembourg, which was admitted to membership of the International

A game for all sizes. The genial giant, the Canadian skip, Hec Gervais, dwarfs his Norwegian opponent, 15-year-old Sjur Loen, at the 1974 Silver Broom in Berne. Sjur, then an outstanding prospect, grew to full stature ten years later when he played third in the Norwegian team which won the 1984 World Championship. The ages of the 1974 Norwegian rink were 15, 16, 17 and 18 – the sum of which equalled the age of the delightful Georg von Krogh, President of the Norwegian Curling Association.

Curling Federation in 1984, is the smallest of the Federation members. Claas van den Houten, President of the Union Luxembourgeoise de Curling, reported in 1984 that the Union had only one active club, the Curling Club Hiversport Luxembourg.

In 1971, Armand Denter and Ernest Juttel tried unsuccessfully to start curling on an open skating rink in the north of Luxembourg. A year later, Armand Denter, a war invalid, was invited to participate in the World Games for Physical War Invalids in Courchevel in France. He bought second-hand curling stones in Switzerland, persuaded three men to join him, taught them the rudiments of the game and, to their astonishment, they won the gold medals with Josy Wagner as skip. This success acted as a spur and Camille Polfer, Luxembourg City sports director, provided two sheets of curling ice in a municipal project in Kockelschever. In 1974, the Hiversport Club was founded.

A national championship is held annually in addition to three international tournaments – Coupe d'Ouverture, Coupe de l'Amitié and Final Season Cup – with entries from Switzerland, France, Germany, the Netherlands, Scotland and Belgium. Teams from Luxembourg regularly compete in Switzerland, Germany and France and occasionally play in the Netherlands and Italy.

Luxembourg teams now participate in the European Championships, the men joining in 1980 and the ladies in 1981.

WALES

In December 1973, a large ice rink was opened as part of the Deeside Leisure Centre in North Wales. The new rink was provided by the local authority for skating but the management offered curling facilities and a group of interested curlers and curlers-to-be met and formed curling clubs.

A 'caretaker committee' was set up with Don Cowen as Secretary, and, in March 1974, Don wrote to the Royal Club reporting that the following proposals had been made: that a minimum of six local clubs should establish the Welsh Curling Association, with the representative members of the clubs forming the Committee of the Association, and that the Welsh Association would then apply for affiliation to the Royal Club.

The Welsh Curling Association was instituted in 1974 and the Council of the Royal Club offered to send a group of Scots curlers to play a match at Deeside. The offer was accepted and, after the Welsh Association joined the Royal Club in 1975, five Scots rinks led by Royal Club President David Duncan played the first Scotland v Wales international match at the Deeside Centre early in 1976, the welcome in Wales being headed by Don Cowen, the first Welsh President. We recall the fellowship of the occasion and playing with a mixed set of stones in a game cut short to allow a platform to be erected for a 'pop' concert in the evening. Welsh curlers travelled to Perth the following season and the match became an annual fixture.

Wales quickly became part of the international scene. The Association joined the European Curling Federation in 1978 and a men's team played in the European Championship in Varese in 1979. Men's and ladies' teams now compete in the 'European'. Wales joined the International Curling Federation in 1980 and participated in challenge matches for the right to play in the 1984 Air Canada Silver Broom, losing to the Netherlands in the final of a preliminary Netherlands-Wales-England play-off.

The scene at home is less encouraging. In 1984, John Stone, Past-President of the Association, Welsh representative on the International Curling Federation and a member of Welsh teams in European Championships, reported that, in the first ten years at Deeside, the Welsh curlers had managed to obtain ice for only two hours per week and that, because of this, the membership had remained constant – approximately eighty members in six clubs.

In the summer of 1984, an offer from the ice rink – for additional ice time from 6.30 a.m. to 10.15 a.m. on Sundays – was accepted. The thought of curling at 6.30 on a Sunday morning becomes even more daunting when you learn that, since Welsh curling started in 1974, Welsh curlers have prepared their own ice!

The Welsh Association holds an annual International Bonspiel, started in 1978, which attracts entries from England, Scotland and, on occasion, from other countries. A Ladies Branch of the Association was formed in 1982 and is now active and gaining in stature. Ann Stone is the Welsh representative on the Ladies Committee of the International Federation.

Visiting curlers are always assured of a warm 'welcome in the hillsides' in Wales.

NOTE: Wales should not properly be listed under 'Overseas Countries' but we include the Principality within the world-wide family of curling nations.
    The history of curling in England, which includes the early experiments with Glaciariums, is listed in the Chapter on the Growth of Artificial Ice Rinks.

WEST AFRICA

The Ivory Coast seems an unlikely curling centre but a curling club was founded in Abidjan on the West Coast of Africa in 1972 and later that

A team from the West African outpost of curling, Abidjan, pictured at a bonspiel in Paris. From *left*, A. Emery, Samuel Kouame, M. Duchastel (Canadian Ambassador), Dominique Mascolo, Guy Chiasson (Air Canada, Europe), Sodogodo Tidiani and J.P. Voutat.

year the club held an international tournament on the new indoor rink of the luxurious Ivoire Hotel.

The prime movers behind the establishment of curling in Africa were: Edwin Kilcher, member of the Curling Club Engiadina in St Moritz and owner of a banana plantation on the Ivory Coast; D. Pasquier, Director of Swissair, Abidjan; Mr Carpentier, General Manager of the hotel; and Mr and Mrs Moshé Meier.

In the first tournament, two teams from St Moritz and one from Paris joined Abidjan rinks – and St Moritz personality Bobby zen Ruffinen skipped the winning team. The second tournament, called the International African Derby, attracted sixty Swiss visitors and twelve visiting rinks – ten from Switzerland (including the winning rink skipped by another Swiss personality, Franz Marti), one from France and one from U.S.A. The American rink was skipped by Robert O. Young, from the Philadelphia Curling Club in Paoli, Pennsylvania, who reported that a Swiss jeweller had presented the Piaget Trophy, that the second prize was an ivory tusk and other prizes were African carvings and that it was fascinating to watch curlers leaving the ice, eating bananas and diving into a lagoon!

Members of the Abidjan Curling Club have curled in competitions in Canada and Europe.

JAPAN

In 1969, commenting on a visit by the American curling ambassador Dar Curtis to teach curling in Tokyo in 1967, we wrote: 'Bearing in mind to what an extent the sports-loving Japanese have adopted golf, we can only surmise what will happen if they take to curling ice'.*

We can now report that the Japanese *have* taken to the ice – in their thousands. At the 1984 Annual Meeting of the International Curling Federation, a deputation from Japan gave a glowing report of curling progress – the Japan Curling Association, established in February 1984, had run the first All Japan Curling Championship, and, in the three regional Associations of Hokkaido, Tokyo and Aichi, there were eight thousand curlers, two thousand of whom were already registered.

Teams from each regional Association played in the first national Championship in Sapporo, site of the 1972 Winter Olympic Games. Two Hokkaido teams contested the final and Yorozu's rink from Ikeda became the champions. It was fitting that the town of Ikeda should provide the winners because the first curling competition in Japan was held there in 1979, with the support of the Canadian Embassy and as part of a programme with the town's sister city, Penticton in British Columbia. In the same year, the Hokkaido–Canada Society purchased a full set of curling equipment from Canada and launched a series of seminars to teach curling to physical education teachers. The Governor of Hokkaido then asked the Province of Alberta to send a qualified instructor and Wally Ursuliak, member of Hec Gervais' World Champions rink in 1961, made the trip, was an immediate success and has been going to Japan annually since. Wally enthuses about his visits and tells of the keenness and dedication of the beginners and how he once supervised the instruction of four hundred High School curlers in one day. He confidently expects Japan to be a major force in world curling in the near future.

The President of the Japan Curling Association is Takeyoshi Morihana

* Following Dar Curtis's visit in 1967, Royal Club President Willie Wilson showed curling films in Tokyo in 1971 and, in 1972, the Royal Club corresponded with Japanese contacts in Tokyo and Sapporo and with Bruce Barnett, First Secretary in the Canadian Embassy in Tokyo.

of Sapporo and the Secretary General is Tetsuo Tanaka from whom the International Curling Federation anticipates an early application for membership. This would add another country to the World Championship line-up and another Continent to the fellowship of the game.*

SOUTH AFRICA

Graham Gardiner, educated in Edinburgh and now living in Johannesburg, represented South African curlers at the 1984 Annual Meeting of the Royal Club as President of the Johannesburg Curling Club. When Secretary in 1983, he sent this report of the Johannesburg Club which was instituted in 1981 and affiliated to the Royal Club the following year:

'We have now completed three seasons of curling in South Africa and I am delighted to report that the Johannesburg Curling Club, the only club in the Republic, goes from strength to strength. Our membership, of approximately fifty, is cosmopolitan with Swiss and Scots predominating but also including Irish, English, Dutch, Canadian and South African members. There is a healthy number of junior members from whom a "Most Improved Junior Curler" is chosen annually.

'The season runs from March to September with curling, indoors of course, taking place on one night per week. Competitions are run within the club each season for the Rigi Trophy, donated by the husband of a club member, and for the White Horse Whisky Trophy. Competition is keen and the standard is high on ice that is very slow by Scottish standards.

'This season, we held our first International Tournament for the Swissair Trophy. Four teams from Switzerland participated playing against four local teams, the final result being a win for the Wengen International team after a closely contested final against a local rink. The tournament was an outstanding success and we look forward to our next International Tournament in 1985 when we hope that teams not only from Switzerland, but also from other countries will be able to make the trip.

'We are deeply indebted to Hedi Roethlisberger of the Wengen Club who was able to organise a supply of stones which were kindly donated by various Swiss Clubs and airfreighted to South Africa by Swissair whose local manager is Kurt Roethlisberger, a club mem-

* Japan was admitted to membership of the Federation in December 1984.

ber. Incidentally, these stones are at present being ground and polished by a grave-stone manufacturer in the western Transvaal!'

At the 1983 Royal Club Annual Meeting, Max Schmieder, then the Johannesburg President, gave a general invitation to curlers to the first International Curling Tournament in Johannesburg in September, 1983 – an event with features not normally associated with a curling competition, including safari trips in the game parks of South Africa.

AUSTRALIA

In an interview in 1960, Jack Gordon, Managing Director of the St Moritz Ice Rink in Melbourne, headquarters of the National Ice Skating Association of Australia, clearly remembered curling with I.M. Moffat-Pender and his fellow Scots, Dr Cyril McGillicuddy and Robert Jackson in the Glaciarium in Melbourne in the 1930s.

Moffat-Pender, a Scottish rugby internationalist and Highland dancer of distinction, launched the Curling Club of Australia and made the event an all-round sporting occasion by inviting Norman Brookes, world lawn tennis champion (Wimbledon 1907) and famous Australian, to become President and throw the first stone on 15 May 1933. The Club lasted from 1933 until 1939, when Moffat-Pender died. The other Scots died during the Second World War and the old Glaciarium was demolished in the 1950s.

In 1980 and 1981, the Royal Club corresponded with ice rinks in Brisbane, Adelaide and near Melbourne, the managers of which were considering the introduction of curling to their ice. In 1983, Dr Alan Woods, a Fifer now resident in Melbourne, visited the Royal Club headquarters and resolved to restart the game in Australia.

Proof of the doctor's resolve came in August 1984, from Jacqueline Lund, daughter of George and Joan Grant of Carrbridge. (In 1984, George ended a total of nine years' service on the Royal Club Council.) Jacqueline reported that curling had started, on Thursday and Sunday evenings, in the Dandenong ice rink in Melbourne and that plans to establish the Australian Curling Association Inc. were well advanced. An advertisement in the *Melbourne Herald* and a notice displayed in the Canada Club in the city had brought an encouraging response.

A newsletter indicated that the ice had been marked by club members and a form of league competition would start in August 1984; that the membership, including Alan and Kirsten Woods, Jacqueline Lund and Secretary Audrey Elston, had risen to twenty (a membership application form was attached to the newsletter); that Gary King would convene a match committee and that a social committee for fund-raising would be established; that attempts were being made to obtain additional curling stones – from New Zealand and Scotland; that a scoreboard would be provided; that the design of an emblem was being considered – and that a special General Meeting would be held on 9 August 1984, to approve the Constitution and Rules of the new Australian Curling Association.

From this side of the world, we send 'Keen and Clear' greetings while waiting and hoping for news of the establishment of curling in Australia.

BELGIUM

The first news of curling in Belgium was sent by Madame Jenny Francis in 1964. She started to curl at Murren in Switzerland, presented a trophy there and returned to Belgium where she launched the Curling Club Liège, which obtained ice on Friday nights in the local ice rink, and organised the first Curling Championship of Liège.

In 1982, the Deurnese Curling Club, the Chairman and Secretary of which were based in Borsbeek, was affiliated to the Royal Club. The first club in Belgium is associated with the Royal Belgian Icesport Federation (formed in 1972) and its members curl in competitions in Luxembourg and other Continental countries.

SPAIN

Ron Fisk and fellow Canadians in Madrid were instrumental in forming the first curling club in Spain. The Madrid Club was instituted on 1 February 1983, and affiliated to the Royal Club the same year, with Christian and Mrs Hardy as Patron and Patroness, Garth Phillips as President and twenty-four members.

Curling has also been played in *Ireland* – in 1839, the celebrated John Cairnie inspired the founding of the Belfast Club, which played home-and-away matches with the Ardrossan Club in Scotland, and later clubs were started in 1879 at Clandeboye and Kiltonga, Newtonards, but no curling news has come from Ireland since 1900; in *Russia* the Moscow Club, which continued until the First World War, was established in 1873 by a Scot, William Hopper, who reported in 1876 that sixteen meetings for play had been held from November to February at Reaumur; Hopper and Lord Dufferin, the British Ambassador at St Petersburg, tried to start a St Petersburg club with the prospect of a 'curling congress' on the Neva; and *China* – in 1966, Ernst Debrunner, Treasurer of the Swiss Curling Association, was astonished to find curling stones in Tientsin (they were used by members of the Tientsin Club, which, founded by Scots in 1890, was active until the Second World War).

Wally Ursuliak, the energetic Canadian who has done so much to launch curling in Japan, forecasts that *Korea* will be the next curling country. The sports-conscious Koreans, who will host the 1988 Olympic Games, will be warmly welcomed to the world-wide community of curlers.

10

The Growth of Artificial Ice Rinks

THERE IS EVIDENCE that Scottish curlers, in revolt against their treatment by the weather, discussed the possibility of playing on an artificial surface in the early years of the nineteenth century. But the first *concrete* move was made by the irrepressible John Cairnie, whose book, *Essay on Curling and Artificial Pond Making*, was published in 1833.

More than 20 years before this, Cairnie suggested to the Duddingston Curling Society, of which he was a member, that artificial ponds should be laid. He started to build a pond but abandoned the idea when he could not find anyone to help him to finance the project. Thoughts of his pond would not leave him, and, after a Duddingston Club dinner in Edinburgh in 1827, he resolved a make a clay pond at his own expense. The pond, built on his land at Curling Hall, Largs, was completed early in January 1828, and, on 11 January, 'after one night's frost, a party of eight gentlemen had the satisfaction of enjoying curling on it in all its perfection'.*

Cairnie constructed his clay pond with small nodules of whinstone pounded into the clay and claimed that almost half of his pond 'exhibited a surface of stone'. He emphasised that the surface had to be level and that, when flooded to the depth of a quarter of an inch, it provided ice after one night's frost.

Cairnie hoped that this pond, which could be made at a trifling cost, would be used in Scots parishes. His paved rink, the idea for which sprang from youthful memories of making ice on pavements, 'to the great annoyance of His Majesty's lieges,' was much more expensive; 46 yards long and six yards broad at the ends, the 20-yard centre section being narrower, only four yards wide. On a base of lime and gravel mixed with gravel and sea sand, four-and-a-half-inch pavement stones were laid, with bevelled kerbs at the edges of the rink so that stones struck against them

---

* The Rev J. Somerville of Currie also claimed the invention and there was much controversy, and acrimonious correspondence, on the subject. It appears to us that Cairnie's claim was fair since his pond was *artificial* while Somerville's had a *natural* base.

would run off the pond without damage. Masons were instructed to dress each pavement stone to a perfect level; Cairnie claimed that the greatest deviation from the level on his pond did not exceed a quarter of an inch. The freestone 'flags' were then flooded with a few gallons of water from a force pump and curling was possible with reasonable frost although the rink was little more than 100 yards from the sea.

Cairnie's invention was adopted and improved by clubs throughout the nineteenth century. Concrete, asphalt and other bases were used but the principle was the same – the laying of a non-porous surface, which, when flooded, provided ice under a few degrees of frost.

The movement was carried a stage further through the genius of John Loudon Macadam (1756-1836), the Scot who invented the tarmacadam system of road-making. No curling history would be complete without a tribute to tarmac, which popularised curling throughout Scotland over eighty years ago.

The first tarmac curling rinks, the forerunners of hundreds in the country, were laid in Edinburgh in 1902 by the Watsonian Curling Club. The rinks, now lost to view under buildings at George Watson's College Playing Fields at Myreside, were laid by Andrew Scott, the Myreside groundsman, who offered his services to other curling clubs in an advertisement in Josh Bowie's treatise, *The Art of the Game* (1904). The tarmac rink soon superseded the concrete rinks which had a tendency to crack and develop bumps. Another reason for the sudden popularity of tarmac was the cost. A concrete curling rink cost over £100 while a tarmac rink could be laid for £20 or £30.

But the greatest advantage of tarmac was the reduction of preparatory work and the frequency of play. On many concrete and other shallow ponds, water lying up to an inch deep required a hard frost before play was possible. On tarmac, only a light spray of water was needed with the temperature a degree or two below freezing point and the game was on.

As the tarmac revolution swept the country, curling clubs vied with each other in providing efficient lighting systems for their ponds. Previously, as twilight merged into night, white handerchiefs were dangled on skips' brooms and candles, lanterns and flares were lit in an effort to prolong the play.*

The new systems of lighting changed the complexion of club activities. Naphtha, paraffin, acetylene and gas, with electricity the crowning amenity, illuminated the Scottish scene and, providing for evening and late

---

* In more recent times, we have heard of outdoor curling being played at nights under the glare of the headlamps of cars suitably stationed round a loch or pond.

night play, doubled the amount of curling.* (Some clubs which did not have their own ponds, negotiated with tennis clubs so that, with a water supply readily available, curling could be played on the courts in winter.)

George Harris, Secretary of the Arbroath Curling Club, wrote in 1910: 'Before this improvement (tarmac), our club could only get a game during very hard frost, but, this season, we enjoyed the pleasures of the roarin' game on forty different occasions, the most interesting games being played in the evenings under electric light.'†

Tarmac gave a fresh impetus to curling in Scotland and literally paved the way towards the advent of the big indoor ice rinks.

INDOOR RINKS
Early attempts to build indoor ice rinks proved abortive and it was a long time before indoor rinks were properly established and curlers could say with the versifier:

> Fare thee well, O fickle frost,
> Thou'rt no more the curler's boast.

The first attempt, made by a Mr Henry Kirk in London as early as 1842, was described in the Royal Club *Annual* of that year: 'A new marvellous feat of science is added to those by which this era has already distinguished, in the discovery of a chemical compound having all the appearance of ice – capable of being deposited in the sheet, and offering to the skater a suface much more agreeable for the purposes of his graceful exercise than that ordinarily supplied by the winter operations of nature upon our park waters. The gentleman who has achieved this victory over the elements of chemistry, Mr Henry Kirk, now exhibits the results of his five years' labour to that end, at a building on the grounds of Mr Jenkins in the New Road near to Dorset Square. The floor of an apartment there is covered with an apparently icy integument – not quite as clear as crystal but like congelation after a white frost – upon which a considerable number of members of the skating club indulged in their

---

*The most ingenious lighting system we have heard of was constructed, on what was called the Model Curling Pond, by Major Henderson, President of Bridge of Allan Curling Club, at Westerton, near Bridge of Allan, 120 years ago. Round the pond, Major Henderson, the proprietor, set up lines of lanterns which were attached by guttapercha tubes to an underground gas pipe which supplied Bridge of Allan. Using the same source of power, the Major lit the pathway leading from the town to the pond with lanterns hanging from a row of trees.

† A sheet of polythene laid on an existing pond holds water well and is much cheaper than making repairs to the pond. The Earl of Elgin, President of the Royal Club from 1967 to 1969, laid polythene on his pond at Broomhall, Dunfermline, and reported that the ice had been good for curling.

evolutions. This substance, seven-eighths of an inch thick, cannot be broken by any concussion short of that by a sledge-hammer.'

The reaction of curlers of the time was cool and critical: 'We know not whether artificial ice can be made available to the purposes of curling. To the really useful ends of curling, considered as a winter amusement to the rural part of the population disengaged from labour, artificial ice cannot be of much advantage.'

Mr Kirk's building, 70 feet long by 50 feet wide, was called a Glaciarium. It did not last and, as far as we know, curling was never played there, but the seed had been planted. There *was* curling in the Rusholme Rink in Manchester in 1877, on ice processed by Professor Gamgee, whose Secretary, Mr Hyde, travelled to Scotland, with a file of testimonials, in an attempt to set up ice rinks in Edinburgh and Glasgow. But nothing further was heard of the project.

The cost of the rink, £20,000, seems excessive in that Mid-Victorian period, but the next Glaciarium, built on the Gamgee principle and opened in Southport in 1879, cost over £30,000.* Edward Holden presented the Holden Challenge Shield, value 50 guineas, for competition twice a year, and the event was played at Southport until 1889. The Shield is now the prize for the Royal Club Rink Championship, a competition open to rinks of four regular members of the same club, which annually attracts an entry of over 400 rinks.

The Royal Club held its Annual Meeting in Southport in 1885, in recognition of the services given to curling by the Glaciarium and, after the Meeting, the Mayor of Southport welcomed over 200 curlers in the Prince of Wales Hotel. But the rink was closed through lack of support in May 1889 and went into liquidation in 1890 with a loss of £25,000, most of which was borne by Edward Holden.

Referring to the failure of the rink, in the curling section of *The Badminton Library* (1892), the Rev John Kerr skated on thin ice, which has since given way under him, when he prophesied. 'As the Southport Rink has had to be closed for want of patronage, it is to be feared that the chances of any further development of this ice-making scheme are very small.'

It was fitting that, when the cannie Scots at last decided to follow the example of their brother curlers in England, their indoor ice rinks, after a hesitant start, should take firm root. It was also natural because the curling population was already there, eagerly looking for outlets for more play.

* The Southport Glaciarium Cup is still played for by the Preston and Dalbeattie Clubs.

The first indoor ice rink in Scotland was the Scottish Ice Rink, at Crossmyloof in Glasgow, opened on 1 October 1907. A small group of businessmen formed a private company and launched a new era in Scottish curling.

The Scottish Ice Rink Skating and Curling Pavilion had a bandstand high up in the centre of the rink, an idea derived from the Moulin Rouge in Paris. The rink contained 'a dining-room, smoking room, kitchen and what not', and 'spectator learners' were encouraged to curl on vacant ice in the evenings at a modest fee. A fire destroyed the rink in 1917 and the existing Scottish Ice Rink was built on the ruins in 1928.

The four-sheet Lochrin Ice Pond at Tollcross, Edinburgh, was the next indoor rink. Opened in January 1912, it was the home of the Edinburgh Corporation, Edinburgh Markets and Edinburgh Masonic clubs and promised well but the venture was short-lived.

The much bigger Edinburgh Ice Rink, beside the Haymarket Station, Edinburgh, was opened on 5 February 1912, by Lord Balfour of Burleigh. When the old Scottish Ice Rink was destroyed, the Edinburgh Rink was the only curling rink in Scotland and, for many years, curlers from all parts of the country came to Edinburgh for their major bonspiels, provincial matches and club games. The rink remained a major centre of Scottish curling until it closed in February 1978, sixty-six years to the day from the opening ceremony in 1912.

Edinburgh was without a curling ice rink for a year until the four-sheet Gogar Park Curling Club was opened in January 1979, through the enterprise and drive of Kenneth Gumley, who reported at the opening ceremony that, five months before, the site had been an overgrown walled garden. In the early years, the club was run with a private membership, like a golf club, but the membership has recently been extended into various categories.

The other modern Edinburgh rink, run by the Edinburgh Curling Club, is alongside the big Murrayfield Ice Rink in the grounds of the Scottish Rugby Union. The older Murrayfield rink was built in 1939 and became a war casualty. It now concentrates on skating and ice-hockey while, alongside it, the new building, officially opened on 4 October 1980 – Royal Club President Philip Dawson throwing the first stone with Marjorie Broatch, Ladies' Branch President, holding the broom – is devoted exclusively to curling. The record of Past-Presidents and the competition boards, containing the names of trophy winners since the early days of Edinburgh curling, are the only reminders of sixty-six years at Haymarket.

Her Majesty The Queen, Patron of the Royal Club, honoured the curling community when she opened the new Aberdeen Curling Rink in 1983. In happy mood, The Queen prepares to receive a presentation from Jane Gray, with Chairman Dr Norman Cooper and Director Philip Dawson in attendance.

An ice rink in Aberdeen – the Aberdeen Winter Recreation Institute in Forbesfield Road – was opened in September 1912, but closed its doors in 1917. After the Second War, Aberdonian curlers played at Donald's Ice Rink, a building converted from a garage to a skating rink in 1939, until the floor collapsed and curling was discontinued in 1982. The new Aberdeen Curling Rink was officially opened on 18 October 1983 by Her Majesty The Queen, Patron of the Royal Club – the best possible augury for the future of the game in Aberdeen. The six-sheet rink is attractively laid out and well appointed. Dr Norman Cooper, Chairman, and his fellow directors have given the curlers in the North-East a centre of which they can be justly proud.

In the mid-thirties, the sister winter sport of ice-hockey gave curlers a helping hand and the game itself the fillip it needed to enter the modern era. The sudden boom of ice-hockey in Scotland attracted businessmen to build ice rinks, with accommodation for spectators, to satisfy the demand for the game. The pre-war boom days are over but the spectacular sport left a legacy to the curling fraternity which curlers gratefully accepted before the war and still acknowledge today.

The estimated cost of Perth Ice Rink (called the Central Scotland Ice Rink) was £26,000, an interesting figure to lay alongside the £30,000 expended at Southport almost sixty years before. The rink, which was opened by the Duke of Atholl on 1 October 1936, offered many new amenities, including seating for two thousand spectators, and advertised 'The Haven' tearoom – 'for Tea, Hot Muffins and a Chat'. The rink, now modernised with new features and splendid viewing facilities, has been the site of many World Championships.

Kirkcaldy Ice Rink, Dundee-Angus Ice Rink in Dundee, Falkirk Ice Rink and Dunfermline Ice Rink all opened in 1938; the Dunfermline rink closed thirty years ago and the Falkirk rink in 1977. Curling was also played at Paisley Ice Rink just before and during the Second World War but there has been no curling in Paisley since.

The Ayr Ice Rink was officially launched on 13 March 1939 and was eventually closed as a curling centre in 1972. But an enthusiastic group (Ayrshire Curlers Ltd.) built a new ice rink at Tam's Brig, an appropriate Ayr address, in 1973, and, in 1982, at a cost of £150,000, a three-sheet rink was added so that Ayr now offers all-the-year-round facilities for skating and ice-hockey and, during the winter season, week-end curling competitions in addition to normal curling. The Dundee-Angus Ice Rink also extended its curling facilities, adding six more sheets of ice in 1984.

After the spate of ice rink building in the 'thirties, there was a standstill for twenty-five years. The 'freeze' was eventually broken by the single-minded purpose of W. D. Wilson of St Boswells, a famous Border curler and an overseas tourist of repute. Willie Wilson, who served as Royal Club President from 1971 to 1973, returned from tours in Canada and the United States determined to build an ice rink in the Borders, a traditional stronghold of the game. He gathered round him an energetic group of keen curlers who were fired with his enthusiasm. A public meeting was held in Kelso in January 1963, and this led to the formation of the Border Ice Rink Ltd., with Willie Wilson as Chairman. The £40,000 four-sheet rink, situated alongside Kelso Golf Course, was officially opened by Royal Club President Major Allan Cameron on 1 October 1964 and was an immediate success.

Before Willie Wilson's inspired move, the eight major ice rinks in Scotland had been bursting at the seams, and it was clear that expansion was vital, but extension meetings broke up in disorder when capital expenditure was mentioned. The Border rink was the spur. Within four years four new indoor rinks made their appearance, the first of which, admittedly, was part of a massive new scheme and not a private venture.

Lord Fraser of Allander, a restless Scots industrialist, was the driving force behind the Aviemore Centre, the £3,000,000 complex within which the luxurious Aviemore Ice Rink is a focal point. The Centre, in its beautiful setting in the Cairngorm Mountains, was opened by Lady Fraser on 14 December 1966,* and the Aviemore Ice Rink, which annually runs the Highland Week of International Curling, with entries from many countries, is a name to conjure with in the curling world.

A month later, on 20 January 1967, the South of Scotland Ice Rink at Lockerbie in Dumfriesshire was opened by Captain Jack Anderson, Royal Club President. The five-sheet rink, with a design similar to the Border Ice Rink, on which it was based, is now one of the busiest ice rinks in the country – a resounding success which is giving valuable service particularly to the South of Scotland and the North of England.

The idea of the Lanarkshire Ice Rink at Hamilton was born in 1964 during a Canadian Tour by a Scottish Rotarian curling team, which included Tom Dickson, who became Chairman of the Board. It was highly appropriate, therefore, that Jack McKimmie, Gerry Boyd, Doug Washer and Bill Miller from Lachute flew from Canada for the opening ceremony for it was at Lachute that a small group of curlers discussed designs and dreamed of a brand new rink. The dream became a reality on 29 September 1967, when the rink was opened by Bill Robertson Aikman, Immediate Past-President of the Royal Club, an internationally famous curler and himself a Hamilton man.

The Inverness Ice Rink at Bught Park, Inverness, joined the growing number of Scottish rinks in 1968. The opening, performed by the Earl of Elgin, was attended by Canadian Air Force curlers from Germany and a group of the popular Chateau d'Oex curlers from Switzerland, who, with Scots personalities, enjoyed the opening bonspiel on lightning-fast ice on the five-sheet rink.

The Stranraer Ice Rink was opened on 31 October 1970, and curlers

---

* We recall that the timing of the opening ceremony was changed slightly – to allow the Earl of Rosebery, famous racehorse owner, and Bill Robertson Aikman, Royal Club President and Clerk of the Course at Hamilton and Lanark, to watch Arkle, the greatest horse of his time, in a race on television.

in the South-West of Scotland are indebted to Hammy McMillan, the dynamic businessman who launched the project. The four-sheet rink is an extension of the North West Castle Hotel and it can be said that Hammy established the concept of week-end bonspiels in Scotland with package-deals which include hotel accommodation and facilities and at least three games of curling at attractive rates. The week-end events, run by Hammy and Janet McMillan, both of whom are excellent curlers, have become so popular that they are oversubscribed. Royal Club President Tom Stewart threw the opening stone at the new rink in the deep South of Scotland, home of two recent Royal Club Presidents, Bob Grierson and Sam McColm.

John Stevenson and his family financed the ice rink at Greenacres, which was opened in 1979 with Tom Dickson, Royal Club President, throwing the first stone. John Stevenson, who supervised the construction of the rink and helped to build a wall with stone from his farm, even sprayed the ice before the opening bonspiel in the four-sheet rink alongside Greenacres Hotel in Howwood, Renfrewshire.

The Stirling Ice Rink, part of a sports complex at Williamfield, opened on 29 September 1980. The rink filled the gap caused by the loss of the Falkirk Ice Rink three years before and it was appropriate that Willie Young, famous Falkirk curler who scored a phenomenal record of major successes in the post-war years, should throw the ceremonial first stone. Ronnie Mayes, the Chairman at Stirling, is a dedicated worker for curling, having inherited his love of the game from his father, Alex, long-time President of Falkirk Ice Rink Curling Club.

Ian Robb was the driving force behind the establishment of the Atholl Curling Rink in Pitlochry and is chairman of the board. The rink, in the geographical centre of Scotland, was opened in October 1982 by the Earl of Mansfield, Minister of State, and Candian tourists Bill Meyer and Mike Gourlay and American national office-bearers Bill and Dorothy Ensign were among the large number of personalities present. Built on the site of the old Pitlochry Theatre, the Atholl rink was financed by a grant from the Scottish Tourist Board, a loan from Perth & District Council and contributions from the directors and a large group of shareholders. The four-sheet rink, set in beautiful countryside, receives solid support from the Pitlochry hotels which include keen curlers in their management teams.

Three new ice rinks were opened in Scotland in September 1984 – at Letham Grange, near Arbroath; in the Forest Hills Estate at Aberfoyle; and in Glenrothes.

Angus businessman Ken Smith master-minded the creation of a sports complex at Letham Grange, comprising hotel and holiday villa accommodation, a golf course (scheduled to open in 1986), riding centre, squash courts, swimming pool – and a four-sheet curling rink. The ice rink consultant, John Foster, is well known to the curlers of Scotland, and beyond, having been manager of Perth Ice Rink for thirty years. The attractive modern rink is beautifully situated in the Angus countryside.

The four-sheet rink at Aberfoyle is part of the new Forest Hills leisure centre in the Trossachs built for their timeshare owners by Barratt Multi-Ownership & Hotels Ltd. The hotel complex offers a wide variety of other sporting attractions, including a swimming pool and jacuzzi, squash and badminton courts, billiards and snooker tables – and, after play, saunas, solaria and Turkish baths.

Walker Contracts (Scotland) Ltd built the Crystals Arena in Glenrothes, to be run by Plimley Estates Ltd. The complex contains a full-sized ice rink for curling and skating, an indoor bowling rink and facilities for snooker and darts in addition to a restaurant and dance floor.

ENGLAND

The situation in England is far less healthy. After the failure of the Southport rink, there was curling at the Prince's Skating and Curling Club in London, and on 27 October 1910 the Manchester Ice Palace was opened. This was the venue for the small but vital group of clubs which comprise the First English Province of the Royal Club – until 1962. Imagine the feelings of the curlers in the Province when the Ice Palace was taken over for other activities and curling in the area was lost!

What can a keen curler do when he suddenly finds he has no ice to play on? To their eternal credit, the English curlers – many of whom are Scots, or have Scots ancestry – did not give up or even contemplate giving up. They rearranged their programme, staged their principal bonspiel in Edinburgh, and carried out a series of raids over the border to keep their hand in. The South of Scotland Ice Rink became an oasis for men thirsty for ice and Lockerbie now figures prominently on the Province fixture list. Preston curlers can reach the rink in under two hours on the motorway.

The First English Province curlers, who have been called 'the keenest of the keen', have a long and strong curling tradition. There is a record of a bonspiel between England and the Border counties of Scotland in 1795. English clubs were formed in the nineteenth century – Leeds (1820), Liverpool (1839), Newcastle (1843), Wigan (1861), Preston (1871),

Huddersfield (1892), Bradford (1895). In more modern times, Willie Kerr, for many years the major figure in England, became known as 'the father of English curling.' Willie was the embodiment of all that is good in the game. His sons, Edward and Dan, worthily maintained that tradition and they, with J. L. Kerr, other members of the Kerr family and a band of real enthusiasts continue to preserve curling as a vital force with few of the benefits enjoyed by Scots curlers.

The Province obtained 'home ice' again in 1965 by a lucky chance. The manager of the Ice Drome at Blackpool, Tony Scott, saw Tom Kerr, Dan Kerr's son, skating on a Sunday in his Preston Curling Club sweater. Their meeting led to regular play at Blackpool where the rinks were a few yards short. The English did not care, rightly believing that the game's the thing. Curling at Blackpool was discontinued in 1970.

In London, curling was played at Richmond Ice Rink, near Twickenham, a world-famous skating centre, for thirty years until 1980. The building was constructed by a Belgian company as a munitions factory during the First World War. The Richmond Ice Rink was founded in 1928, and, by strange coincidence, Ronald Alpe, Secretary at Richmond for many years, first visited the site when it was a car components factory prior to becoming an ice rink.

Two Scots, Harry Rule and Willie Blair, father of Sandy Blair, President of the English Curling Association (instituted in 1971),* were prime movers in a drive which led to the formation of the Richmond Curling Club in 1951, Harry Rule becoming the first President.

Eight clubs in the Province of London of the Royal Club curled once a week, on Tuesday evenings, at Richmond. A Scot, Mr J. B. Duncan, was Chairman of the rink and was sympathetic to curling requests, regularly attending the dinner after the Scotland *v* England international match – arranged every second year in London by Alex Kirkbright, curling Secretary for the final ten years at Richmond.† When a new company was formed, curling was dropped from the ice rink programme in the 1979–80 season.

In May 1983 Sandy Blair, the popular English Association President, travelled to the ice rink at Peterborough – one hundred miles north of London – with twenty London curlers. They took their own stones and played a demonstration game for an hour and then invited interested

---

* Sandy's grandfather, Alexander Blair, an architect, was one of the founders of the Scottish Ice Rink and the Alexander Blair Trophy is played annually in Glasgow.

† The 1982 international was held at Streatham Ice Rink.

spectators to join them. Forty volunteers, most of whom had never seen a curling stone, took their first uncertain steps on the rink.

A month later, a meeting was held and the Peterborough Curling Club was formed. Donald Barclay, who used to curl in London and before that with the Paisley St Mirren Club in Glasgow, was elected President. Nan Rains, who courageously accepted the post of Secretary, had never curled but Sandy Blair reported that she had curling in her blood, being a niece of Willie Wilson of St Boswells! Nan is now a Committee member and the Secretary is Terry Nicholls.

Helpful co-operation from Paul French, the rink manager, and his staff consolidated the early efforts, and on 26 November 1983 the Peterborough curlers welcomed visitors from Wales, London and the Preston and Glendale clubs at the first Peterborough Johnnie Walker Bonspiel. The final score was Peterborough 44, Visitors 40 and the joint winning rinks, which were skipped by Sandy Blair and Eric Hinds, contained curlers who had thrown their first stones only a few months before.

11
Overseas Tours

IN FORMER TIMES, Scottish curlers undertook the perilous journey on foot over the snow-capped hill or travelled by cart or trap to play a bonspiel against the neighbouring parish. In 1847, Charles Cowan, a distinguished curling administrator, urged curlers to travel by train in an article, *Prospective Advantages of Railways for Curlers*, in which he advised that 'sheets of shallow water be procured in juxtaposition with leading lines of railways'.

Now we fly in comfort to all parts of the curling world and travel to Switzerland more quickly than many an old-time curler took to reach the bonspiel in the next valley. The growth of overseas curling tours constitutes a revolution in the history of the game which ranks in importance with the rounding of the stone and the invention of artificial ice.

'The curlers of Canada would be glad to play a friendly game against players from Scotland, if such a match could be arranged for next winter, and to ascertain on what terms such a challenge would be acccepted.'

This invitation, from the Canadian Branch of the Royal Club, was sent to Scotland as long ago as 1858. A Scottish committee was formed, and, the following year, one of its members wrote: 'Our brethren in Canada appear to be disappointed that we have not yet accepted their challenge, but they may rest assured that nothing could give us more pleasure than having a meeting with them, and we hope a good time is coming, either for us going *there*, or for them coming *here*.'

David Mair, Secretary of the Canadian Branch, sent another letter, couched in more challenging terms: 'It surely cannot be that the Scotchmen are afraid of us! I am confident we could find two rinks in Canada who would be willing to cross and try what they could do.'

There was talk but no action. The Canadians, joined by the Americans, persisted, and in 1878 the Secretary of the Ontario Branch of the Royal Club and the President of the Grand National Curling Club of America sent separate invitations for Scots teams to tour Canada and the United States. Circulars were sent to Scottish clubs but, again, no tour materialised.

On the financial side, Mr Russell of the Ontario Branch of the Royal Club estimated in 1884 that a three-month tour would cost about £50 per curler. In 1892, a recommendation that a sum not exceeding £200 be provided by the Royal Club to meet expenses was rejected by the Annual Meeting. Transatlantic correspondence continued until 1900 when Dr Barclay and the Rev Dr Campbell, representing the Canadian Branch, came from Montreal to make a personal plea at the Royal Club Annual Meeting in Glasgow. This spurred the curlers of Scotland into action.

A 'Meeting of Gentlemen interested in the Proposal to send Curling Teams to Canada and the States'* was held in the Royal Club offices in April 1902, and the fourteen Gentlemen, with Hugh Gilmour of the Waverley Club in the chair, adopted the following resolution: 'The meeting, being unanimously of opinion that the visit proposed is highly desirable both from a curling and Imperial point of view, appointed all the gentlemen present to form a committee, with power to add to their number, to gather further information, arrange ways and means and generally to take any further steps with a view of carrying the matter through successfully; and also to prepare a report to be submitted to the next annual meeting of the Royal Club; it being understood that any team going out shall be under the auspices of the R.C.C.C.'.

The proposals were approved and an advertisement calling for volunteer tourists was inserted in the Press. Over two hundred applicants embarrassed the selection committee who, after much heart-searching, chose twenty-eight curlers and appointed the Chaplain, the Rev John Kerr, as captain of this first-ever Scottish team to tour overseas. The team sailed for Canada in December 1902.

After a three-month tour, the captain reported on the overwhelming hospitality received from Canadians at every stage of the journey and added that, wherever the tired Scots went, they found a fresh relay of Canadian curlers waiting to receive them 'with their feet, as it were, upon their native heath'. It has been the same ever since. It is why the curlers of the host country will always start favourites.

The captain gave one interesting reason for this first Canadian victory: 'Our curling stones, while being transferred from place to place in the railway trains that were heated to such a high temperature, became themselves over-heated and required a considerable time to cool down. On more than one occasion the members of the team were surprised to find

* The Minute of the Meeting was presented to the Royal Club in 1982 by Sir John Gilmour, Royal Club President in 1956-57. His grandfather was Vice-President of the Royal Club in 1902 and President in 1912-13.

The Scottish team which made the first overseas curling tour – to Canada in 1902–03. The Rev John Kerr, the team Captain, is seated fourth from the right.

their curling stones settling down half-way up the rink when they had given them sufficient impetus to carry them into the "parish", and on going up to find out the reason for such conduct, it was found that by their extra warmth the stones had embedded themselves to a considerable depth in the ice.'

The Canadians made their first tour to Scotland in 1909 and reports of the occasion indicate the excitement caused by the arrival of the thirty-seven tourists in Edinburgh. The atmosphere of anticipation was heightened by Mr Maitland, the station master at Waverley Station, who placed fog signals on the rails leading to the main platform and loud reports heralded the approach of the visitors.

Amid scenes of wild enthusiasm, a pipe band led a long procession into Princes Street *en route* to the North British Hotel. The next day, a specially decorated train took the Canadians to Peebles, where they planted a maple tree in the public park. They marched in torchlight procession with members of the Upper Strathearn Province. Novel and elaborate plans were made at every stopping point of the tour to welcome the visiting team.

Over five hundred curlers attended the tour banquet in the Music Hall, Edinburgh, under the chairmanship of Lord Strathcona and Mount Royal, President of the Royal Club, who presented the Strathcona Cup for competition between the two countries.*

There were two particular personalities in that first Canadian team – the team captain, the Hon Duncan Cameron Fraser, Lieutenant-Governor of Nova Scotia, 'an exceptionally tall figure with strong Celtic features, whose splendid oratory touched all hearts and set the whole gathering aglow with enthusiasm;' and C. W. Macpherson, 'possibly the cheeriest tourist,' who travelled seven thousand miles to reach Scotland from Dawson City in the Yukon, starting his journey on a dog sledge!

A Royal Club team, captained by the President, John Watson, went to the United States in 1955, following the first tour by American curlers in Scotland in 1952. John Watson and the nineteen members of his team were, in John's words, 'photographed, televised, feted, bagpiped and generally overwhelmed with kindness'. Team members called the tour 'the experience of a lifetime'. The Scots won the trophy, presented for competition between the countries by Commander Herries Maxwell, Royal Club President in 1950–51, and gained countless admirers with the accuracy *and speed* of their play. Glenn Harris, editor of *The North American Curling News*, reported: 'The Scots curl concisely, quickly – and no foolin'. No time-consuming decisions in the "head", no lengthy consultations on the shot to play.' Tours with the United States are now on the same basis as tours with Canada – a five-year home-and-away programme – and American curlers will visit Scotland again in 1987.†

The lady curlers of Scotland made history when they toured in Canada and the United States in 1958.‡ Captained by Jean Gow, wife of the reigning Royal Club President, Brigadier Jack Gow, and with Mamie

---

* The beautiful cup, the most valuable of many trophies owned by the Royal Club, has been won eight times by Canada, seven times by Scotland. The countries now play home-and-away every five years and the Canadians will make their next tour in Scotland in January 1988.

† The Scots were unbeaten in the first six Herries Maxwell Trophy matches, having won in Scotland in 1952, 1962 and 1972 and in U.S.A. in 1955, 1967 and 1977. The 1982 U.S. team in Scotland, under the joint captaincy of Bud Chandler and Bill Ensign, scored their first victory – and carrried the trophy back to America in triumph.

‡ Three years before, in 1955, eight Canadian and eight American ladies made the inaugural ladies' tour when they came to Scotland under the joint captaincy of Mrs H. L. Liffiton (Canada) and Mrs Horace Vaile (U.S.A.).

Highet as Vice-Captain, the sixteen Scots became front-page news. These newspaper 'quotes' give a hint of the atmosphere of that first ladies' tour, in which the Scots beat Canada by 486 shots to 396 and U.S.A. by 403 shots to 264:

'Perhaps it was the bagpipes, perhaps the fine dinner and certainly the entertainment by Peterborough lady curlers which helped the Scots to relax and later show their natural vivacity as eight of them clicked heels and hooted in a Scottish reel. Jenny Nicol from Fife sang *Mary's Wedding*, with her countrywomen joining her in each chorus.'

'The Ottawa Curling Club became a wee bit of Scotland when the team of Scots was entertained to lunch. These ladies from the land where curling originated were colourfully arrayed in tartan skirts, heavy sweaters and tam o'shanters trimmed with pins. The ladies all wore their own tartans, which, unlike their names, do not change with marriage.'

Muriel McPherson, the Scottish Secretary, echoed the sentiments of Arthur Frame, Secretary of the 1957 Team in Canada, who remarked on his return: 'All tourists should pack a case of sleep!'

At the invitation of the Royal Club, tours by overseas countries in Scotland were made by Sweden and Switzerland in 1963, Norway in 1965, France in 1968, Germany in 1972* and New Zealand in 1973.

Acting on a proposal by Ian Turnbull, 1983–84 President, the Royal Club initiated a tour programme with countries on a ten-year cycle – home-and-away tours every five years with the various countries – and established January as the official touring month. The future programme is:

> 1986 – Germans in Scotland. New Zealanders in Scotland in February/March.
> 1987 – Scots in U.S.A.
> 1988 – Canadians in Scotland.
> 1989 – Scots in Switzerland.
> 1990 – available for a tour if offered.
> 1991 – Scots in Germany.
> 1992 – Americans in Scotland.
> 1993 – Scots in Canada.

The first large-scale international match in history was played between

---

* The two closest tour results have been in Scottish tours in Germany. In 1975, David Duncan's team finished equal in games (17½ each) and lost by 296 to 294 shots. In 1982, Robin Brechin's team won by 19 games to 18 and by 248 to 245 shots. The results of both tours depended on the last shot!

Canada and the United States at Buffalo, Lake Erie, on 5 January 1865, with over two hundred curlers involved in a five-hour struggle. James S. Lyon, the chairman at the dinner after the memorable day said: 'Battle was fought on the dividing waters between the United States, during the Presidency of Abraham Lincoln, and Canada, in the twenty-ninth year of the reign of the glorious matron, Queen Victoria.'

The following day, the *Buffalo Express* reported: 'The watery line which separates us from our Canadian neighbours is bridged over by reciprocal friendship. We gracefully accept a handsome defeat. True, it may be that the superior practice of our Canadian friends resulted in our discomfiture, but what of that? The result has been a genial meeting, beneficial to both States, and pleasant to all curlers.'

Genial meetings, beneficial to both sides and pleasant to all curlers. The Buffalo newspaperman summed up not only the first tour but the succeeding tours by all curling nations. An overseas tour is, truly, 'the experience of a lifetime', in which curlers feel the glow of fellowship, and enjoy the fun and rich humour which goes with it, including the inevitable *faux pas* which the perpetrator is never allowed to forget!

12

International Curling Federation

AN ATTEMPT TO form an International Curling Federation – a prerequisite for an application for curling to be included in the Winter Olympic Games – was made in June 1957, when a meeting was called by the Royal Club in Edinburgh. Royal Club President Sir John Gilmour chaired the meeting which was attended by Collie Campbell (Canada), Walter Rhodes (U.S.A.), a representative from the Italian Curling Association and a Royal Club Committee of Bill Piper, Alex Mayes, Gilbert McClung and Robin Welsh. The meeting agreed to make an application to participate in the 1960 Winter Olympics. The International Olympic Committee acknowledged the application, stating that it would be discussed at a meeting in Sofia in September 1957, but nothing further was heard.

In 1965, because of the tremendous growth of the game in the world, the Royal Club again initiated plans for international meetings, and, during the World Championship for the Scotch Whisky Cup in March 1965, invited office-bearers from overseas Associations to 'A Meeting of Administrators and Personalities' in Perth. At this meeting, the President of the Royal Club, Major Allan Cameron of Allangrange, proposed that an International Committee of the Royal Club be formed. At a second meeting three days later, it was agreed that the new body should be called the International Curling Federation and that a draft Constitution should be prepared.

The first meeting was attended by Major Allan Cameron, Chairman, Bill Robertson Aikman, President-Elect, and Robin Welsh, Secretary of the Royal Club; Collie Campbell, Chairman, Programme Committee of the Dominion Curling Association; Rolf Christensen, President of the Norwegian Curling Association; Per Odlund, President, and Sven Eklund, Secretary of the Swedish Curling Association; Elmer Freytag of the U.S. Men's Curling Association; and Charles Schenkel, President, and Johnnie Tschappeler of the Swiss Curling Association. Theo Welschen substituted for Johnnie Tschappeler at the second meeting which was also attended by Brigadier Jack Gow, Past-President of the Royal Club.

Representatives of seven nations – Scotland, Canada, U.S.A., Sweden, Norway, Switzerland and France – met during the Scotch Whisky Cup in Vancouver in March 1966, and it was agreed that, subject to the approval of at least three member countries, the Federation would be deemed to be established as from 1 April 1966.

When the representatives met in Perth in 1967, the establishment of the Federation was confirmed and an amended Constitution was ratified. Rules for International Competitions, prepared by a sub-committee of Collie Campbell, Sven Eklund and Robin Welsh, were considered, and, at the next meeting, held in Pointe Claire, Quebec – site of the first Air Canada Silver Broom – in March 1968, these rules were approved and adopted for the World Championship.

Founder members of the Federation were the Royal Club and the national Associations of Canada, Norway, Sweden, Switzerland, France and Germany. A letter of support was received from the New Zealand Province of the Royal Club and a verbal application to join was accepted from the United States Men's Curling Association.

Major Allan Cameron, who had called the first meeting, was appointed first President of the Federation. He served for two years and was succeeded by Brigadier Collie Campbell, a famous figure in world curling, who, in addition to his contributions as administrator and international ambassador, carved a special niche in curling history as the creator of 'morning class', at which, between 7 and 9 each morning, resplendent in special apron, he dispensed his particular elixir of life – a ceremony which required cases of gin, crates of lemons, bags of sugar and considerable expertise. 'Collie's class' was acknowledged by curlers the world over as the best possible way to start each day.

Collie Campbell's diplomacy, learned in a life of wide experience, including service as a Minister in the Canadian legislature, was a crucial factor in the formative years of the Federation. Early meetings were exploratory and fraught with difficulties as administrators from varied curling backgrounds propounded their strongly-held views. When meetings were in danger of reaching an impasse, Collie would break the deadlock by delivering a historical treatise, stressing the importance of fellowship – or would announce a brief recess and invite representatives for a gin and tonic!

In his inimitable way, Collie guided and strengthened the Federation. When he died in 1978 in his tenth Presidential year, he was succeeded by Sven Eklund who had represented Sweden since the formation of the Federation. As a curler, he had played in the Scotch Whisky Cup (1963).

As Secretary of the Swedish Curling Association,* he had extensive administrative experience. As linguist, he was able to clarify contentious points and his excellent English was enhanced by a wide knowledge of colloquial terms. Sven, who served the Federation with distinction, had many verbal battles with Secretary Robin Welsh, with whom he shared interests outside curling. After one lengthy session, conducted in true curling spirit, Sven pointed out vehemently that he couldn't understand Robin's Anglo-Saxon sense of humour! The wry remark indicated a difference of interpretation which is a feature of meetings of the international forum of curling.

After Collie Campbell's death, the Federation ruled that a President could serve for a maximum of three years, and, in 1982, Clif Thompson, like Collie a Past-President of the Canadian Curling Association, was elected President – and grasped the reins of office with authority and skill. Coincidental with his election, Air Canada, sponsor of the Silver Broom World Championship, asked the Federation to assume more responsibility in the organisation of the top world event and it was fortunate that the President was able to supervise the complex division of responsibilities in a series of meetings in his own country prior to meetings with the Federation's Executive Committee.

Clif's own responsibilities extended far beyond the meetings with Air Canada.† In a feverish schedule, he ranged over a wide series of issues – sponsorship and televising of three World Championships; minimum standards and challenge matches for world play; credentials for membership of the Federation; a development plan, which he initiated, to take curling into new countries; meetings and correspondence about the inclusion of curling as a demonstration sport in the 1988 Winter Olympics in Calgary. His work load set a standard which will be difficult to follow and all is done with quiet efficiency and a rational approach – exactly the blend needed to steer the destinies of the Federation through the torrent of words generated by the representatives of sixteen countries. There were eight Federation meetings during the week of the 1984 Silver Broom in Duluth. With so much talking at so many meetings, rationality, commonsense and a sense of humour are attributes, in Shakespeare's words, devoutly to be wished.

A controversial issue at Duluth was the approval, by the narrowest of

* Sven Eklund was Secretary of the Swedish Curling Association for twenty years from season 1961–62.
† In August 1984, Air Canada gave notice of withdrawal from sponsorship of the World Championships (see chapter on World Championships).

margins (a single vote), of a new penalty system which gave the Chief Umpire at World Championships powers (a) to warn players about the hog-line delivery rule at the players' meeting, (b) to instruct the playing side to remove a stone after a clear infraction of the rule, (c) where there was a further infraction by the same player, to order the removal of the stone plus the suspension of the player for the remainder of the game in progress and (d) where there was a further infraction by the same player, to order the removal of the stone plus the suspension of the player for the remainder of the game - and to make a report which would render the player subject to suspension for the remainder of the competition, such suspension requiring the approval of the Federation. (It was noted that, where there was doubt about the release point on delivery - what was called the 'grey area' - the player would be cautioned but no other action would be taken.)

The unfortunate feature of the controversy was that the system was proposed as a 'working model'. Without notifying the Federation, the chief umpires at the 1983 European Championships at Vasteras had introduced the system for the Championships and then reported their action to the Federation on the third day of play. Clearly, the revolutionary new system, which included the final sanction of suspending a player, should first have been submitted to the elected representatives of the Federation who hold the ultimate authority on international affairs.

Fredy Collioud from Berne, who skipped the Swiss rink in the World Championship in 1978, is the Federation Vice-President and the Federation is composed of representatives from the Royal Club (Scotland), Canada, U.S.A., Sweden, Switzerland, Norway, France, Germany, Denmark, Italy, England, the Netherlands, Wales, Austria, and Finland and Luxembourg which were accepted as members in the 1983-84 season. The number of representatives and votes per country is dictated by the curling population in the country. The Royal Club headquarters are the Federation headquarters and the Royal Club Secretary is the Federation Secretary. Robin Welsh, Secretary of the Federation since its inception, retired in 1984 and was succeeded by his successor in the Royal Club, Jim Aitken.

The Executive Committee of the Federation is composed of the office-bearers and representatives from Canada, U.S.A., United Kingdom, Scandinavia and Continental Europe - and a member of the Ladies Committee when matters concerning ladies' curling are on the agenda.

The Ladies Committee, containing single representatives from each of the member countries, works in co-operation with the Executive Committee to deal with sponsors of Ladies World Championships and other matters concerned with international ladies' curling. Christine Black, the English representative, is Secretary of the Ladies Committee which holds an annual closed meeting with the Federation.

INTERNATIONAL CURLING FEDERATION

1984–85

President – G. Clif Thompson (Canada)
Vice-President – Fredy Collioud (Switzerland)
Secretary – Jim M. Aitken (Royal Club)
2 Coates Crescent, Edinburgh EH3 7AN
Treasurer – Art J. Cobb (U.S.A.)

REPRESENTATIVES

Royal Caledonian Curling Club – Ian Turnbull, Willie Sanderson, Bill Muirhead
Canadian Curling Association – Mike Chernoff, Ralph Boyd, Clyde Opaleychuk
United States Curling Association – Art Cobb, Don McKay, Don Barcome
Swedish Curling Association – Axel Kamp, Hakan Sundstrom
Swiss Curling Association – Peter Scheurmann, Pierre Thuring
Norwegian Curling Association – Peter Lange
French Curling Committee – Gerard Alazet (successor to Pierre Catella)
German Curling Association – Charles Heckmann
Danish Curling Association – Sten Willer-Andersen
Italian Curling Association – Ivo Lorenzi
English Curling Association – Sandy Blair
Netherlands Curling Association – Eric Harmsen
Welsh Curling Association – John Stone
Austrian Curling Association – Gunther Hummelt
Finnish Curling Association – Osmo Anttila
Luxembourg Curling Association – Claas van den Houten

THE INTERNATIONAL CURLING FEDERATION RULES FOR INTERNATIONAL COMPETITIONS

1   INTERPRETATION

In these rules, umpires' rulings, and other official documents of the Federation and its officers:

(a)   'competition' means a playdown by any number of teams playing games to determine a winner;

(b)   'end' means that part of a game in which the two opposing teams each deliver eight stones alternately and then determine the score;

(c)   'Federation': the International Curling Federation;

(d)   'game' means play between two teams to determine a winner;

(e)   'house' means the area within the outside circle at each end of the rink;

(f)   'match' means play between two or more teams on one side against an equal number of teams on the other side

to determine a winning side by the total number of
shots or games;

(g) 'rink' means an area of ice marked in accordance with
Rule 3.

2   APPLICATION

These rules apply to games:

(a) within the jurisdiction of the Federation; or

(b) to which they have been made applicable by the curling
body having jurisdiction.

3   RINK

(1) Where possible, the rink shall be drawn on the ice in
accordance with the diagram (page 50).

(2) Two rubber hacks of a style and size approved by the
Federation shall be placed on the foot line with the
inside edge of each hack 7·62 cm. (3 inches) from the
centre line and on opposite sides of the centre line. The
length of the hack shall not exceed 20·32 cm. (8 inches).
The rubber of the hack shall be attached firmly to wood
or other suitable material and the hack shall be recessed
into the ice as much as is practical, but no more than
5·04 cm. (2 inches) in depth. There shall be no obstruc-
tion behind the hack structure.

4   STONES

(1) Curling stones shall be of circular shape.

(2) No stone, including handle and bolt, shall be of greater
weight than 19·96 kilograms (44 lbs.) or of greater circumference than 91·44 centimetres (36 inches) or of less
height than 11·43 centimetres (4·5 inches).

(3) If a stone is broken in play, the largest fragment shall
be counted in that end, the player using another stone
thereafter.

(4) A stone that rolls over in its course or comes to rest on
its side or top shall be removed immediately from play.

(5) Where the handle of a stone quits the stone in delivery,
the player is entitled to replay the shot.

(6) A stone that does not clear the farther hog line shall be

removed immediately from play, except where it has struck another stone lying in play.

(7) A stone that passes the back line and lies clear of it shall be removed immediately from play.

(8) A stone that hits a side board or comes to rest biting a side line shall be removed immediately from play.

(9) A stone that touches or crosses a side line and finishes within the rink remains in play.

(10) No stones shall be measured by instrument until the last stone of the end has come to rest except by the umpire, when requested by a skip, to decide whether or not a stone is in play.

5 TEAMS

(1) At the start of a competition, every team shall be composed of four players and each player shall deliver two stones in each end alternately with his opponent.

(2) No player shall use footwear or equipment that may damage the surface of the ice.

(3) The rotation of play established by a team during the first end of a game shall be observed throughout the game.

(4) The teams opposing each other in a game shall settle by lot the team that will lead at the first end, after which the winner of the preceding end shall lead.

(5) Where a player because of illness or accident or for any other valid reason is unable:

(a) to continue to play in a game; or

(b) to play at the start of a game, his skip may

(c) finish the game then in progress and start any subsequent game with the remaining players, in which case the first two players shall play three stones each; or

(d) bring in a qualified substitute for the game then in progress or at the start of any subsequent game.

(6) A player who was unable to continue to play in a game or to play at the start of a game may not resume play until the start of a subsequent game.

(7) No team shall play more than two substitutes in a competition.

(8) A team shall not play under any circumstances with fewer than three players.

6 SKIPS

(1) The skip has the exclusive direction of the game for his team.

(2) Subject to Rule 5 (3), the skip may play any position in his team that he chooses.

(3) When it is the skip's turn to play, he shall select one of his players to act as skip in his place who shall remain in that capacity throughout the course of that game. The skip may, however, return to the house for brief consultation.

7 POSITION OF PLAYERS

(1) Only the skips or acting skips in charge of the house for the time being may stand within the house and the skip of the playing team has the choice of place and shall not be obstructed by the other skip, but behind the tee line the privileges of both in regard to sweeping are equal.

(2) The players, other than the skip and acting skip, shall not stand behind the house, but shall place themselves along the sides of the rink between the hog lines, except when sweeping or about to deliver a stone.

8 DELIVERY

(1) Right-handed players shall play from the hack on the left of the centre line, and left-handed players from the hack on the right of the centre line.

(2) In the delivery of the stone, the stone shall be clearly released from the hand before the stone reaches the nearer hog line. If the player fails to so release the stone, it shall be removed from play immediately by the playing team. If the stone has struck another stone, the played stone shall be removed from play by the playing team and any displaced stone shall be placed as nearly as

possible where it originally lay to the satisfaction of the opposing skip.

(3) A stone that has not been released from the player's hand and that has not reached the nearer tee line may be returned to the hack and re-delivered.

(4) Each player shall be ready to deliver his stone when his turn comes, and shall not take an unreasonable time to play. Where the chief umpire considers that play is unnecessarily slow, he shall notify the skip of the team at fault that if their next stone is not delivered within 30 seconds from the time he gives a signal, he will order the stone to be removed from play immediately.

(5) Where a player delivers a stone belonging to the opposing team, a stone belonging to his team shall be put in its place.

(6) Where a player delivers a stone out of proper rotation it shall be removed from play immediately by the playing team and returned to the player to be delivered in proper rotation, but where the mistake is not discovered until after the stone has come to rest or struck another stone, the end shall be continued as if the mistake had not occurred, and the missed stone shall be delivered by the player missing his turn as the last stone for his team in that end.

(7) Where the skips agree that a stone has been missed but are unable to agree as to which player missed his turn, the lead of the team that made the mistake shall play the last stone for his team in that end.

(8) Where two stones of a team are delivered in succession in the same end, the opposing skip shall remove the stone played by mistake, replace to his satisfaction any stone displaced by the stone played by mistake, and continue the end as if the mistake had not occurred, and the player who delivered the stone played by mistake shall re-deliver it as the last stone for his team in that end.

(9) Where a player delivers three stones in one end, the end shall be continued as if the mistake had not occurred

and the fourth player of the team that made the mistake shall deliver one stone only in that end.

9 SWEEPING

(1) Between the tee lines, a running stone, or a stone set in motion by a running stone, may be swept by any one or more of the team to which it belongs.

(2) Behind the tee line the skip or acting skip of each team is entitled to sweep any stone but neither of them shall start to sweep an approaching stone until it reaches the tee line.

(3) The sweeping motion shall be from side to side across the entire running surface in front of the stone and clearly finish to either side of the stone, and no sweepings or other debris shall be left in front of a running stone.

(4) When sweeping with a brush no part of its handle shall be over the stone.

10 TOUCHED RUNNING STONES

(1) If a running stone is touched by any of the playing team or by his equipment, the burned stone shall be removed from play immediately by that team. However, if in the opinion of the opposing skip, removal of the stone would be beneficial to the offending team, then he may place the stone as nearly as possible to the position where he considers it would have come to rest had it not been touched. He may also reposition any stone or stones that would have been displaced had the running stone not been touched and been allowed to continue.

(2) If a running stone is touched by any of the opposing team, or by his equipment, the stone shall be placed where the skip of the team to which it belongs considers it would have come to rest if it had not been touched.

(3) If the position of any stone is altered by a burned stone, the skip opposed to the team at fault may elect:
(a) to remove the burned stone and replace all other

altered stones to the position where he considers they originally lay; or

(b) to leave the burned stone and all altered stones where they came to rest.

11 DISPLACED STATIONARY STONES

(1) If a stone which would have altered the course of a running stone is displaced by the playing team, the running stone shall be allowed to come to rest and may be left there or removed from play immediately at the discretion of the opposing skip.

(2) If the running stone is removed from play then all displaced stones shall be placed where the opposing skip considers they originally lay.

(3) If the running stone is left where it came to rest, then displaced stones must remain where they came to rest.

12 SCORING

(1) Games shall be decided by a majority of shots and a team scores one shot for each stone that is nearer the tee than any stone of the opposing team.

(2) Every stone that is within 1·83 metres (6 feet) of the tee is eligible to be counted.

(3) Measurements shall be taken from the tee to the nearest part of the stone.

(4) An end shall be considered as decided when the skips or acting skips in charge of the house at the time agree upon the score for that end.

(5) If two or more stones are so close to the tee that it is impossible to use a measuring device to determine the scoring stone, the end shall be scored as a blank end.

13 UMPIRE

(1) The umpire has the general superintendence of, and shall govern, any game to which he is assigned.

(2) The umpire shall determine any matter in dispute between opposing skips, whether or not the matter is covered in the rules.

(3) The umpire shall not intervene in any game or determine any matter in dispute unless requested to do so by one of the opposing skips.

14 CHIEF UMPIRE

(1) The chief umpire shall hear and determine appeals from decisions of umpires. His decision is final.

(2) Where the chief umpire has been so authorised, he may intervene at any time in any game and give such directions concerning the conduct of the game as he considers proper.

(*Note:* The Royal Club rules are included in the Chapter on the Royal Caledonian Curling Club.)

13

World and European Championships and European Curling Federation

JOCK WAUGH, INTERNATIONAL tourist and personality, whose 'Churchill' and 'David and Goliath' monologues delighted curling gatherings in many parts of the world, will be remembered in the annals of curling for two historic events, both of which occurred in 1959.

First, he was instrumental in transferring the T. B. Murray Trophy from the Edinburgh Ice Rink to the Royal Club so that the trophy could revert to its original purpose as the principal competition for the junior curlers of Scotland. This imaginative move led to the Scottish Junior Championship, the winners of which now compete annually in the Uniroyal World Junior Championship.

Second, he was a main driving force in the introduction of the Scotch Cup, the international competition sponsored by The Scotch Whisky Association between the champion rinks of Scotland and Canada, which quickly grew into the World Championship. Ken Watson, three-time Canadian champion and world curling figure, came to Scotland, at the invitation of the whisky directors, a month before the start of the competition, and publicity functions were held in Edinburgh and Glasgow. Jock Waugh formed a small committee composed of James Woodhouse (Secretary, The Scotch Whisky Association), James B. Alexander (transport), Norman Tod (accommodation) and Robin Welsh (publicity). Brigadier Jack Gow, the live-wire Royal Club President, led the Scottish welcome.

The famous Richardson rink beat Willie Young's Scottish team 5–0 in the first Scotch Cup games in Edinburgh, Perth and Falkirk. To say that the Canadians caused a stir in Scotland understates the case, their tactics and skill leaving hard-headed Scots gasping for a drink. The Richardsons were also outstanding sportsmen; after the series, William Reid, Chairman of The Scotch Whisky Association, sent this telegram to the Mayor of Regina: 'Understand Richardson rink receiving civic reception today.

Please convey kindest regards of all our members to Ernie, Arnold, Garnet and Wes. Great display of curling thrilled everyone here. Their bearing and modesty on and off the rink made them friends of all. Saskatchewan may be proud of her sons.'

In 1961, the United States champions joined the competition – and, after a great performance, Willie McIntosh and his Scots team lost in the final to Hec Gervais – and Sweden joined in 1962. In 1964, when Switzerland and Norway entered the lists, the event was played in Canada for the first time, in Calgary, where Alex Torrance and his young Scots rink failed gallantly at an extra end in the final. France made the competition, now called the Scotch Whisky Cup, a seven-nations contest in 1966, and, the following year, Germany brought the world line-up to eight nations.

Jock Waugh, Scotch Whisky Cup Director, and James Woodhouse gave dedicated service to the world competition and they will always be associated with the event. When The Scotch Whisky Association, an ideal sponsor, withdrew in 1967, the Royal Club negotiated for a replacement sponsor, and on 15 January 1968, the Royal Club and Air Canada

Jock Waugh, the dynamic Scotch Cup Director, giving one of his celebrated Churchill impersonations during the 1964 Scotch Cup World Championship in Calgary.

The start of the World Championship. The famous Richardson family rink from Canada
– from *left to right*, Wes (lead), Sam (2nd), Arnold (3rd) and Ernie (skip) – in Edinburgh
before the first Scotch Cup games against Scotland in 1959. At back, Bobby Young (lead),
Jimmy Scott (2nd), Brigadier Jack Gow (Royal Club President), William Reid (Chairman,
The Scotch Whisky Association), John Pearson (3rd) and Willie Young (skip).

announced that the world event would now be called the Air Canada
Silver Broom. The debt owed by the curling world to The Scotch Whisky
Association was stressed by Air Canada when they assumed sponsorship.

In the nine years of Scotch Cup play, the competition was held in
Scotland seven times. Air Canada changed the policy, taking the big
event to many parts of the curling world. Denmark and Italy joined in
1973 to bring the World Championship to its present strength and now
other countries wishing to participate must challenge the lowest-placed
countries in the previous world event.

We acknowledge the co-operation and fellowship received from Air
Canada in their long association as sponsor – and, from personal experi-

ence, we do so with conviction and gratitude.* It is impossible to assess Air Canada's massive contribution to world curling in terms of international friendship and quality of play. In the early years of world competition, Canadian rinks dominated, but each year, the other nations learned more and more of the winning Canadian ways and the new tactics and techniques permeated from the top rinks to the competitive scene in many countries. The standard of play improved dramatically throughout the world. Canada failed to win the Silver Broom for seven successive years (1973 to 1979) and now the competition is closely fought with seven or even eight of the competing countries being possible winners.

Air Canada executives have been good friends to curling. We think we will be forgiven for mentioning only three who have had a long connection with the Silver Broom – Claude Taylor, President of Air Canada, a tower of strength at the head; Don McLeod, who did so much in the formative years of the Silver Broom; and Pierre Jerome, the tireless and ever-cheerful former Chairman of the Silver Broom Committee.

Robin Brechin, the 1985 Organising Chairman, and his committee have brought the World Championship back to Scotland for the first time in ten years – and, by providing ice and seating in the Kelvin Hall during the week before the event, the Glasgow committee has opened a new field of opportunity for prospective World Championship bidders who previously have been inhibited by the availability of large existing ice arenas.

WORLD CHAMPIONSHIP SCOREBOARD

1959–1984
for the
SCOTCH WHISKY CUP
(sponsored by The Scotch Whisky Association)

Date	Venue	Winner	Countries competing
1959	Scotland	ERNIE RICHARDSON (Canada)	Canada and Scotland
1960	Scotland	ERNIE RICHARDSON (Canada)	same

* By strange coincidence in August, 1984, one day after writing this page, we heard the sad news that Air Canada had intimated their withdrawal from sponsorship, to take effect after the 1985 Silver Broom. Like The Scotch Whisky Association, Air Canada forged a strong and happy relationship with the governing body, achieving the all-important balance between publicity and the proper running of the event – and, of course, the international airline was the ideal sponsor for the World Championship.

Date	Venue	Winner	Countries competing
1961	Scotland	HEC GERVAIS (Canada)	Canada, Scotland and U.S.A.
1962	Scotland	ERNIE RICHARDSON (Canada)	Canada, Scotland, U.S.A. and Sweden
1963	Scotland	ERNIE RICHARDSON (Canada)	same
1964	Canada (Calgary)	LYALL DAGG (Canada)	same plus Switzerland and Norway
1965	Scotland (Perth)	BUD SOMERVILLE (U.S.A.)	same
1966	Canada (Vancouver)	RON NORTHCOTT (Canada)	same plus France
1967	Scotland (Perth)	CHUCK HAY (Scotland)	same plus West Germany

for the
SILVER BROOM
(sponsored by Air Canada)

Date	Venue	Winner	Countries competing
1968	Canada (Pointe Claire)	RON NORTHCOTT (Canada)	same
1969	Scotland (Perth)	RON NORTHCOTT (Canada)	same
1970	U.S.A. (Utica)	DON DUGUID (Canada)	same
1971	France (Megeve)	DON DUGUID (Canada)	same
1972	Germany (Garmisch-Partenkirchen)	OREST MELESCHUK (Canada)	same
1973	Canada (Regina)	KJELL OSCARIUS (Sweden)	same plus Denmark and Italy
1974	Switzerland (Berne)	BUD SOMERVILLE (U.S.A.)	same
1975	Scotland (Perth)	OTTO DANIELI (Switzerland)	same

Date	Venue	Winner	Countries competing
1976	U.S.A. (Duluth)	BRUCE ROBERTS (U.S.A.)	same
1977	Sweden (Karlstad)	RAGNAR KAMP (Sweden)	same
1978	Canada (Winnipeg)	BOB NICHOLS (U.S.A.)	same
1979	Switzerland (Berne)	KRISTIAN SOERUM (Norway)	same
1980	Canada (Moncton)	RICK FOLK (Canada)	same
1981	Canada (London)	JURG TANNER (Switzerland)	same
1982	Germany (Garmisch-Partenkirchen)	AL HACKNER (Canada)	same
1983	Canada (Regina)	ED WERENICH (Canada)	same (with Austria in place of France)
1984	U.S.A. (Duluth)	EIGIL RAMSFJELL (Norway)	same

LADIES WORLD CHAMPIONSHIP

'How would you like to sponsor a Ladies World Curling Championship?' The direct question from one member of the Stewart clan to another – put by 'Dinky' Stewart to Les Stewart, Public Relations Officer of the Royal Bank of Scotland – was the start of Ladies World Curling sponsorship. The Bank, which sponsored the world event for the first three years (1979 to 1981) and firmly established it on the world curling map, took up sponsorship again when the Championship returned to Scotland in 1984.

'Dinky' Stewart, the highly popular President of the Edinburgh Area of the Ladies Branch of the Royal Club, discussed sponsorship with the Ladies Branch President, Frances Brodie, before asking her direct question which changed the course of international ladies' curling. Mike Keohane, Public Relations Manager, Royal Bank of Scotland, represented the sponsor from 1980 onwards. A tall, commanding figure, who looks like the Army officer he was prior to entering the Bank, Mike was also a commanding and courteous figure in the early years of the Ladies World Championship.

Before sponsorship was considered, ladies made their first appearance

The first winners of the Royal Bank Ladies World Championship – in Perth in 1979. From *left to right*, Rosi Manger, Linda Thommen, Gaby Casanova (skip) and Betty Bourquin.

at a meeting of the International Curling Federation – in Duluth, Minnesota, in March, 1976 – and Mabel de Ware, Minister of Labour in the New Brunswick Legislature who was later to win the Elmer Freytag Award for her services to curling, reported on discussions between Scottish and Canadian ladies which had led to a firm proposal to launch a Ladies World Championship. The meeting agreed that the ladies would try to find a sponsor and then make a formal presentation to the Federation.

In 1977, the International Curling Federation approved the formation of a Ladies Committee of the Federation, and at Winnipeg in 1978 Dorothy New of Canada, the elected Chairman of the Committee, reported that it was hoped to start 'an international ladies' competition' in 1979. Frances Brodie, Scotland's lady representative at the meeting, reported that the venue would be Perth and that there was a possibility of sponsorship. Frances Brodie and 'Dinky' Stewart then acted, in the naval term, with despatch, and the Royal Bank of Scotland agreed to act as sponsor. The first Royal Bank Ladies World Championship was held in

The 1980 ladies world champions – in front, Marg Mitchell (skip) and Nancy Kerr, and, at back, Wendy Leach and Shirley McKendry, the Canadian champions.

The Swedish winners of the Ladies World Championship in 1981, *left to right*, Karin Sjogren, Birgitta Sewik, Carina Olsson and Elisabeth Hogstrom (skip). Elisabeth's team – in which Katarina Hultling later came in at third in place of Carina Olsson – was generally recognised as the world's top ladies' rink.

The Canadian team which won the 1984 ladies world title – from *left to right*, Janet Arnott, Corinne Peters, Christine More and Connie Laliberte (skip).

Perth in 1979 and the Swiss team skipped by Gaby Casanova decisively beat Birgitta Torn's Swedish rink in the final.

At a Federation meeting in Berne in 1979, Frances Brodie, who had played the leading role in the build up to the world event, was appointed Convener of the Ladies World Championship Committee. The ladies of the Perth committees gave superb support to ensure the success of the Championship which is now one of the major events of the curling world.

The Ladies World Championship went overseas in 1982, to Geneva, and in 1983 to Moose Jaw, Saskatchewan, where the attendance was easily the biggest in the history of the event. The Championship, sponsored by the Pioneer Group of Companies, attracted over twenty-five thousand spectators in the week.

Scottish ladies' teams have not excelled at world level. Isobel Torrance won the bronze medals in 1982 and Beth Lindsay (1979) and Betty Law (1980) reached the semi-finals.

LADIES WORLD SCORESHEET

Date	Venue	Winner
1979	Perth (Scotland)	Gaby Casanova (Switzerland)
1980	Perth (Scotland)	Marg Mitchell (Canada)

Paul Gowsell, one of the most brilliant exponents of the modern game, and his Canadian rink which won the 1976 Uniroyal World Junior Championship in Aviemore. From *left to right*, Kelly Sterne, Paul Gowsell, Neil Houston and Glenn Jackson.

The Scots on the victors' platform after the 1980 Uniroyal Championship in Kitchener-Waterloo. From *left to right*, Richards Adams, Hugh Aitken Jr., Norman Brown Jr. and Andrew McQuistin (skip) from Stranraer.

Date	Venue	Winner
1981	Perth (Scotland)	Elisabeth Högström (Sweden)
1982	Geneva (Switzerland)	Marianne Joergensen (Denmark)
1983	Moose Jaw (Canada)	Erika Mueller (Switzerland)
1984	Perth (Scotland)	Connie Laliberte (Canada)

UNIROYAL WORLD JUNIOR CHAMPIONSHIP

In 1967, members of East York Curling Club, Toronto - Willis Blair, David Prentice, Jack Manley, Bob Kennedy and Jimmy Brown - launched an invitation junior bonspiel. The event grew in popularity, and, in 1970, the title was changed to International Junior Masters. The following year, Scotland and Germany entered teams and Sweden sent a rink in 1972.

The title changed again when Uniroyal assumed sponsorship in 1973 and the Uniroyal International Junior Championship attracted further entries from Norway and Switzerland. In 1974, the high success of the competition was recognised by the International Curling Federation and the title was changed yet again - to the Uniroyal World Junior Curling Championship.

A second Stranraer rink won the 1981 Uniroyal event in Megeve to maintain an outstanding Scottish record in the World Junior Championship - *left to right*, John Parker, Roger McIntyre, Jim Cannon and Peter Wilson (skip).

Appropriately, the first official world event, for male curlers under the age of twenty-one at midnight on 30 June prior to the start of each season, was held in 1975 at the East York Club, where it had all started, with nine countries participating – Canada, Scotland, U.S.A., Germany, Sweden, Switzerland, Norway, France and Italy. Jan Ullsten of Sweden beat Canada's Rod King in a spectacular final. Playing third in Peter Wilson's Scottish rink (with Neale McQuistin and John Sharp) Andrew McQuistin won a bronze medal and this was the first stage of the best Uniroyal record by any player – bronze, silver and gold medals won by Andrew in 1975, 1979 and 1980.

Curlers who later became major names in world curling started their international careers in the Uniroyal event, including Jan Ullsten and Soren Grahn of Sweden, Paul Gowsell of Canada, Sjur Loen of Norway, Jurg Tanner of Switzerland and Andrew McQuistin, Colin Hamilton and Mike Hay of Scotland.

The Scottish victories in the 'Uniroyal' were scored, in 1980, by Andrew McQuistin, Norman Brown, Hugh Aitken and Richard Adams; and in 1981 by Peter Wilson, Jim Cannon, Roger McIntyre and John Parker. Both rinks were from Stranraer, where the young lions were fêted on their triumphant return.

UNIROYAL SCORESHEET

Date	Venue	Winner
1975	East York (Canada)	Jan Ullsten (Sweden)
1976	Aviemore (Scotland)	Paul Gowsell (Canada)
1977	Quebec City (Canada)	Bill Jenkins (Canada)
1978	Grindelwald (Switzerland)	Paul Gowsell (Canada)
1979	Moose Jaw (Canada)	Don Barcome Jr (U.S.A.)
1980	Kitchener-Waterloo (Canada)	Andrew McQuistin (Scotland)
1981	Megeve (France)	Peter Wilson (Scotland)
1982	Fredericton (Canada)	Soren Grahn (Sweden)
1983	Medicine Hat (Canada)	John Base (Canada)
1984	Cornwall (Canada)	Al Edwards (U.S.A.)

EUROPEAN CURLING FEDERATION AND EUROPEAN CHAMPIONSHIPS

Jean Schild of Geneva, Past President of the Swiss Curling Association, former representative to the International Curling Federation* and restaurateur of repute, was the man mainly responsible for the start of the European Championships. Jean dreamed of a major European competition, and at a meeting of European Presidents and representatives in Perth on 19 March 1975 he reported that, during a Six-Nations Tournament in Zurich in November 1974, he had presided at a meeting which discussed the idea of a European event. Representatives of the six nations – Switzerland, Sweden, Norway, Germany, France and Italy – had agreed to place the proposal before the International Curling Federation.

The Perth meeting, with Royal Club President Alan Johnston in the chair, agreed to recommend to the Federation that European Championships for men and ladies be established; that the first Championships be held in Megeve, France, in December 1975; that English would be the official language; that the Federation rules would be used; and the procedural rules for the competition would be prepared by Hans Maeder of Switzerland and Robin Welsh of the Royal Club.

At a meeting of the International Curling Federation the following day, the proposals were approved – and the first European Championships were held in Megeve in December 1975, Knut Bjaanaes of Norway and Betty Law of Scotland being the first winners. Jean Schild, the leading figure in all the preparatory negotiations, became the first President of the European Curling Council with André Viscolo as his Secretary. A European Committee of Jean Schild, Sven Eklund of Sweden and David Duncan of Scotland, with a representative of the country hosting the next Championship, was appointed.

In 1978, a simple constitution for the European Curling Council was adopted. When Eric Harmsen was appointed European President, at Vasteras in Sweden in 1983, one of his first acts was to call meetings of his newly-elected Executive Committee – Ian Turnbull (Royal Club), Axel Kamp (Sweden), Peter Scheurmann (Switzerland), Charles Heckmann (Germany) and Sten Willer-Andersen (Denmark) – to up-date the Constitution and to provide more comprehensive rules for the Championships.

The Presidents of the European Curling Council have been Jean Schild of Switzerland (1975 to 1977), Bob Grierson of Scotland (1977 to 1979)

---

* In Winnipeg in 1978, Jean Schild stopped a Federation meeting in its tracks when he stated that he had seen a press photograph of a Canadian smoking a cigar during play and added that, in order to build the image of curling in Switzerland and Europe generally, smoking on the ice was not permitted in major Swiss events – and that this would apply at the 1979 World Championship in Berne. Jean's views, which created a buzz of excitement for the remainder of the Silver Broom week in Winnipeg, have now been accepted world-wide.

and Birger Mortensen of Norway (1979 to 1983). When Birger retired, the title, European Curling Council, was changed and the reigning President of the European Curling Federation is Eric Harmsen of the Netherlands. The Secretaries have been André Viscolo of Switzerland (1975 to 1977), Robin Welsh of Scotland (1977 to 1980) and Stanley Flostrand of Norway (1980 to 1983) and the present Secretary is Annemie de Jongh of the Netherlands.

With men's and ladies' teams from fourteen countries, the 'European' is the world's most representative international event.

EUROPEAN SCORESHEET

Date	Venue	Winners
1975	Megeve (France)	Knut Bjaanaes (Norway)
		Betty Law (Scotland)
1976	Berlin (Germany)	Peter Attinger (Switzerland)
		Elisabeth Branäs (Sweden)
1977	Oslo (Norway)	Ragnar Kamp (Sweden)
		Elisabeth Branäs (Sweden)
1978	Aviemore (Scotland)	Jurg Tanner (Switzerland)
		(Inga Arfwidsson (Sweden)
1979	Varese (Italy)	James Waddell (Scotland)
		Gaby Casanova (Switzerland)
1980	Copenhagen (Denmark)	Barton Henderson (Scotland)
		Elisabeth Högström (Sweden)
1981	Grindelwald (Switzerland)	Jurg Tanner (Switzerland)
		Susanne Schlappbach (Switzerland)
1982	Kirkcaldy (Scotland)	Mike Hay (Scotland)
		Elisabeth Högström (Sweden)
1983	Vasteras (Sweden)	Amédée Biner (Switzerland)
		Elisabeth Högström (Sweden)
1984	Morzine (France)	Peter Attinger (Switzerland)
		Almut Hege (Germany)

EUROPEAN JUNIOR LADIES CHAMPIONSHIP

The Uniroyal World Junior Championship gives the junior male curlers a chance to play at world level. As yet there is no world event for junior ladies and, with this in mind, the European Curling Council launched the European Junior Ladies Championship. The inaugural event was held in Helsingborg, Sweden, in February 1983, with five nations competing – Sweden, Germany, Denmark, Norway and Scotland. Isobel Torrance, a top lady skip in Scotland for many years, travelled to Sweden to watch her daughter, Isobel, who skipped the Scottish rink. The Scots lost in the final to a strong Danish rink skipped by Helena Blach – and the new Championship was off to a splendid start.

Switzerland joined the competition to make the second Championship, sponsored by the Bank of Scotland at the Gogar Park Curling Club, Edinburgh, in 1984, a six-nations event. Eric Harmsen, President of the European Curling Federation, flew from Holland to attend the opening ceremony, performed by the Rt Hon Tom Morgan, Edinburgh's Lord Provost. Katarina Hjorth and her Swedish team deservedly won the Championship. Norway, skipped by Mette Halvorsen, took the silver medals and the bronze medallists were Susan McLean's Scottish rink.

14

How to Curl and the Curling Courtesies

WHAT IS CURLING? The first historical description is still the best. Two hundred years ago, a non-curling English tourist called Pennant wrote a paragraph about the game in *A Tour in Scotland and Voyage to the Hebrides* (1772):

'Of the sports in these parts, that of Curling is a favourite and one unknown in England. It is an amusement of the winter, and played on the ice by sliding from one mark to another great stones of 40 to 70 pounds weight, of hemispherical form with an iron or wooden handle at top. The object of the player is to lay his stone as near to the mark as possible, to guard that of his partner, which has been well laid before, or to strike off that of his antagonist.' For simplicity and clarity, that last sentence cannot be bettered.

The game is played by two teams of four players, each using two stones and playing them alternately with his opponent. A curler throws 40-pound stones over 40 yards to circles marked on the ice, and often coloured. The playing of all sixteen stones constitutes an 'end' and the teams then play the same ice in the opposite direction at the next end. The aim is to count more stones than your opponents nearer the centre of the circles (the tee) at the conclusion of each end.

There are many ways of achieving this, the most important being that you play better than the opposition and that you have the last stone, but, to start from scratch, or, more appropriately, from rock bottom, the first move is to go to the nearest ice rink to watch good curlers, preferably very good curlers, and to soak up the atmosphere. The second move is to ask the Curling Club Committee about coaching.

The Royal Club's national coaching scheme involves the Scottish ice rinks, representatives of which have been trained as instructors. National courses are held annually and prospective instructors undergo practical and written examinations, the successful candidates going back to their ice rinks to train curlers locally. At the head of the national scheme are

Chuck Hay* (National Instructor), Bill Muirhead (Assistant National Instructor) and Senior Instructors Keith Douglas, Bob Cowan and Jane Sanderson. Each year, new names are added to the next category, Club Instructors, and the build-up of this corps represents the main hope for Scottish gold, silver and bronze medals in the future.

Skilled instruction is the sensible way for all beginners to start. A solid grounding in the mechanics of the delivery of a stone is essential and the intelligent initiate will go to trained instructors to learn the rudiments of the game. There are far too many 'contortionist' curlers who cannot rid themselves of bad styles and habits evolved unaided in their early games.

In the old days, experienced curlers were the 'coaches' for new club members, many of whom had to fend for themselves. It was common to see curlers taking the ice with a variety of unsuitable shoes, or ill-fitting galoshes, and to watch stones rumbling forward unsteadily, like the throwers, to cause alarm in the next rink.

Beginners often find that, instead of throwing stones, the stones throw them; instructors will instil confidence. Beginners, particularly school-boys, are strongly tempted to throw heavy stones, to make spectacular strikes; instructors will tell them to resist the temptation and concentrate on draw weight because, at all levels, from club to world championship play, the draw is the shot that matters most, the basic shot in curling.

When the lessons end, it is time to ascertain when spare ice is available in the ice rink and to practise - and practise - and, as you practise, to learn to become a proficient sweeper. You will also be able to enlarge your repertoire of shots, with guards, wicks, raises, strikes, while sticking mainly to draw weight and perhaps finishing on a high note with the satisfaction of a cold draw round guards to the tee.

The new curler will now be ready to join a club. There are about six hundred and fifty clubs in Scotland and the beginner will be warmly welcomed, particularly if he or she has been a good learner in the instructional and practice stages. The initiate will probably start as a lead like many respected Scottish skips who proclaim proudly that they played lead for the first five, eight or ten years of their curling careers. Top-class players make the position their own and become specialist lead players. Now the hours of practice will pay dividends and the newcomer will be able to show club members how the first stones at each end should be played.

The beginner will graduate to become an average player. The much

_____

* Chuck Hay resigned in 1984 and Bill Muirhead is now National Instructor.

more difficult transition from an average to a first-class player is a matter of natural ability, application, will-to-succeed and other qualities which are entirely the responsibility of the individual.

THE CURLING COURTESIES

The responsibility for this all-important feature of international curling – the unwritten laws which curlers obey as if they were in the rule book – should rest primarily with club office-bearers and skips, who should advise and guide new curlers along the proper lines. Sadly, in too many cases, clubs do not fulfil their obligations.

The curling courtesies are, in simple terms, the good manners of the ice. Properly observed, they bring order and a sense of well-being. Properly observe, therefore, the following customs:

Do not move when a player is about to deliver his stone. When waiting behind the hack to play, do not talk or stand close to your opponent when he is about to play – and keep clear of your opponents when they are sweeping. Equally, a skip should stand still behind the rings when his opposing skip is directing. In Canada, and now elsewhere in the world, it is normal for skips to stand directly behind the house – to watch the complete course of the opposing stone – while some Scottish skips still observe the old Scottish custom of standing to a side until the opposing stone is thrown. The important thing is to stand still while the opposing skip is directing.

While the skip stands still behind the house, the sweepers should take their places along the side of the rink and be ready to sweep the next stone for their team. Sweepers should never have to rush back to the hog to sweep; they should be already waiting there.

Never cross the middle of the ice when a player is on the hack ready to play.

The second player should keep an accurate record of the score after each end and adjust the scoreboard accordingly. This prevents any possibility of later confusion and an up-to-the-minute scoreboard is a courtesy to spectators.

Arrive on time on the ice, and, during the game, be ready to play when your turn comes. Waste of time, one of the bugbears of the game, sets the nerves of both sides on edge.

If the luck runs against you, keep cool. If you have a temper, control it. Because of the variation in ice sufaces, the expression, 'Take the rough with the smooth', has a special significance for curlers.

When a member of your side is off form, encourage him and humour him – a humorist is a decided asset on any rink. Curling is essentially a team game, so strive to foster team spirit.

Be quick to compliment a good shot – from either side – and never pass adverse comments or smile at an opponent's misfortune.*

Finally, we have an old curling saying in Scotland – 'the one thing you must do is to do what you're told'. Curlers who think that their skip is giving wrong directions should follow the wise advice given by J. D. Flavelle of Lindsay, Ontario, in 1896: 'Speak to your skip quietly between the heads, suggesting where you think he is in error. If you fail to convince him, waive your judgment and carry out his instructions to the best of your ability.' A practice adopted by some curlers – to play for the skip's right or left leg instead of his broom – is not recommended. Far better to have a private word with the skip than to take your own ice. The simple rule is: obey your skip at all times, even when he is wrong!

Commenting on the conduct of curlers in *The Saturday Magazine* (10 December 1842) the editor wrote: 'It is affirmed that, not only upon the grand occasions of parish spiels but even on less important *rencontres*, there appears always to be infused into the minds of the participators a kind of honourable and gentlemanlike feeling which, in many of them, may not be remarkable on other occasions'.

The worthy editor let his pen run away with him but his heart was in the right place. The curling courtesies can be summed up more succinctly in two words – good sportsmanship. In these days when bad sportsmanship on television is commonplace, it is more important than ever to guard and maintain the good name and sporting reputation of curling.

* A Regulation framed by the Peebles Club in 1821 still applies: 'When a member falls and is hurt, the rest shall not laugh but render him every assistance to enable him to regain his former erect position.'

15

The Delivery

LET US NOW consider the method of *throwing* a stone – for you must throw it and not slide it or push it. This is the first law of the delivery.

The Rev John Kerr wrote: 'The swing is to convey life to the stone and the eye must communicate the information by which the mind of the player determines what kind of life is needed. The hand is worked by the head and the head by the eye.' This is the second delivery law: Keep your head up and your eye on the skip's broom and never look down at the ice, or, as some players do, pick a line or patch on the ice to aim at.

These two basic laws apply to all varieties of the delivery – sliding, modified sliding, standing and all types in between. A number of other features also apply to all deliveries:

1   Clean the underside of the stone carefully before delivery.
2   Grip the handle of the stone firmly but not tightly. A fierce grip will result in a wristy turn of the stone on delivery and will destroy the all-important delicacy of touch.
3   Keep the body in a square position facing the broom, at right angles to the direction of the stone.
4   Sole the stone properly so that it is delivered smoothly without any rocking movement. Bad soling spreads unhappiness all round; if the stone is bumped on delivery, the player is unhappy with his shot and the other seven players are unhappy with the hole left in the ice!
5   Maintain balance in a straight line and follow through smoothly with the throwing arm. The follow through is often neglected by curlers who complete the other movements admirably but spoil their performance with a poor last act.

The secret of consistent accuracy in curling is to continue to do the same thing time after time, in practice and under stress in big games.

THE 'TURN'

The crucial matter of importing the in-turn or out-turn to the stone – to make it curve to the right or left – is the last stage before the curler releases the stone. The old expressions, 'elbow in' and 'elbow out', are the most misguided terms that could have been used to describe the turn of a stone. Bent arms may have been common in the old outdoor days but elbows should play a minor role in the modern delivery action.

The far more accurate 'in-hand' and 'out-hand' or 'in-turn' and 'out-turn', are activated in different ways. We believe that, at the start of the delivery, the handle of the stone should be pointing up and down the rink, and that, when the stone is soled, the handle should be in the same position. But there are no hard and fast rules on this and top-class curlers set the handle at various angles for delivery.

The important feature is that the 'handle' or 'turn' should be given to the stone at the very last moment before the handle is released and that the movement should be so natural that it becomes instinctive. In other words, the turn to be played will be noted when sizing up a shot and not consciously considered during delivery.

Constant practice will make perfect this 'turn' technique, and, in addition, will impart to the stone the *amount* of turn which will bring the greatest control to the shot. For example, the handle of the stone should make approximately three complete turns between delivery and the far tee to give maximum draw with a drawing shot. (This applies to stones delivered direct from the hack, not stones released further up the ice by long-sliders.)

It is well known that a 'birling' stone – that is, a stone which is rotating quickly or spinning – does not draw nearly so much as a stone with the correct amount of handle. Again, a stone with too little turn imparted to it tends to lose its handle, or change its handle, and consequently, the shot is missed. This happens frequently with beginners and occasionally with all curlers and is a humbling experience, especially if the stone has left the hand on target!

On outdoor ice, with its rougher patches and bumps, more handle is often required to keep a stone on its proper course and the experienced curler will adjust accordingly.

One last observation on the 'turn'. Because it is generally supposed that the in-turn or in-hand shot is the easier to play, it is assumed to be the natural turn. It is true that almost all beginners are taught first to play the in-turn and the majority of skips start an end by directing their leads to play in-turn shots. But here, despite writings and arguments to the contrary, we agree with the old-time Scottish skips who, when they shouted to team-mates to play the 'natural hand', meant the out-hand. When first studying the contradictory evidence, we handed miniature curling stones to our two sons, then aged about ten and eight, and asked them to throw the stones along the drawing-room carpet to circles marked in chalk at the far end of the room. Knowing nothing about curling, nothing about stones and certainly nothing about 'turns', both boys threw out-hand shots.

I must complete this section on the delivery of a curling stone with a personal conviction which lies near to my heart. Whatever styles have been suggested, whatever shoulds and should-nots have been stated, it remains true that almost all games-players have their individual idiosyncrasies, little quirks of style all their own which, in the case of better-known players, become their trademarks. A recurring theme propounded by that great golfer and teacher of golf, Henry Cotton, is: 'Get the club face square to the back of the ball and forget about the dogmatic theories of there being one correct way to swing a golf club'. There are many other sporting analogies.

Many first-class curlers place the right foot at a sharp angle on the hack or perform an elephant-like shuffle with the left foot on the back-swing; many lift the stone almost head-high to show, in the words of the old saying, the bottom of the stone to the sun, while some 'ride' the stone or push it; many add extra movements for which there appears to be no point except to satisfy the players themselves.

Instructors offer guidelines towards the ideal type of delivery but do not expect them to be followed in every aspect. There are very few curlers with deliveries we can call classical. All the others vary one or other of the movements to some extent and the player with a real talent, even genius, for the game may vary more than the others.

But all good curlers, including those with that little extra who play in the rarified atmosphere at the pinnacle of the game, have attained their position with styles which are soundly based on the first principles of the delivery. Beginners should bear this in mind in their early struggles with stones.

16

The Sliding Delivery and Take-out Technique

THE SLIDING DELIVERY was introduced to the curling world by Canadians. Ken Watson, the first internationally-famous curler, who won the last of his three Canadian Championships in 1949, has been called the first long-slider and it is certain that he and his rink were the pioneers of the 'slide' and that his successes inspired young curlers to follow his example.

Ken Watson, who now lives with his memories in Winnipeg or Hawaii, has corresponded with us at the Royal Club headquarters over many years, and it is fascinating and of historical value to have his views on the subject – propounded at the time of the first Scotch Cup matches:

'The type of stone propulsion, which takes the player from his starting point on the hack a distance of thirty-three feet to the hog line, requires a firm footing, a snap of the right knee for leg drive and in many cases synthetic material like teflon, polythene, neolite, arborite or liquid solder on the sole of the sliding foot.

'The long slide was born in 1930 in the St John's Curling Rink in Winnipeg. In those days, Gordon Hudson was the king of curling in Canada, and, being hero worshippers, four of us tried to imitate his every move, even his mannerisms. Hudson used a short slide and, with his strong ankles, could coast out twelve to fourteen feet in front of the hack. We tried to copy him but to no avail as our metatarsal bones were weak. One night, in a practice session, our lead man, in a moment of caprice, removed his left rubber before delivery and skidded crazily with the stone a distance of twenty feet. The idea was born. Soon we were sliding in great glee much to the consternation of some of the older onlookers. In 1936, we won our first Canadian Championship, and, as three of us were pedagogues, we were dubbed *The Sliding Schoolmasters*.

'The new style caught on and soon thousands of sliding curlers littered the ice rinks in Canada. The gliding delivery also drew schoolboys into curling rinks. The agile adolescents were fascinated by the slide and today we have a national Schoolboy Championship for the seventy-five thousand kids who love to curl. The long slide is a lethal weapon in the hands of youthful curlers but its effectiveness can be reduced by both obesity and advancing years'.

Ken Watson admits that, in his best years, he released the handle of the stone no more than a foot or two beyond the centre of the rings and that his slide took him halfway between the front ring and the hog line.*

As Ken indicates, the slide started a youthful curling boom in Canada. Attracted by the grace and athleticism of a balanced long slide, young Canadians developed more and more leg thrust from the secure Canadian hacks, and, with sliding soles on their shoes, vied with each other for length of slide. In their competitive enthusiasm, many of them concentrated more on the slide than on the quality of their play.

An air of unreality clouded the Canadian game as the young men tilted at the 'establishment' and hit the headlines. Games of curling became acrobatic circus acts and the final comedy was staged in February 1955, at the Town of Mount Royal Curling Club in Montreal, when, in an exhibition game, Stan Austman of Saskatoon, third player in Saskatchewan's school championship rink, astounded the gallery by sliding the whole length of the rink to deposit his stone on the tee while still retaining enough momentum to slide on through the house!

This was clearly going over the score! The Canadian legislators, who had previously defended the long slide because it had brought so many schoolboys into the game, were forced to act, and, a month later, the wording, 'and the player shall not slide beyond the hog-line nearest the hack from which the stone has been delivered' was introduced to the rule book (see the Chapter on Rules for the modern rule).

The slide is now taught universally. What must be guarded against is the exaggerated slide with excessive leg thrust from the hack which forces the player to hurry the release of the stone before the hog line. The delivery rule is clear: 'In the delivery of the stone, the stone shall be released from the hand before the stone reaches the nearer hog line'. (But note the new powers given to chief umpires in the Chapter on the International Curling Federation.)

Of itself, the long slide is not a passport to better curling. Many expert curlers use the standing delivery or a modified slide and the main reasons

---

* After his spectacular successes, Ken Watson put back a great deal into the game by organising schools curling and clinics in Canada.

The classic delivery style of Ron Northcott, three times a winning skip in the Canadian and World Championships.

why long-sliders are the top competitive curlers are that they are lithe, athletic players with the keen eyes of youth.

The advantage of the sliding delivery is that curlers can slide low on the ice and get the eye, arm and the skip's broom in transit, thus adding to the chances of accuracy. The problems of the slide are loss of balance, riding the stone and a final push instead of a smooth release on delivery.

The long-sliding delivery and the wide-open take-out type of game which goes with it were brought to Scotland by the Richardson family rink – Ernie Richardson (skip), Arnold Richardson (third player), Garnet (Sam) Richardson (second player) and Wes Richardson (lead). Ernie skipped his rink to a record four wins in the Canadian Championships and four wins in the World Championship for the Scotch Whisky Cup, a performance which has rightly earned for the Richardsons a place among the immortals of the game.

The clear-cut victories of this famous Canadian rink over Scottish teams in the early Scotch Whisky Cup games, from 1959 to 1963, sent Scots curlers home in pensive mood. The new take-out technique, played by curlers of the calibre of the Richardsons, seemed unbeatable. Strong criticisms were voiced, particularly (a) that long-sliders gained an unfair advantage by sliding yards up the ice before delivery, and (b) that they delivered in the position, with the head directly behind the stone, of a billiards player and could thus adjust the direction of slow shots while sliding. The long-sliders made the counter-claim that they committed themselves to the shot with their action while leaving the hack and that any attempted adjustment while sliding would hinder rather than help the shot.

Whatever the secret weapon, there is an answer to it. It soon became obvious to students of the game in Scotland that the answer to the top-class take-out game was – the take-out game. Attempts to draw to the face of opposing stones were not practical; no players in the world could be expected to 'freeze'* consistently against stones, and, if the attempted 'freezes' were an inch or two short or strong, narrow or wide, the next strike by opponents as accurate as the Richardsons destroyed the tactic. As the strike, on the other hand, was the easiest shot in curling, the answer, undoubtedly, was to play the Canadians at their own game.

The first Scottish rink to make a positive effort to adopt the new technique was Chuck Hay and his team, who acknowledge their debt to Ernie Richardson for help and encouragement. They realised that the Canadian wide-open game was the winning game. How well they applied themselves to learn the new type of play can be gauged by the rink's wonderfully consistent record in World Championship play, culminating in their dramatic victory in the Scotch Cup in 1967. The winning rink was Chuck Hay, John Bryden, Alan Glen and David Howie – all Perthshire farmers.

The take-out game sets a premium on accuracy, fitness and nerve because one miss can be more costly than in other types of play. There are many different tactics, the basic plans being to take off stones and keep the ice clear when ahead, and, when down, to lay stones short of the circles and, if they are missed by attempted opposition strikes, to draw behind the front stones to gain shots.

For a time, strict take-out with few variations was all-too-common in top-class play but, happily, in recent years, a more positive and aggressive game has been adopted in which the uncompromising take-out has been discarded in favour of mixing stones, gambling occasionally and even, when ahead, trying to 'steal' another shot when without the last stone.

---

*The freeze shot, acknowledged to be the most difficult shot in the game, is to draw a stone alongside another stone and directly in front of it, without touching it or only just touching it. When played perfectly, the stone cannot be removed by a strike because it is completely checked by the other stone. The old Scottish instruction for the shot is 'crack an egg on it'.

Peter Attinger, brilliant Swiss skip, shows his spectacular delivery action. He has won two European titles and has twice skipped the running-up rink in the World Championship.

We know that curling is a participation sport but it is certainly true that this aggressive game is much more interesting than strict knock-out for spectators. Misses can count dramatically and the strain imposed on each player is a feature of the take-out game. The strain on the skip, particularly towards the end of a close game, is obvious; the skip will often try to 'blank' an end to retain the vital last stone in the closing stages.

Another feature is bare houses* with few stones in play, which reduces the possibility of lucky rubs and wicks to a minimum. This is a source of further controversy among Scots who have been bred on the traditional type of draw game which includes all the shots. ('Apartments to Let' was the term once used to describe an empty house.) The argument against the take-out game is that, on good ice, the players concentrate on two shots, the strike and the draw, and the many 'kittle' or delicate shots – like the angled guard, the six-foot raise to the tee, the wick past other

---

* 'When the order of the day is "Strike, strike", bare rink-heads are the consequence and no opportunity presents for wicking, cannoning, drawing, porting and guarding, which bring out the science of the combatants and constitute that beauty and fascination in the spiel which alike invigorates the body and braces the mind.' From *Memorabilia Curliana Mabenensia*, by Sir Richard Broun, Bt 1830.

stones, the draw through a port or even a double port – are lost to the game; and that, because of this, the whole character of the game is being adversely affected.

On difficult ice, or ice affected by weather, television lights or crowds, it is not possible to achieve the accuracy needed for the straight take-out game, and, on such occasions, curlers are forced to play a greater variety of shots. In this connection, we believe that tricky, even bad ice is no bad thing for a major competition.* It separates the men from the boys, and, while giving all curlers the opportunity to use their brains, gives the top-quality striking rinks – as against the strikers who cannot adapt when the ice beats them – the chance to prove that they can win on any ice. Good 'strikers' in top-class rinks, of course, are also masters of the basic draw shot, and, in addition, many of them use little more than hack-weight for take-out shots.

A positive argument against the draw game is that its exponents tend to become obsessed with draw weight. The extreme case is expressed in the claim: 'Did you see that great end with all sixteen stones in the house?' The ignorance of such a remark is exposed when it is shown how many striking chances were missed. Without doubt, an aggressive draw game is the only successful type of draw game.

An unattractive facet of the striking game is the 'tactical' stone which is deliberately thrown through the house to leave the opposition nothing to work on. There are misgivings on both sides but there is no doubt that the take-out game is the winning game at the highest level.

To sum up, the take-out school aim to simplify the game, to cut the number of stones in play to a minimum – to reduce the chances of lucky shots – to place a greater premium of accuracy on all shots played, and, consequently, to set all players a more challenging test of nerve and skill. The supporters of the aggressive draw game aim to create more 'heads' of stones, to play all the shots known in curling, and thus enjoy a greater variety of satisfying situations, and to accept the 'rubs' for or against as part of the game.

Many curlers claim that the draw game is far more interesting to watch and that the take-out game, with its concentration on strike and draw to the virtual exclusion of all else, is poor value for the spectators. This point, as we have said, is irrelevant when you consider that curling has always been a participation sport. Certainly the draw game, with more

* It is almost sacrilegious to talk of bad ice when we think of the superb ice prepared for Air Canada Silver Brooms and other major events by ice-maker extraordinary Don Lewis.

stones in play, presents a greater general interest to spectators, but, while a succession of hits – or misses – can make the take-out game deadly dull, it can promote high excitement in the galleries if the two rinks hit form together and feelings of suspense are built up as the audience waits for the misses which count.

The controversy continues and it is good for the game. Curling has become a young man's game at the top and this is also good for the game. A small percentage of the world population of curlers play straight take-out and the rest play a draw, aggressive draw or modified take-out game; and, remember, the long-sliders, who now dominate the highly-competitive scene, will become short-sliders as they grow older.

There are good and bad players of all types and the sensible approach to 'draw' and 'take-out' is that there is room for both in a game in which crack players and rank bad players equally enjoy themselves within the brotherhood of the broom.

17

The Art of Sweeping

'Soop, lads, so-o-o-p!'

CURLING HAS BEEN described as 'bowls on ice'. We prefer the description of bowls as 'curling on grass', but however you judge the two games, the comparison between them is valid. The number of players per side, the rotation of play and the scoring system are the same. Bowls take 'bias', stones take 'the hand' and skips direct team members to play roughly similar shots although striking is less certain at bowls because of the elliptical shape of 'woods'.

But there are two major differences in play. The first, and less important, is that, while early bowls at an end are generally played behind the jack, which may be struck towards them, stones are more valuable if they are short of the centre of the circles and 'in the way of promotion' to the tee. The second, and all-important, difference is that, because of sweeping, all four players in a rink take an active part in every stone played – the skip skipping, the player playing and the two sweepers sweeping.

We look back with awe to the hardy Ayrshire curlers one hundred and seventy years ago who played on the lochs in their stocking soles, and, when short of besoms, plied the ice with their Kilmarnock bonnets. Today's equipment is infinitely more efficient than a bonnet, and, with the modern tools, it is the workman who is at fault if his sweeping in ineffective.

Good sweeping, satisfying to the curler and a delight to watch, adds greatly to a player's stature and is a match-winning factor. The recipe is simple for it is much easier to be a first-class sweeper than a first-class curler. The main ingredients are power and rhythm.

But, first, let us dispose of the argument which crops up periodically, even in the best-informed circles, that sweeping is so much wasted effort. It is true that on wet ice or ice heavy with hoar frost, sweeping has little or no effect. It is also true that mechanical tests – in Canada, Professor Harrington (1923), R.M. Werlich (1950s) and J.C. Muirhead (1960s); in Switzerland, Dr Edgecombe (1924); and in U.S.A., Edwin O. Martinson (1970s) – proved inconclusive, there being too many imponderables for scientific conclusions on the value of sweeping.

One of the strongest sweepers of his day, George Fink, third player in Ron Northcott's Canadian rink which won the 1966 Scotch Cup World Championship in Vancouver, provides a portrait of power with a Canadian broom.

A friend of R.M. Werlich, the international tourist Bill Meyer, took the Werlich test machine to Megeve for trials during the 1971 Silver Broom and reached two conclusions – that sweeping kept a stone on a straighter course, reducing draw, and that brushes were more effective than brooms in sweeping.

The lack of scientific conclusions has no effect whatever on *our* conclusion – that sweeping works. We believe the evidence of our own eyes. With much less assurance, we give reasons for the value of sweeping:

1 Burnishing the ice removes dust and impurities from the path of the stone.
2 The atmospheric pressure in front of the stone is reduced, creating a minor vacuum which draws the stone on.
3 The increased temperature causes a temporary melting of the ice which reduces the surface friction.

These are reasoned conjectures. What is certain is that sweeping must be powerful. The broom is not for leaning on and it is no use whatever rubbing lightly or tickling the surface of the ice. Good sweepers should feel their muscles tingling after a game; in boxing parlance, they should know they have been in a fight. Rhythmical sweeping is far less tiring than jerking movements and this means that leg and body movements should be allied to the actions of the arms.

In Scotland, the two sweepers generally work one on either side of the stone and as close together as possible while both sweepers in top Canadian rinks operate on one side. Sweeping with the Canadian corn broom is more spectacular than sweeping with Scottish brushes – sweepers of the calibre of Bernie Sparkes and Fred Storey of the Ron Northcott rink (three times Canadian and World Champions) were a joy to watch as they pounded the ice in perfect unison.*

Less attractive as a spectacle, Scottish sweeping is more economical in style, less wasteful of effort, and, for this reason, we believe that the Scots brush is more effective than the Canadian broom, which flaps in the air to the left and right between strokes while the effort of brush strokes is

---

* In his *History of the Sanquhar Curling Society* (1874), James Brown gives us a graphic description of 'tall, strapping young men' at Wanlockhead, whose sweeping discipline was 'absolutely perfect' at the time when there were eight players in a rink: 'Arranged three and three on each side of the rink, they waited with the greatest attention till the stone was delivered, followed it quietly but eagerly in its course, till, at the call of the skip, "soop her up", down came the besoms like lightning, hands were clasped, the feet kept time to the rapid strokes of the besom and no exertion was spared until the stone was landed at the desired spot, when, a good long breath being drawn, the player was rewarded with a universal shout, "weel played, mon!"'

Alex Torrance and his Scottish rink (Bobby Kirkland, Jimmy Waddell and cousin Alex Torrance) display the strength of their sweeping with Scottish brushes.

concentrated on the spot which matters – on the ice directly in front of the stone.

A sweeping practice which is not recommended is the skip running out from the house to join his sweepers to achieve that extra inch or two which, he feels, could mean so much. Games have been lost through this sort of over-enthusiasm and skips should stay in the house except where there is clearly no danger of over-sweeping.

Always sweep at right angles to the direction of the stone, not at an angle, and in front, not to the side, of a stone. This is common sense but a study of sweepers will show that this sense is not so common! The practice of sweeping at an angle from behind a stone became so widespread that the International Curling Federation recently inserted new wording in the rule book: 'When sweeping with a brush, no part of its handle shall be over the stone.'

Be careful also not to touch the stone, but, if you do, immediately declare the fact that you have 'burnt the stone'* and remove it from play.

---

* 'To burn: one is said to be burnt when he has suffered in any attempt. Ill burnt: having suffered severely. To derange any part of a game by improper interference, as in curling, to burn a stane.' Excerpts from Jamieson's *Scottish Dictionary*.

Encouraged by Scottish skip Jimmy Sanderson (*left*) and third player Iain Baxter (*right*), the sweepers, Colin Baxter and Willie Sanderson, bring a stone into the house during the 1978 World Championship in Winnipeg. Willie Sanderson was elected President of the Royal Club in 1984.

This is a rule but it is the sporting instinct of a curler more than the written word which prompts him to act, even if his broom has only just touched the stone and has not appeared to affect the course of the stone in any way.

One final point which should prove helpful to apprentice sweepers. Beginners will find that some of their fellow curlers prefer to sweep on one side rather than the other. The simple solution to a possible clash of interests between 'one-sided' curlers is to practise sweeping to the left and right so that you become equally proficient on either side.

'It is the broom that wins the battle,' wrote the Rev John Kerr, and no experienced sweeper needs proof of this 'sweeping statement'. A good sweeper does not need tests to convince him of the value of his efforts. He already *knows* because he can *see* the stone surging forward and *feel* its added impetus behind his broom.

18

Curling Dress

THIRTY YEARS AGO, we were asked by a Canadian curler for a report on the curling dress in general use in Scotland.* The answer, devastating to the clothes-conscious Canadian, was like a naval signal, brief and to the point: 'There is no curling dress in Scotland.'

At that time, Scotsmen curled in their business suits, farm clothes or sports jackets. Some took off their jackets and curled in their waistcoats while others played with light cardigans in conservative colours, usually grey or lovat green, over their waistcoats. Knickerbockers and the less attractive baggy plus-fours used by golfers were in evidence. The starched white collars of the business world were common on the rink, and, for a spell midway between the two Great Wars, one rink wore hard 'pot hats', a distinctive if severe uniform which prompted an opposition skip to remark, after a heavy defeat, that he had just attended his own funeral!

A number of curlers actually wore special jerseys but a jersey with a club badge was a talking point and four men in the same uniform stopped the game on adjoining rinks.

Historical references are more exciting. The Minutes of the Rosslyn Club report that, one hundred and forty years ago, the mother of Colonel Wedderburn knitted worsted vests and presented them to the members of the five rinks in the Club. In the same period, the Abdie Club decreed that every member, except the Chaplain, must wear the club uniform – a blue coat with sixteen large buttons and a buff vest with eight small buttons, each button engraved with the club crest. In 1850, the Royal Club itself proposed a uniform for curlers initiated at Curlers' Courts, the uniform to be 'coat, vest and trousers of one pattern and quality, the groundwork of the cloth to be as nearly as possible of a granite colour, checked with blue and green bars, the blue being the royal colour and the green emblematic of the broom'. The material was to cost

---

* For many years before this, Canadian curlers dressed as rinks and the Canadian Championship was, and is, a blaze of colour with the rinks representing all the Provinces dressed in their own sweaters and crests. Canadians and Americans were talking of well-dressed curlers when Scots were taking off their jackets and draping them over the barricade at the end of the ice before a game.

4s. 6d. per yard and the cost of making the uniform 32s. but trade was poor for John Piper, the Royal Club's official clothier, and this granite, blue and green creation is, mercifully, heard of no more.

At the turn of the century, members of the Pitlochry Club were obliged to wear Atholl tartan trousers, red waistcoats with brass buttons, double-breasted blue reefer jackets with buttons, on which the motif was a curling stone, and balmorals. The Breadalbane Aberfeldy Club members wore Breadalbane tartan trousers, red vests, blue coats with Breadalbane buttons and blue balmorals edged with tartan.

There were many other club uniforms in the days when curling was exclusively an outdoor sport, the most famous being the dress worn by members of the Dunkeld Club. The dress – Atholl tartan trews, blue waistcoat with red piping, blue jacket with red collar and red cuffs and the Atholl bonnet which is the same as that worn by the Scottish Horse – has added colour to many Grand Matches and is still used by a number of members on these occasions. The bonnet was designed by the Atholl family and the late Duke of Atholl, the founder and Commanding Officer of the Scottish Horse, adopted the bonnet for use by the Dunkeld Club, of which the present Duke of Atholl is President.

Club uniforms faded from the scene with the spread of indoor ice rinks and a survey in 1954 revealed that only a few clubs had their own dress, among them the Gangrels Club in Ayrshire and the Glendoick Club in Perthshire, the members of which created a new badge for the 1950 Canadian tour in Scotland. Two famous skips, John Robertson of Glasgow and Alex Mayes of Falkirk, took the ice with rinks wearing jerseys of the same colour. In Glasgow, the Crossmyloof Club* had a cloth badge and the Carmunnock and Rutherglen Club had just designed one.

The 1954 survey, published in *The Scottish Curler* magazine, was quickly followed by a circular from the Royal Club announcing that 'a measure of uniformity in dress' had been agreed for the Royal Club tour in the United States in January 1955.

The twenty Scots who made that first Scottish tour in U.S.A. wore dark blue blazers, and, for curling, light blue sweaters with crests. Mrs Horace Vaile, Chicago, who met the team as she was leaving to be joint-captain of the first group of Canadian and American ladies to tour in Scotland, said, on arrival at Prestwick: 'The Scots, in their smart

---

* An excerpt from the *Ordnance Gazetteer of Scotland*, edited by Francis H. Groome, is interesting. 'Crossmyloof: at a council of war here, according to a popular myth, Queen Mary, on the morning of the battle of Langside, laid a small crucifix on her hand, saying "as surely as that cross lies on my loof (hand), I will this day fight the Regent" – hence the name Crossmyloof'. The centrepiece of the Crossmyloof Curling Club badge is a cross on a hand.

uniforms, were wonderful and made our lady curlers swoon.' Having waved bon voyage to the twenty Scotsmen only a few days before, we told Mrs Vaile that she must have met a different team!

The year 1955 was the turning point. From this time on, 'curlers' claes'* changed out of all recognition in Scottish ice rinks. Dozens of clubs prepared cloth badges to sew on club jerseys. Jimmy Neilson of the Dippool Club and his highly-successful rink were among the leaders with yellow jerseys and other top-class rinks followed their lead. A Royal Club tie, designed by Colonel William Drummond, was first seen in all the rinks in 1955. The Glasgow Province tie, introduced two years before, was followed by other Provincial ties.

In the immediate post-war years, the standard dress for the lady curlers of Scotland was the tartan skirt. The ladies have now changed their skirts and donned curling trousers, and, like the men, take the ice in club colours with insignia.

And what of the kilt for men? In his book, *The Complete Curler* (1914), J. Gordon Grant said on the subject of clothes: 'Well, that is a matter of taste, and sometimes very bad taste at that. Possibly, for freedom of action, the kilt is the best curling dress extant.' We are not sure that Gordon Grant was right, nor are ninety-nine per cent of the curlers of Scotland.

Today, Scottish curlers dress for curling and the vast majority of Scottish clubs now have special uniforms and badges which bring colour to the game and contribute to that best of all sporting feelings – team spirit. The importance of club play cannot be stressed too strongly; despite the growth of major events throughout the world, it remains true that club curling is the backbone of the game.

As in every sport, the beginner should aim to be comfortably dressed. Clothes should fit and sweaters and cardigans should not be too heavy because new curlers, who will play lead or second, will constantly be called upon to sweep and sweeping is hot work; after a hard game, beginners will find aches in all sorts of new places.

On the question of neckwear, we stick our neck out – for the benefit of the many occasional club curlers who rush from their offices for league or friendly games – to counsel the use of a sports shirt without a tie, or, if a tie is worn, that it should be worn loosely. The eyes must be clear and relaxed when the curler goes down on the hack.

---

* The words, 'Dress: Curlers' Claes', are traditionally inserted on tickets for curling suppers and functions in Scotland.

Each to his taste is the rule when choosing footwear for curling. A hole is clearly seen in the right boot of Don Duguid, twice a winning skip in the World Championship.

19

Footwear

FOR HUNDREDS OF years since the dawn of the game, curling stones were the curler's most prized possessions. Now that matched sets of stones have been introduced to the ice rinks and Scottish curlers do not use their own stones,* the most important items of personal equipment are curling shoes or boots.

In making a choice, beginners should bear in mind that, in the initial stages, a left sole with too much slide will make a difficult series of movements even more difficult. There are a number of well-known makes of curling footwear on the market or the beginner may choose to fit special soles to existing shoes. It is a purely personal choice.

Older Scottish curlers will remember the palmy days in the early 'fifties when Scottish ice rinks charged three shillings for a three-hour curling session, sixpence to hire stones (if required) and threepence to hire galoshes. Curlers used to arrive early to search through the bundles of galoshes for good-fitting pairs and I remember one farmer, a giant of a man, who managed with difficulty to fit on the largest pair available – size fourteen! Now the charge for a session of between two hours and two and a half hours is approximately £3 and galoshes are not on offer.

A curler wearing certain types of rubber soles will find that, when the ice is sticky or the pebble has been worn flat, his left foot will grip and he will stumble awkwardly instead of sliding forward on delivery. This affects performances and destroys confidence. In former days, some curlers used to change to another shoe in such a situation and a number of well-known players slipped a sock over their shoe before delivery.

In the Chapter on the Sliding Delivery, Ken Watson gives details of types of sliding soles introduced over fifty years ago in Canada. Shoe manufacturers have standardised footwear for curlers to a certain degree but Canadian Don Duguid, twice a winning Silver Broom skip, played with a hole in the upper part of one shoe, because he liked it that way, and there are still fifty-seven varieties of approach to curling footwear. The object is to curl in comfort, to play the game on a sensible footing!

* Matched sets of stones were first used in the Canadian Championship in 1940 – and were introduced to Scottish ice rinks in 1961.

20

Curling Prizes

IN THE YEARS of competitive play in the indoor ice rinks in Scotland until 1939, the greatest rink in the country was undoubtedly the famous Jackson rink from Symington, Lanarkshire, skipped by W.K. Jackson with his two sons, Laurence and Elliot. The lead, Johnnie Plenderleith, used 44-pound stones and the rink was consistently brilliant with outstanding sweepers.

Willie Jackson, who died in 1955, aged eighty-four, was the best-known Scottish curler of the inter-war period. He skipped his all-conquering rink to success in no fewer than fifty-nine competitions in Edinburgh Ice Rink alone and scored many other triumphs. He was the top performer in the 1924 Scottish touring team in Canada. In the same year, he skipped the British rink which scored a runaway victory in the Winter Olympic Games in Chamonix, the only time curling has been included as a participating sport in the Games. Willie Jackson (skip), Robin Welsh (third), Tom Murray (second) and Laurence Jackson (lead) took the gold medals for Britain with easy wins over Sweden and France. The British curling deputation at Chamonix was led by Colonel Robertson Aikman, President of the Royal Club, who attended a Curling Congress during the Games.

In the immediate post-war era, John Robertson, Bob Dick and Hugh and Jimmy Neilson of Glasgow; Laurence Jackson, Jimmy Sellar, Willie Scobie and James Sanderson Sr of Edinburgh; Bill Piper and Tom Morris of Perth; Willie Young and Alex Mayes of Falkirk; Bill Forbes, 'Bunty' McWhirter and Charlie Carnegie of Ayr were top skips in an ever-widening competitive field. Willie Young and his rink – John Pearson, Jimmy Scott and Bob Young – amassed a record of wins in major events which elevated them to the peak position held by the Jackson rink in the pre-war period. The team experimentally switched Willie Young from lead to skip in 1949, won thirteen trophies in the 1949–50 season and then won everything in sight in Scotland.

Later, George Lindsay of Waterside* was recognised as one of the

* George Lindsay, Bob Grierson (Loch Connel) and John Hutchison (Kirkmabreck) lost to Willie Young in a play-off for the right to represent Scotland in the first Scotch Cup matches in 1959.

The only Scottish team to win the World Championship – up to 1985. The rink of Perthshire farmers who won the Scotch Cup on their home ice in Perth in 1967. From *left to right*, Chuck Hay (skip), John Bryden (3rd), Alan Glen (2nd) and David Howie (lead).

most dominant figures in the Scottish game and then the Perth rinks skipped by Chuck Hay and Bill Muirhead and Alex Torrance's Hamilton and Thornyhill Club rink established themselves as the leading teams in Scotland. Since the institution of the Scotch Cup in 1959, the Scottish skips in World Championship play from then until 1984 have been Willie Young (twice), Hugh Neilson, Willie McIntosh, Chuck Hay (five times), Alex Torrance (three times), Bill Muirhead (three times), James Sanderson Jr (twice), Jimmy Waddell (three times), Kenneth Horton, Barton Henderson, Colin Hamilton (twice), Graeme Adam and Mike Hay. In 1984, Mike Hay represented Scotland in both the World and World Junior Championships within the space of three weeks.

All these high-class teams, and others too numerous to mention – with successful ladies' teams spearheaded by Betty Law and supported by many others – have left prize-giving ceremonies in Scottish ice rinks loaded with cups and prizes. It was once said of Willie Young at a closing function in Edinburgh: 'He'll need one of J.B. Alexander's lorries to take his trophies home!'

But trophies are returned for the competitions the following season and the winners are left with their individual prizes as memories of their victories. For this reason, we make a plea to all ice rink and curling club committees to give prizes which, while not valuable items in themselves, will become valued mementoes to the winning players.

The legendary Canadian, Ken Watson, reports that, when he surveys his trophy room, 'filled with a conglomeration of loot', he treasures the medals and miniature trophies and, in retrospect, is saddened by the lack of imagination shown by the donors of lamps, chairs, luggage, blankets and gift certificates.

A replica of the trophy is excellent. So is a medal, suitably inscribed, containing the badge of the ice rink or club. If glass or silver prizes are chosen, they assume curling significance if the name of the competition and the year is inscribed on them. Bear in mind that prizes will be placed in glass cabinets or trophy rooms in the winners' homes and that, in the years to come, old curlers will show their collection to friends, children and grandchildren who will be much more impressed if the titles and years of competitions can be read. A number of jewellers display a wide range of attractive items with curling motifs and a gift of framed photo-

Alex Torrance's rink from Hamilton, shown in Calgary in 1964 when they lost at an extra end in the final of the World Championship to Canada's Lyall Dagg. *Left to right*, Alex F. Torrance (skip), Alex Torrance (3rd), Bobby Kirkland (2nd) and Jimmy Waddell (lead).

Scotland's top team which scored a remarkable series of successes, starting with a dramatic victory in the 1982 European Championship at Kirkcaldy. The Perth rink – David Hay (3rd), Mike Hay (skip), David Smith (2nd) and Russell Keiller (lead) – followed this by winning the Scottish Championship, and, with Gregor Smith substituting for David Hay, the Scottish Junior Championship in 1984. They represented Scotland in the Silver Broom and Uniroyal events that year.

graphs of the winning team is another thought for committees who are preoccupied with problems of prizes.

There is a growing tendency to give bigger and 'better' prizes, often unconnected with the competition or the game of curling. The extreme cases are the Canadian car and cash bonspiels which, we hope, will fade from the scene or at least remain as an isolated feature on the fringe of world curling. Curlers should take a long, hard look at lawn tennis and other sports which have been soured by cash; there are few smiles on the modern tennis circuit.

The practice of giving expensive and exhibitionist prizes is out of keeping with the traditions of the game. Curlers have always taken the view that the honour of winning should be great, the prize small. They admire the cup but treasure the prize, which has little intrinsic value, but, later, much sentimental value.

The worst feature of the expensive prize is that, if one club offers it, the next club will feel that, to attract the best entry, it must follow suit

The Olympic gold medal and certificate won by the British curling team at the 1924 Winter Olympic Games at Chamonix. Curling will be included as a demonstration sport at the 1988 Winter Olympics in Calgary.

and the insidious practice, once started, will spiral as clubs vie with each other in matters of finance and prestige, neither of which has anything to do with curling.

To the claim that bigger prizes make better curlers, we say that commercialisation may make the competition fiercer but there is bound to be a corresponding loss in the spirit of fun traditionally associated with curling events. To the question, 'but where do you draw the line?' we answer that those who cannot see the huge gulf between cars and cash on the one hand and tasteful mementoes on the other must find it difficult to discern between the in-hand and the out-hand.

We are happy to think that the Jacksons, Youngs, Hays, Muirheads, Torrances and other names of the curling world have sideboards groaning with miniature trophies, medals and mementoes – perennial reminders of their prowess on the ice and of last-end, last-gasp victories – and that their cars are their own. For the rest of us, with one or two medals, or none at all, it's still a great game!

21

The Skip

THE SKIP DIRECTS the game – in front of 'plate-glass skips' who feel they could do better – and his three players, whom he must inspire with confidence. It is a heavy responsibility and he should discharge it in a variety of ways:

1   By being decisive. Any uncertainty in giving directions is transmitted to his team. He should maintain the tempo of the game and not become involved in lengthy discussions or 'committees'. The rule states: 'The skip may, however, return to the house for brief consultation' – and the interpretation of the word, 'brief', has been a contentious point for years. Slow play is one of the bugbears of the modern game.*

2   By making each shot clear to his players. There should be no doubt what is required.

3   By nominating simple shots. He should not confuse a player with 'show' shots except in emergencies. To give a simple example, if there are three opposition stones in the house, a double take-out should be nominated (if all three stones go, so much the better).

4   By giving credit to his players for good shots *and* good attempts which fail, and by commiserating with and encouraging players who are off form.

Most important of all, the skip should never lose his temper with his players (for their misses), with himself (for his misses) or with his opponents (for their successes with outrageous flukes). He must have fight-

*A touring Scottish skip reported that, on one occasion, he lit a cigarette and finished it while the opposition decided what shot to play. A skip at the 1983 World Championship in Regina took three minutes, fifty seconds to study every angle of his next shot. By no stretch of the imagination can many curling 'committees' be described as brief. Ten ends of play should be attainable in two hours and easily attainable in two and a quarter hours. Twenty years ago, before 'committees' were heard of, a survey of Scottish competitive play over three-hour sessions showed that sixteen to eighteen ends were common and twenty-one ends were rare but possible!

ing spirit and a keen determination to win but must also be patient, calm and 'unflappable' or he will not be a good skip.

If he is a keen sportsman and has a sense of humour, all the other qualities should follow and he will also be a 'personality' who will keep team morale at a high level and earn the respect of his players. He will earn further respect if, after losing a game, he accepts responsibility and does not lay the blame elsewhere.

Encouragement of his team should be a skip's first aim. I have heard skips shouting, 'och, you're no' half-way,' and other terms of abuse to players after bad shots; have seen them throwing their arms to left or right to show how wide the shots were or throwing up both hands in despair; and have even seen them turning their backs on players.

Bad play is no excuse for a skip's bad manners which will also adversely affect his chances of victory. When trying hard to give of their best, players become anxious if they play badly and peevishness or ridicule will make them more anxious and less likely to recover their confidence.

In addition to encouraging his team members, a skip carries heavy responsibilities which weigh upon him from the very first stone. The first end is often vital. An opening offensive may take the opposing rink by surprise and a count of two or more shots can often dictate the whole course of the play.

A skip must study the run of the ice at the early ends and quickly learn how stones run on either side of the rink and how the runs vary with different speeds of shot. Knowledge of the ice and strategy are the weapons used by the opposing skips in their personal war of nerves, and, given reasonable equality of play, games are won 'on the head' by skips who can 'read the ice' and apply their knowledge in strategic moves.

A ridge on the ice - once called a 'sow's back' - may force a skip to give minus-ice directions to his players. This means that a stone will fall back against the turn of the handle, and thus, in order to hit an opposing stone, the skip will place his broom in a position which appears to be on the wrong side of the stone. Such shots are normally played wide by beginners who find it difficult to believe that the fall-back, which seems unnatural to them, will be so considerable. Eventually, they will overcome this handicap and play the skip's broom with confidence.

The ability to read strange ice - away from their home ice rink, where they know every ridge and hollow - and knowing exactly when to sweep are other qualities of a good skip. One responsibility has been lifted from his shoulders. In the days before matched sets of stones, he had to learn the different properties of each pair of stones in his rink, one pair being duller than the others, one taking less turn and so on. But the skip must still learn the favourite shots, and the fads, of all his players and give instructions accordingly. Even top-class curlers, who, in theory, should be able to play all the shots with equal facility, prefer to strike, for example, on the in-turn, or have a predilection for a wick and roll rather than a draw.

The strategy of the skip is made up of a wide range of subjects, like switching from a striking to a drawing game and vice versa, cutting down on weight on swinging ice, ascertaining and playing to an opponent's weakness. And we need not stress such elementary items as striking the front stone if two opposing stones are in the house and the truth of the old adage, 'the best guard is second shot'.

Skips develop their own signs to direct play and curlers who play regularly together immediately understand words and gestures. Skips have never been a silent race and their shouts and gesticulations add to the fun and fellowship of the ice. Laurence Jackson, famous Symington curler, told the story of one exceptional rink which played against John Robertson of Glasgow, who christened his opponents, the 'Silent Four'. None of them spoke a word and the skip made signs to indicate his requirements. John Robertson's lead, Tom MacFarlane, tried without success to coax a word out of his opposite number, who, half-way through the game, eventually came up to Tom and asked: 'Have ye electric light?'. Tom replied, 'Aye, we have', but there the conversation ended until the very last end, when the lead again approached Tom and said, slowly: 'Ye're damned lucky, we've only got candles!'

We cannot imagine what the 'Silent Four' would have made of 'wee' Alex Torrance, elected Junior President-Elect of the Royal Club in 1984, who was a crowd favourite at World Championships because of his un-inhibited zest for the game which manifested itself in cries of anguish or delight and acrobatics on the ice. Alex was at his irrepressible best at the World Championship in Regina in 1973 when, after a series of brilliant last stones, he finished with a superb wick and roll at the extra end of the semi-final only to lose to an equally spectacular last stone by Canadian champion Harvey Mazinke.

A skip has so much to think about that we hesitate to add to his problems and will close this treatise on the duties of skips with one 'don't' and one 'do'.

Don't interfere with your third player or acting skip in any measurements or decisions needed at the conclusion of an end.

Do try to forget your previous misses during a game. Worrying about them is not worth a docken. Concentrate on the shot in hand and try your best; you can do no more.

Let us finish with toasts to two skipping giants of the past – Bailie Hamilton of Douglas and Deacon Jardine of Lochmaben. On a 49-yard rink, the Bailie drew through a 10-inch port three times running and the cheers of the onlookers alarmed 'The Douglas' in his castle hall. The Deacon could 'birse a needle'; having attached birses with wax to two stones, laid to form a port, and, similarly attached needles to two stones directly alongside and in line, he could draw so scientifically that, in grazing through the port, his stone would impel the birses forward through the eyes of the needles! This must surely be the best curling 'yarn' ever spun.

22

Concentration and Nerves

... Low o'er the weighty stone
He bends incumbent, and with nicest eye
Surveys the further goal, and in his mind
Measures the distance, careful to bestow
Just force enough.

From *Poems on Several Occasions* by
James Graeme (Edinburgh 1773)

IN THE FINAL of the first Scottish National Schools Competition for the John Monteith Trophy, in 1967, Neil Turner, skip of the Glasgow High School rink, shouted at his players as they settled in the hack: 'Now, concentrate!'

Neil had the right idea, for concentration can be called the key-stone of curling. Many players are blessed with a natural ability, some have inherent 'touch', but a conscious effort is still required to play *every* shot.

It was said of Napoleon that he had many boxes in his mind and that he could close all but the one required to do the job in hand, eventually closing all to sleep. It was why his concentration was so intense, so remarkable even in the history of great men.

To apply such a mental approach is invaluable in all games, because each shot is then played as a separate entity unencumbered by thoughts of the bad shots which have gone before, the state of the game and what might follow. In the heat of a game, application of this kind is clearly difficult, but, with training, a curler can achieve a measure of detachment.

The first step towards this objective is to immerse yourself completely in your own game – not on the games on the adjoining rinks. Ken Watson, famous Canadian skip, reports that one of the highest compliments ever paid his rink came from his opposite number in an important game: 'Gosh, Ken, I wish my men would quit watching the game on the next sheet. Your men are so busy watching every shot we make, I'll bet they don't know who is winning alongside us.' When asked, Ken's second player, Lyal Dyker, had to look at the scoreboard before answering.

Other aids-to-concentration are:

When you settle on the hack, clearly understand the shot required.

Keep your eyes fixed firmly on the skip's broom. (For 'keep your eye on the ball', the curler substitutes 'Look at the mark with all your een'.)

Swing the stone straight back, and, on the back-swing, sense the weight required for the shot.

Aim the throwing arm at the broom in a full and relaxed follow-through.

In other words, concentrate on the simple mechanics of delivering a curling stone.

Glenn Harris, former Editor of *The North American Curling News*, wrote on the subject: 'If a man will go through some sort of remindful ritual each time he prepares to deliver his stone, that will suggest concentration on the shot in hand, he'll improve his game at once.' *A remindful ritual.* The expression should become an essential curling term!

An apparently contradictory feature of concentration in any sport is that it must be allied to relaxation for tenseness cramps the style in every sense. But the anomaly is more apparent than real. To become immersed in a concentrated effort to produce your best is of itself a means of reducing tension.

All sportsmen worthy of the name have nerves. Without them, a champion could not lift his game to fit the occasion. Heroes are those with nervous temperaments who conquer or come to terms with their nerves.

Nervousness has little to do with lack of confidence. A good curler, for example, knows he can accomplish a given shot; he has done it dozens of times before. It is when the shot is called for in a crisis that nerves take over and panic ensues. The Canadians call shots of this nature pressure shots or 'the big ones' and we have heard many other names for them, some of them unprintable! Whatever name you use, they are the shots which win championships.

Conceit is a word we don't like in curling but the value of self-confidence cannot be stressed too strongly. If you look at a shot and feel you can do it, you very often will do it.

What can be done to help a curler when the crunch comes, when he faces the shot which matters more than any others in a game? The answer is nothing. He must help himself, by training and experience, so that, when the time comes to play the all-important shot, he is mentally equipped to meet the challenge.

Experience is the best-known cure for curling nerves but here are three hints which may prove helpful to curlers who feel nervous about a vital shot.

1 Be philosophical. After all, the worst that can happen is that the shot is missed.

2 Size up the situation calmly and resolve to make as good a shot as possible.

3 *Visualise* a successful shot.

23

It's a Slippery Game
and the Eight-End

IN THE MODERN game, with its accent on high-powered play, the aim at the top level is to eliminate the element of chance. As few stones as possible are left in play – in case of a lucky rub or wick – unless a side is trailing, when, in need of shots, a skip must mix stones in the house in search of a big end.

But, at whatever level, curling retains the essential charm for which it is famous – the quick change of fortune which transforms a game and carries a team from the brink of defeat to dramatic victory.

The moral to be drawn, and it is one which curlers follow more and more as they gain in experience, is *never give up*. There are many aspects of a successful curler's make-up, but, if he is not imbued with an iron determination to fight on against the odds, he will never be a true champion.

The late Bob Dick, famous Glasgow curler whom we reckoned to be the best player of his age anywhere – in his eighties, he was still a redoubtable skip – followed a curling philosophy which should be adopted by all curlers: 'When you're up, don't smile too much; when you're down, keep smiling – you'll aye bob up again'.

When a very young curler, I played in a rink with three realists who gave us no chance in the final of a minor trophy against a crack rink. I quoted a line from one of John Masefield's poems: 'And the gold cup won by the worst horse at the races.' A poor line of poetry, it was a good line for the three realists. We won at the last end.

The history of curling is punctuated by stirring stories of victory against all the odds. When, more than one hundred and seventy years ago, the Currie Club first drew up the system of play for the eight-points Points Competition, the Club President, the Rev Dr Somerville, inventor of an improved form of crampit in 1833, said: 'we have now placed the Points Medal beyond the reach of duffers'. But in the very first competition the Medal was won by Willie Drum, whose distinction that day has been tarnished since as he appears in the record books as 'admittedly, the worst player in the Club'.

In our own day, there are memories which keep recurring, like the astonishing come-back by Bill Piper, Past-President of the Royal Club and three times a winning skip in the former Scottish Championship at Perth, in a Perth *v* Edinburgh inter-city match in Edinburgh Ice Rink in 1956. Bill lost a six at the first end and was 18-0 down after little more than an hour's play. Then, aided by cavalier play by the opposing skip, the 'impossible' happened, and with a six at the last end Bill won 21-19! The banter after that memorable game included this gem from the winning lead, Dr John MacDougall: 'We would have annihilated them if we had found the weight of the ice earlier!' The riposte from the losing skip was worthy of the occasion: 'Bill is leaving in a month to captain the 1957 Scottish Team in Canada, and, as a true Scot, I let him off the hook for the sake of the country I love!'

Horace Bell of the Panmure Club learned a salutary lesson – in the Dundee-Angus Ice Rink in the 'thirties – when, well ahead and lying two 'comfortable' second shots. Horace sent us a cutting from the *Dundee Courier and Advertiser* which reads: 'A league game between Carnoustie Panmure and Dundee on the Dundee Ice Rink had an amazing finish. Panmure, skipped by Horace Bell, led 16.8 with one end to go. Dundee, skipped by P.T. Roberts, played a sensational last end, lying all eight shots to force a draw.' This may be the only example of a last-end '8' to peel a game but it proves the truth of the saying, 'you're never beaten until the last stone is played or you're nine down with an end to go'.

When down, even when well down, never give in. Often, late in the game, a chance comes for a big end, and, if you can take it, you will be back in the fight. Once there, it's the other side's turn to worry.

These examples of the two imposters, triumph and disaster – and every curler has his stock of miraculous escape stories – make the wise curler wary of an early lead, soon to be dissipated by the *laissez-faire* attitude of his own side or the inspired play of his opponents; and once on the slide how difficult it is to regain control!

The moral of this aspect of curling is *never let up*. When six shots up, try to become eight shots up. Don't relax. One careless stone can be the turning point in a game.

The ups and downs of curling build character. It was what the old curler meant when, admitting defeat at the hands of a much poorer rink, he said: 'Aye, it's a slippery game but it makes you stand on your own two feet!'

EIGHT-ENDS

Horace Bell sportingly told the story against himself about losing an 8-End and drawing his game. In 1954, playing for Edinburgh against Falkirk, the Cooper family rink from Carnwath lost an 8-End and still won their game 16–12. Most curlers have 8-End stories. We have scored two 8-Ends in a lifetime of curling, one in an inter-city match. Jimmy Sellar, Edinburgh Ice Rink Manager and famous curler, who had a habit of capping our stories, had the last word when he reported that, playing with Dan Tudhope, he scored two 8-Ends in one game! The name of the opposing skip was not mentioned, nor ever should be.

In October 1983, with the approval of the Royal Club, John Walker & Sons, the Scotch whisky distillers, introduced the Johnnie Walker Eight-End Black Award for curlers over eighteen years of age whose team scored the 'perfect fluke' in international, national or official club or inter-club play, including outdoor competitions; the award is not for friendly or 'bounce' games.

At a lunch prior to the launching of the scheme, Nigel Shattock of Johnnie Walker asked Royal Club President Ian Turnbull and Secretary Robin Welsh how many 8-Ends might be scored in Scotland in a season. Being cannie Scots and considering the incidence of the take-out game, they suggested that six or seven awards could be anticipated. They were well wide of the broom! In the 1983–84 season, thirteen teams applied and were awarded commemorative ties (scarves for ladies), certificates, sweater badges – and bottles of Black Label, which fits in perfectly with the Black Award, so called because black has always been used in winter sports to designate the most exacting ski or bob runs.

The scheme, which fills a long-felt need, was also introduced by Nigel Shattock to Europe – at the 1983 European Championships in Vasteras – and to the North American continent – at the 1984 Silver Broom in Duluth – at international parties arranged by the Royal Club and generously stocked by Johnnie Walker.

24

The Ladies

ON HIS RETURN from the first Scots tour to Canada in 1903, Major Scott Davidson of Cairnie, Fife, was given an enthusiastic welcome-home dinner in the Marine Hotel, Elie. Headed by a piper, a procession of fifty curlers, led by Sir Ralph Anstruther and Sir Archibald Campbell, marched into the dining-room to honour the returning hero in the name of the Hercules Club, in which he was a prominent skip.

In a survey of his tour, the gallant Major said: 'The ladies were particularly attentive. Indeed, I might have been married three or four times! He read out telegrams received *en route* through Canada, to prove the point:

'Absence makes the heart grow fonder' (from Maudie, Halifax); 'Will ye no' come back again? All hearts bowed down' (from lady curlers, Montreal); 'None but the brave deserve the fair' (from Ethel, Winnipeg); 'I am still trusting' (from Mary).

It was particularly apt that the members of the Hercules Club should hear of the activities of lady curling enthusiasts in Canada for the Hercules Ladies Club, the first all-ladies' curling club in Scotland, was formed on 13 February 1895, with Major Scott Davidson's wife as Vice-President – and an annual subscription of two shillings and sixpence.*

Only five years before, the Rev John Kerr stated: 'Ladies do not curl. The Rational Dress Association has not yet secured for women the freedom that is necessary to fling the channel-stone ... and the majority find the stones too heavy for their delicate arms.'

John Kerr himself pointed out that there were several exceptions. There was a ladies' bonspiel on Loch Ged in the Parish of Keir in 1840, when two rinks of the maidens of Capenoch played two rinks of the maidens of Waterside, and an enormous concourse of spectators watched the maidens finish the match up to their ankles in water. Club Minute Books contain records of matches last century between married and unmarried ladies and between the married ladies of neighbouring parishes.

* In Canada, the Ladies' Branch of the Royal Montreal Club was established on 1 December 1894. The Quebec Ladies (1898) and Lachine Ladies (1899) followed and the Ladies Curling Association was formed in 1904 to regulate ladies' curling in the Canadian Branch of the Royal Club.

In 1884, the Hon Mrs Fergusson opened the Pitfour Curling Pond 'with a stone of 36 pounds weight and delivered the same in true curling style, sending it the full length of the rink with such unerring aim that it drove a stone on the tee to the bank and lay itself a perfect pat-lid'. Mrs Fergusson's chap-and-lie shot was greeted with a vociferous cheer – and rightly so, for, apart from the excellence of the shot, she must have been a good sport to 'have a go' at what was then almost exclusively a man's game.

As John Kerr inferred, the long dresses of the Victorian era must have been an encumbrance even for lady athletes, and, for many years of the present century, ladies were regarded as something of a novelty on the curling rink.

Bertram Smith, in *The Shilling Curler*, wrote: 'For ladies – I am told – a straight-cut, fairly tight skirt is almost a necessity, otherwise the swing will be impeded.' This casual approach, in 1912, indicates that little attention was paid to lady curlers before the First World War.

Now there are World, European and National Championships for ladies. The ladies make overseas tours to many lands. There are ladies' inter-city matches, competitions, leagues. There is no distinction between men and ladies on the ice and the curling programmes for men and ladies are the same.

The tremendous upsurge of ladies in international sport is a phenomenon of the twentieth century. Ruth Menzies, who started curling in 1919, gave another reason for the growth of ladies' curling. She became Secretary of Edinburgh Ladies Curling Club – believed to have been founded in 1912 although the first records start in 1915* – in 1922, when club members played with small black Crawfordjohn stones, some of which weighed less than thirty pounds. Edinburgh and Glasgow started inter-city matches in 1930, stones were standardised and Ruth Menzies credited Glasgow with the change from small to standard stones, which, she believed, was a fundamental reason for the expansion and improvement of ladies' play.

Scottish ice rink managements love the ladies! The large and ever-growing number of ladies' clubs fill the ice in the morning and early afternoon sessions and make a valuable contribution to healthy balance sheets.

In 1958, Irene Cleland, all-round sportswoman and skilful curler who

---

* In 1915, Lady Marjorie Mackenzie presided over forty-five members of Edinburgh Ladies C.C., the first ice rink ladies' club in Scotland. Lady Marjorie, Mrs Alan Menzies, Mrs Sang and Mrs Archie Leslie formed the nucleus of the club. The Glasgow Ladies C.C. was formed in 1928.

The first-ever Scottish ladies' team to tour overseas - to Canada and U.S.A. in 1958. Seated from *left to right*, Janie Love, Maimie Highet (Vice-Captain), Mary Niven, Norah Hart, Jean Gow (Captain), Dorothy Gordon, Muriel McPherson (Secretary), Pretzel Stirrat and Margaret Liddell. Standing, Belle Aitken, Mary Forrester, Ann Niven, Jenny Nicol, Mary Murray, Sheila Alexander and Irene Glen. At back are Royal Club office bearers John Smith and Alex Mayes at the send-off ceremony.

scored the record number of six wins in the prestigious Henderson Bishop Trophy, proposed that a Ladies' Committee of the Royal Club be formed. She organised the first Committee, prepared a Constitution and chaired an open meeting of ladies clubs on 1 December 1958. In 1961, the Ladies Branch of the Royal Club was formally established under the Presidency of Jean Gow, who was succeeded in 1963 by Irene Cleland (later an Honorary President) and in 1965 by Janie Love. All were leading lady skips as were many of the Presidents who followed – Jenny Nicol, Norah Hart, Margaret Motherwell, Chris Gardner, Marguerite Roberts, Frances Brodie, Lucy Fleming, Ella Reid, Marjorie Broatch, Betty Grierson, Sandra South, Betty Wilson and Jessie Whiteford – Helen Caird being the 1984–85 President-Elect.

The reigning President, Jessie Whiteford, played her full part in the best international performance by a Scottish ladies rink when Betty Law (skip), Jessie (third), Beth Lindsay (second) and Isobel Ross (lead) won the first European Ladies Championship in Megeve, France, in 1975. In a nerve-racking final against Sweden, the Scots led 7–2 but lost a four-end and a single to go into an extra end, where Betty Law played a great last draw for victory with two shots lying against her.

The indefatigable Anna Smith served as Ladies Branch Secretary from 1973 to 1984, eventful years in which the volume of ladies' business greatly increased. Anna rightly received plaudits all round when she retired and, as stated in the Chapter on the Royal Club, the Ladies Branch business was then transferred to the Royal Club headquarters and Jane Gorrie* was appointed the Branch Secretary and Assistant to Royal Club Secretary Jim Aitken. The 'delicate arms' of the ladies, if no less feminine than in 1890, have taken a firm grasp of curling affairs.

* When Jane married, Sharon Gray was appointed to the post.

25

Youth and Age

ONCE CALLED, WRONGLY, an old man's game, curling is now, at the top level, essentially a young man's game. But the important thing is that, at many different levels, it is a game for all ages.

Old curlers continue to curl, sweeping less but using their heads more, until very late in life and there are many instances of curlers playing when over 90 and a few cases of centenarian curlers. 'In our club's history,' wrote Robert Goodwin of the Kirkintilloch Club in 1889, 'we have *conclusive evidence* that the game of curling tends to a life of good health and length of days.'

In Edinburgh in the 'thirties, there was an annual match – for walking sticks! – between the over-65s and over 70s, many of whom were over 80. A curling span of fifty or sixty years is common in Scottish curling. It is the same overseas; twenty-five years ago, at a bonspiel in Milwaukee, a photograph was taken of five American curlers, all of whom had curled for more than fifty years – David Bogue, Portage (64), Stephen Dooley, Milwaukee (58), Louis Ehlert, Milwaukee (55), Ferge Ferguson, Milwaukee (54) and Robert Stevenson, Waltham (52).

We know of many excellent old curlers but give the palm for the best performance by a curler of advanced age to Bob Dick of Lanarkshire who skipped the winning rink in the old 'World's' Championship in Edinburgh in 1961 – in his eightieth year! The achievement is even more remarkable when you consider that, at the end of the week-long competition, he maintained his form while playing two games on the Friday and the semi-final and 14-end final on the Saturday – a total of more than twelve hours play in two days. No wonder Bob was carried shoulder-high from the ice after his victory by the two top curlers in Scotland at that time, Willie Young and George Lindsay.

At the other end of the scale, Scottish curling history contains a fair number of references to early attempts to encourage youth, the prime examples coming from the Sanquhar, Kilmarnock and Wanlockhead Clubs, all in the South-West of Scotland, for long a hot-bed of curlers. In his *History of the Sanquhar Curling Society* (1874), James Brown records that, in addition to the regular rinks in the early years of the Society (founded in 1774), there was a 'corps-de-reserve', composed of youngsters who were presided over by an experienced officer appointed at annual meetings.

A Kilmarnock curler wrote, in 1833, that his club had long been distinguished 'for the urbanity of its demeanour towards its juniors' and that the Junior Club had, from its formation, 'been remarkable for its indomitable perseverance and daring'. He added that the more recent Morning Star Club, an aptly named school 'for training the youth of our town at once to habits of early rising and the mysteries of the curling craft', met on the ice at 7 a.m., broke for coffee at 8 a.m. and curled until 10 a.m. when the members returned to business so that their elders could take over on the ice.

In 1912, at a dinner of the Wanlockhead Curling Society (founded in 1777), a speaker remarked that the Wanlock men were good curlers because they *learnt young*. Schoolboys had always been encouraged, he added, but the junior club, formed in 1883, had taught them to play regularly and properly and they now played like men and gentlemen. The St Moritz Club in Switzerland formed a Junior Club in 1922.

The youthful urge in the country clubs faded with the advent of the big indoor ice rinks. In 1961, I wrote: 'Our only answer to the immense reservoir of youthful talent in Canada is the T.B. Murray Trophy and the recent introduction of schoolboy curling in Glasgow'.

The Murray Trophy was presented in 1929 by Tom Murray, Royal Club President in 1936–37 and one of Scotland's best curlers. It was presented to the Royal Club by the Edinburgh Ice Rink C.C. in 1959 and reverted to its original purpose as the main competition for curlers of twenty-five years and under. The winning skip in 1959 was Robin Campbell and we well remember presenting the trophy to Robin and his team, which included Moira Craig at lead, and the prizes to the runners-up, a Hamilton team destined for greater things – Alex F. Torrance (skip), Alex Torrance, Bobby Kirkland and Jim Waddell.

Arthur Frame, Secretary of the Glasgow Province and Secretary of the 1957 Scottish team which toured Canada, led boys from his old school, Hutchesons' Grammar School, to the ice in Glasgow in the early 1950s. Pupils from Glasgow High School joined the Hutchesons' boys and Scottish schools curling was born.

Edinburgh followed this lead in September 1961. A deputation of Watsonian Curling Club members met Roger Young, now Sir Roger, headmaster of George Watson's College, who readily agreed that a Watsonian curler, who had been a naval officer with him in a destroyer during the war, should address the senior boys after Prayers on a Monday morning – an ordeal, the curler later confessed, far more nerve-racking than throwing the last stone on which all depended. The response was at once a source of encouragement and embarrassment, fifty-seven boys handing in their names for the school curling club. Watsonian curlers, given valuable assistance by Gilbert McClung, President of the Royal Club in 1962–63, Willie Scobie of the Corstorphine Club, and David Kennedy, Ice-Master at the Edinburgh Ice Rink, took eager groups of boys to the hacks. Gilbert McClung described the activity on the ice as 'the bravest sight in Edinburgh for many years'.

The first schoolboy inter-city match in Scotland was played between Glasgow and Edinburgh in December 1961, Hutchesons' rinks beating Watson's in the Scottish Ice Rink, Glasgow, which provided what was described as 'a regal high tea' to round off a happy day.

Since that historic meeting, schools curling has shot to the forefront in Scotland. There are schools leagues in most ice rinks. In Edinburgh an inter-schools competition was built up by Bob Christie, former manager of Edinburgh Ice Rink, for a trophy donated by George Crabbie, President of Edinburgh Ice Rink C.C. In the early days of schools curling at the South of Scotland Ice Rink in Lockerbie, pupils from Lockerbie Academy turned up in such numbers that one group of beginners threw stones half-way up a rink, the other group using the other half of the rink from the hack at the far end.

In the 1966–67 season, the National Schools Competition – carefully named so that schoolgirls, who had also been encouraged to start, would not be precluded from the event – was introduced by the Royal Club. The trophy, purchased in Canada, was presented by John Monteith, a Grand Old Man of Scottish curling. Appropriately, Hutchesons' curlers, skipped by Campbell Dick, were the first winners, and, in 1968 and 1969, Colin Baxter, later to make two Silver Broom appearances, skipped the winning Watson's College rink.

We can say with some certainty that the growth of Scottish schoolboy play came roughly twenty years after the High School boom in Canada. When news of the training schemes for Scottish youth reached Canada in 1962, Burd McNiece, Chairman of the Canadian School Curling Committee, wrote a letter of encouragement: 'This activity will expand rapidly. You are starting as we did nearly twenty years ago, since when School Curling has expanded beyond our fondest hopes until we have had for the past twelve years a Canadian Competition between rinks from each Province in round-robin play. It is estimated, now, that the competitions at School, Primary, Provincial and Canadian levels attract approximately 60,000 boys of High School ages.'

Burd McNiece's prediction was accurate. In his country, the first inter-provincial schoolboy competition was held in 1947 between boys from Manitoba, Saskatchewan and Alberta. In 1948, British Columbia and Quebec joined, and, in 1949, eight Provinces were represented. The first National Schoolboy Championship was held in Quebec City in 1950.

An interesting historical aspect of boy and girl curling in Canada was the Jam Tin bonspiel, played by youngsters with jam tins filled with cement and with a rough handle attached, on quarter-size outdoor rinks. Jam tin curling was firmly rooted in Saskatchewan and was also played in other parts of Canada.

A new category of curlers has joined the Scottish curling community. It is a wonderful opportunity for experienced curlers to pass on their experience and to put back something into the game they love. They can do this by teaching the traditional customs and courtesies and by stimulating the interest and enthusiasm of the young curlers with practice sessions, film shows, quiz evenings, and, if possible, the biggest thrill of all to a youngster – an away-from-home match against total strangers who will soon become friends.

26
Curlers' Courts and Beef and Greens

A WORD OF warning for the new curler! 'You're a born curler' is a compliment seldom given – but all curlers should be 'made'. 'My Lord' will be in the chair, and, at his bidding, 'My Lord's Officer' will fence the Court for your benefit. You will be instructed in 'the mysteries' and you must listen carefully. There will be fun and frolic, and fines for doing wrong, and, often, for doing right! The proceeds are auctioned at the end of the evening and are generally given to charity. Fines are exacted for all sorts of reasons, almost none of them pertinent. Historical examples are: for marrying – one shilling; for marrying an heiress – one guinea; for making hay while the sun shone – threepence. Then there was the unfortunate curler who was fined a shilling for not attending the Court and the next year was fined five shillings for attending. At a recent Court occasion, the poor photographer, who was only doing his duty, was fined for 'flashing'!

You will be given the 'word' and shown the 'grip'. But we will say no more about this ancient ceremony – except to advise you to bring small change to pay the fines and not to put on your best suit!

> In canty cracks, and sangs, and jokes,
> The night drives on wi' daffin',
> And mony a kittle shot is ta'en
> While we're the toddy quaffin'.
>
> From *Cauld, Cauld, Frosty Weather* by
> the Rev James Muir of Beith.

At Curlers' Courts and many curling suppers, the principal dish is 'Beef and Greens', the true curlers' fare. This excerpt from a Minute of the old Edinburgh Club in 1840 gives a fair indication of the eating habits of our ancestors: 'The bill of fare consisted of boiled salt beef and greens, haggises, sheeps' heads and broth, cockie-leekie and roast beef. The charge was 4s. 6d. each, including small beer and a bottle of whisky to each two members to be made into toddy.'

Another bill of fare, supplied to the members of the Noodle Club in Ayrshire in 1823, is even more formidable: 'hare soup, fried whitings, a large turbot, a joint of corned beef, roasted beef, corned pork, two tongues, chickens, a fine goose, four grouse, and vegetable, dumplings, pudding, custard, jam and jellies. A moderate proportion of wine was given and ale, porter and a modicum of drams'. In 1831, forty-seven members of one of Scotland's oldest clubs, Strathallan Meath Moss (instituted 1736), ate sixty-seven pounds of beef at their annual supper.

Our stomachs are less demanding in these straitened times! At a Beef and Greens supper, modern curlers are more likely to be offered Scotch Broth, Boiled Beef and Cabbage or Haggis and Neeps, followed by Biscuits and Cheese and Coffee.

But the spirit, and spirits, will be the same!

27

Poetry and Literature

IT IS GENERALLY accepted that the earliest record of the word 'curling' is contained in *The Muses Threnodie, or Mirthfull Mournings on the Death of Master Gall*, by Henry Adamson (1638). An edition, with notes by James Cant, was published in Perth in 1774 and the poem, set in Perth, contains many interesting references to the Fair City. Adamson, George Ruthven, a doctor and surgeon, and James Gall were close friends, and, when Gall died young of consumption – despite the efforts of Ruthven, who collected and administered herbs from the hillsides at Kinnoull and Moredun – Adamson wrote an *In Memoriam* in which the following lines appear:

> 'His cougs, his dishes, and his caps,
> A Totum, and some bairnes taps;
> A gadareilie, and a whisle,
> A trumpe and Abercorne mussell,
> His hats, his hoods, his bels, his bones,
> His allay bowles, and curling-stones,
> The sacred games to celebrat
> Which to the Gods are consecrat.'*

In the same year, 1638, Robert Baillie, Minister at Kilwinning, wrote: 'Orkney's process came before us; he was a curler on the Sabbath day.' (The 'Orkney' mentioned, George Grahame, Bishop of Orkney, was deposed by the General Assembly on 11 December 1638.)

Any reference to curling poetry, or curling literature in general, makes the reader immediately aware of the debt owed by the curling community to Ministers of the Church.

> Frae Maidenkirk to John o' Groats
> Nae curlers like the clergy.
> *Old Proverb.*

---

* The poem is generally known as 'Gall's Gabions', the word gabion meaning a collection of odd items or bric-a-brac.

Ministers not only played the game, with skill and enthusiasm, but also wrote books about it, composed poetry about it and added vitality to it with penetrating and humorous remarks on the ice and from the pulpit. A typical story tells of the Minister who dismissed his congregation with the words: 'My brethren, there's nae mair harm in saying it than in thinking it; if the frost hauds, I'll be on the ice the morn's morning at nine o'clock.*

Many curling clubs elect chaplains and the Chaplains of the Royal Club now serve for five-year periods. The Rev A. Gordon Mitchell, a prolific curling writer and poet, was Royal Club Chaplain from 1920 until 1939. The present holder of the office, the Rev Dr John Cameron of Broughty Ferry, is a keen curler who played in the Scottish team which toured Germany in 1982, a skier and an accomplished golfer and member of the Royal and Ancient Golf Club. He regularly attends Royal Club functions with his wife, Jill.

The celebrated William Guthrie of Fenwick, Ayrshire, author of the *Christian's Great Interest*, was ordained at Fenwick in 1644 and eventually driven from his Kirk in the persecutions of the Covenanters in 1665, just before his death. But, in those twenty-one years, he left an indelible mark on the parish. His loofie stone (1645), which is still preserved, was well known on the ice in Ayrshire, and, says his biographer, 'he used the innocent recreations which then prevailed – fishing, fowling and playing on the ice – which, at the same time, contributed to preserve vigorous health'.

Dr Alex Pennecuik (1652–1722) also praised the health-giving properties of curling. The doctor, the 'Laird of Romanno', published his prescription in 1715:

> To Curle on the Ice does greatly please,
> Being a Manly Scotish Exercise;
> It Clears the Brains, stirrs up the Native Heat
> And gives a gallant Appetite for Meat.

Allan Ramsay (1685–1758) followed the same theme in his poem, *Health*, dedicated in 1724 to the Earl of Stair, four lines of which cover three sporting activities:

---

*The Rev John Kerr estimated that, of the twenty thousand Scottish members of the Royal Club in 1890, five hundred, or one in forty, were clergymen.

> Then on the links, or in the estler* walls,
> He drives the gowff or strikes the tennis-balls,
> From ice with pleasure he can brush the snow
> And run rejoicing with his curling throw.

Ramsay's best-known curling verse occurs in his Epistle to *Robert Yarde of Devonshire*:

> Frae northern mountains clad with snaw,
> Where whistling winds incessant blaw,
> In time now when the curling stane
> Slides murmuring o'er the icy plain.

James Hogg, the Ettrick Shepherd (1772–1835), famous poet and fiddler, was also a keen curler who was President of the Ettrick Club and a member of the Duddingston and Peebles Clubs. His poem, *The Channel Stane*, begins:

> Of a' the games that e'er I saw,
> Man, callant, laddie, birkie, wean,
> The dearest, far aboon them a',
> Was aye the witching channel-stane.

> Chorus.
> Oh! for the channel-stane!
> The fell good game the channel-stane!
> There's no a game that e'er I saw
> Can match auld Scotland's channel-stane.

The Ettrick Shepherd's poem *Curling*, is also well-known. One verse testifies to the democratic nature of the game:

> Here peer and peasant friendly meet,
> Auld etiquette has lost her seat,
> The social broom has swept her neat
> Beyond the pale o' Curling.

Sir Walter Scott (1771–1832) used curling as a backcloth for one of his descriptive passages in *Guy Mannering*: 'On the frozen bosom of the lake itself were a multitude of moving figures – some flitting along with the velocity of swallows, some sweeping in the most graceful circles, and others deeply interested in a less active pastime – crowding round the

---

* Hewn stone – a reference to the enclosure of a real tennis court.

spot where the inhabitants of two rival parishes contended for the prize at curling: an honour of no small importance, if we were to judge from the anxiety expressed both by the players and bystanders.'

The most famous of all verses on curling were written by Scotland's national poet, Robert Burns. Extolling the virtues of his friend, Tam, as a curler, Burns wrote, in his *Elegy on Tam Samson* (1786):

When winter muffles up his cloak,
And binds the mire like a rock;
When to the loughs the curlers flock
   Wi' gleesome speed,
Wha' will they station at the cock?
   Tam Samson's dead!

He was the king o' a' the core,
To guard, or draw, or wick a bore,
Or up the rink like Jehu roar
   In time o' need;
But now he lags on Death's 'hog-score'
   Tam Samson's dead!

(The 'cock' is an old Scots word for 'tee'.)

In *The Vision* (1786), Burns also referred to curling:

> The sun had clos'd the winter day,
> The curlers quat their roarin' play.

The literature of the game is full of poetry – some good, some interesting and some plain doggerel. We will add three often-quoted verses from last century:

> When biting Boreas, keen and snell,
>   Wi' icy breath and a' that,
> Lays on the lochs his magic spell,
>   And stills the streams and a' that.
> For a' that and a' that,
>   Cauld winter's snaw, and a' that;
> Around the tee, wi' mirth and glee,
>   The curlers meet for a' that.

From 'Curling Song', by Henry Shanks, Bathgate, the blind poet.

> Aye may we play with social glee,
> Devoid of strife and snarling,
> Sae put it round, wi' three times three,
> To freedom, love, and Curling.

From 'White Winter on Ilk Hill', by Rob. Hetrick, Dalmellington.

Now fill ae bumper – fill but ane,
And drink wi' social glee, man,
May curlers on life's slippery rink
Frae cruel rubs be free, man;
Or should a treacherous bias lead
Their erring steps a-jee, man,
Some friendly inring may they meet
To guide them to the tee, man.

From 'The Music of the Year is Hushed', by the
Rev Dr Henry Duncan of Ruthwell.

The first book on curling, *An Account of the Game of Curling*, was written by the Rev John Ramsay (1811), and Ministers of the Scots kirk also contributed the two other major books published last century – *Curling, The Ancient Scottish Game*, by the Rev James Taylor (1884) and *History of Curling* by the Rev John Kerr (1890) – Kerr's scholarly book remains the best available* on the history and growth of the game.

Curling has its own terminology. Sayings like 'Rather a hog than dae damage' and the traditional curlers' greeting, 'Keen and Clear', are well known in the game and there are many old toasts, relics of the days when club dinners lasted for six or seven hours and almost all the members stood up to propose a Toast. Examples of these are 'Our old friend John Frost', 'Curlers' wives and sweethearts', 'The Land o' Cakes (Scotland) and her Ain Game o' Curling' and the one which every curler will drink to with special resolution, 'The Tee – what we all aim at!'

Curlers still write poetry on their favourite game, although to a much lesser extent than in the more leisured hours in past centuries, and we must give extracts from two modern poems, both of which are full of the native humour which is an integral part of curling. The first, written by Albert Mackie, a poet of high repute in Scotland and a non-curler, commemorated England's victory over Scotland in 1958 in the annual international match, their first win for thirty-two years – and could be called an elegy!

Ach, sound the pibroch in lament!   Auld Scotia greets, as efter Flodden,
They're laughing frae Carlisle to Kent;   The biggest setback since Culloden,
The Sassenachs the taunts are hurling,   That England has achieved sic fame
They've beaten Scotsmen at the curling.   At Caledonia's native game.

---

*The diminishing number of curlers who own a copy of the book do not let it out of their sight. The book is now rare, and, if a copy finds its way to a bookshop it is quickly resold.

The second was written by John Hamilton, a keen Ayrshire curler whom we reckon to be the best Scots curler-poet of his time. The extract is the first verse from his *Winning of the Alton Cup*:

> But let us no' forget our freen';
> James Gibb, the skip, was unco keen,
> But sic a hash ye never seen
> Tae draw a shot;
> He stood and gaped and blinked his een
> Like some auld goat!

A year or two after the winning of the Alton Cup, we played against John Hamilton and James Gibb in an inter-city match* at Ayr and recited the verse to James. He sat back in his chair, roared with laughter and called for a round of drinks! A delightful companion, he was also a much better drawer of a shot than John Hamilton gave him credit for!

As curlers often ask for the Curler's Grace, to use at their annual suppers, we add it now, with a shorter alternative, to end this chapter, while realising that Grace should have been said at the beginning!

> O Lord, whase luv surrounds us a'
> And brings us a' thegither,
> Wha writes your laws upon oor herts
> And bids us help each ither;
> We thank Thee for thy bounties great,
> For meat and hame and gear,
> And thank Thee too for sna' and ice
> Although we ask for mair;
> Gie us a hert to dae what's richt,
> Like Curlers true and keen,
> To be guid freens alang life's road
> And soop oor slide aye clean.

Or this alternative:

O. Power abune whose bounty free
Our needs and wants suffices,
We render thanks for Barley Bree
And mate that appetises.

Be Thou our Skip throughout life's game
An' syne we're sure to win,
Tho' slow the shot and wide the aim
We'll soop each ither in.

* John played an outrageous long raise with his last stone to peel our game!

28

Keenness and Fellowship

ENTHUSIASTS IN ALL branches of sport are described as 'keen'. There are keen golfers, keen shinty players, keen anglers. But only curlers are 'keen, keen'. The two adjectives have a special significance.

'I promise to be a keen, keen, curler' is the vow taken by all who are 'made' curlers at initiation ceremonies. What do the words mean? They can be explained in three short sentences: 1. A curler is not a true curler if he is not a keen, keen curler; 2. A curler should play the game to the utmost of his ability; 3. A lackadaisical approach is anathema to the game.

To enlarge on the theme, we sometimes hear the claim: 'I don't mind whether I win or lose, the game's the thing.' The words do not ring true and the man who uses them would not be welcome on our side, or, for that matter, on the side against us.

A game of curling should be played at one tempo – flat out – and with one aim – to win. Teams imbued with the will to win are rewarded with the most enjoyable and exciting play. This does not mean that curlers should be tensed-up and inhibited with thoughts of victory; that they should mount hate campaigns against their opponents and play with tight lips and without humour. Quite the opposite. A sense of humour is part and parcel of the game and the best sportsmen are those who respect sport sufficiently to want to play the game the best way they know how.

The Rev A. Gordon Mitchell, a dedicated Chaplain to the Royal Club, preached a Curlers' Sermon in Woodside Parish Church, Glasgow, in 1937. He used as his text: Chronicles', chapter 12, verse 2 – 'Hurling Stones' – and delivered a stone which deserves to be remembered:

'Not to be keen to win is an injustice not only to the curler's own side but also to the side that opposes him. The true curler never queers his pitch, never pulls his course, but strains every nerve to win, and thus, whether he wins or loses, preserves his own self-respect and the respect of his own rink and that of the rink playing against him. Not to be in earnest in the game is not to play curling but only to play *at* curling. If that is the spirit in which anyone plays, I would remind him that, although it may not matter very much whether we win or lose, it does matter very much whether we play the game, and we cannot play the game without being loyal to our side; in other words, without doing our utmost to come out on the winning side.' The mental approach to curling is a study in itself. At the competitive level, a desire to win separates the players at the very top from the players very near the top. The urge for victory, the exercise of mind over matter, undoubtedly works, in the same way as a golfer can 'will' a crucial putt into the hole.

It follows naturally, and is perfectly consistent with a positive will-to-win attitude, that curlers must be good losers. To lose gracefully is essential in curling, as in all games, and, if that virtue is not inbred in a curler, he must develop it. Undoubtedly, the best way to achieve this is to play more and more games because, as a popular skip remarked, when congratulated on accepting defeat with a smile: 'Oh, I'm a good loser all right; I've had plenty of practice!' In this context, many competitive-minded curlers advise me that the game is all about winning – while exactly half of it is about losing.

To sum up, a player has a much better chance of being a good loser if he has fought every inch of the way and given all he knows to win. He could not have done more.

Take your defeat like a man! Nothing looks worse on the ice than a losing curler who throws down his broom in disgust. It is *he* who is disgusting. Fortunately, very few let themselves and the game down in this way. The handshakes all round, which end every game of curling in every curling country in the world, are followed by a friendly drink, laughter and perhaps a song later. The social glass tastes even better after a hard, keenly-fought and sporting game.

Dr John Renton of Penicuik, proposing the toast, 'A' Keen Curlers,' at the Grand Caledonian Curling Club Dinner in 1843, said: 'On Keen-ness the great value of curling depends. It is the principle of action, and intercourse too, and forms the great charm of attachment, not only to the game but which brings and binds curlers together. This attachment I neither can nor is it necessary for me to describe. It must be felt and it is not confined to the time we are engaged in the game nor to the season we enjoy it in; it lasts all the year through and dies only with the curler himself.'

The Doctor was referring to the *spirit* of curling, that elusive force which cannot be captured and enjoyed unless the curler gives himself completely to the game. The moral is clear: be a competitive or social curler, short or long slider, draw player or striker, man or woman, but, for goodness sake, be keen. And, in the words of the old Duddingston battle cry, 'Strain ilka nerve, shouther, backbane and hough'* to win. Then, win or lose, enjoy yourself. *That* is the spirit of curling!

> For on the water's face are met,
> Wi' mony a merry joke, man,
> The tenant and his jolly laird,
> The pastor and his flock, man.†

THE FELLOWSHIP OF curling is the hallmark of the game. The tradition was established in the far reaches of the first clubs. Old minute books are full of charitable intentions and decisions to help the needy sections of the community, the earliest acts of curling fellowship being the playing of matches for bolls of meal for the poor.

The first regulation of the Duddingston Society was: 'Resolved that the sole object of this institution is the enjoyment of the game of curling, which, while it adds vigour to the body, contributes to vivacity of mind and the promotion of the social and *generous* feelings.'

Penalties and fines were imposed on curlers for a long list of offences, from swearing on the ice to introducing a political topic. Some of the money collected was diverted to the needy but most of the gifts to the poor were the result of challenges between parishes and clubs. Charitable funds were created and food and eldin (fuel) were distributed to widows, orphans and those in need. Benevolence was a feature of old-time curling.

Politics has always been a forbidden subject in curling. Among the rules of the Ardoch Club in Upper Strathearn, instituted in 1750, was: 'No politics of Church or State to be discussed.' Many other clubs followed this example in their printed rules.

Dr Norman McLeod's curling song, first published in *Blackwood's Magazine*, underlines the point:

> It's an unco' like story, that baith Whig and Tory
> Maun aye collyshangy, like dogs owre a bane;
> An' that a' denominations are wantin' in patience
> For nae Kirk will thole to let ithers alane.
> But in fine frosty weather, let a' meet thegither,
> Wi' brooms in their hauns an' a stane near the 'T';
> Then, ha! ha! by my certes ye'll see hoo a' pairties
> Like brithers will love and like brithers agree.

---

*From a song, composed by Sir Alexander Boswell and sung by him at a Duddingston Society dinner in 1817.

† From *The Music of the Year is Hushed*, by the Rev Henry Duncan, D.D., of Ruthwell.

Chaff and banter is the stuff of curling. At the bicentenary dinner of the old Cupar Club in 1975, the Chairman, Captain Jack Anderson (1978-79 Royal Club President) announces to the company that the photographer has just caught him with his spectacles down! His top-table companions are Robin Welsh, Lord Elgin (who was principal speaker) Royal Club President-Elect David Duncan and William Bell (Scotscraig Curling Club).

The democratic nature of the game is aptly summed up by a famous parody on Burns:

> Ours is a game for duke or lord,
> Lairds, tenants, hinds, an a' that;
> Our pastors too, wha preach the Word,
> Whiles ply the broom for a' that.
> For a' that and a' that,
> Our different ranks an' a' that,
> The chiel that soops and plays the best
> Is greatest man for a' that.
>
> Old Song.

The easy and natural intermingling of all classes on the ice led to chapters of happy accidents, volumes of humour. The stonemason was directing the Sheriff who had more than once sent him to prison for poaching. 'Noo, Shirra,' shouted the skip, 'dae ye see that stane?' 'Aye, Jock', answered the Sheriff. 'A weel, just gie that ane sixty days!'

At the Jubilee Dinner of the Royal Club in 1888, Lord Balfour told of a conversation on the train to a Grand Match at Carsebreck. A curler looked up from his morning newspaper and said: 'I see, Geordie, that you are drawn against a lord today.' Geordie thought for a moment before answering quietly: 'Maybe I'll be the lord before night!'

The Earl of Eglinton was directed by a famous curler, Hugh Conn, to strike out a stone. Watching the Earl's stone with anxious excitement, the redoubtable Hugh was heard to shout: 'Bravo, my Lord; Bravo my Lord; Bravo, —— oh Lord, I declare ye wad miss a haystack!'

We cannot stress too strongly, for the benefit of beginners who do not yet know and older curlers who may have forgotten, that curling is fun and that any curler who does not enjoy himself is missing the whole point of the game. When once asked on television, 'And why do you curl?' our impromptu answer was 'To have fun'. On reflection, we would not change it.

The banter and wit among curlers has created a literature of its own, which is nurtured and enlarged by overseas tours. The fun and *faux-pas* of a tour are remembered for a lifetime. When the 1957 Scottish team returned from Canada, we invited six of the tourists to reminisce and placed a tape-recorder behind a sofa. The tape, 45 minutes of gentle chaffing, hilarious story-telling and conclusive evidence of international friendship, remains a treasured record of the real stuff of curling tours.

> True feelings waken in their hearts,
> An' thrill frae heart to hand,
> O! peerless game that feeds the flame
> O' fellowship in man!
> The Rev T. Rain.

What more can we say about the camaraderie of curling? New curlers, who listen to speeches at dinners and presentations, will hear a great deal about it – and it is all true. We state this categorically and in the certain knowledge that it is the most important statement in this book: fellowship is the highest point, the greatest virtue in curling. The life blood of the game, it flows through every company of curlers, from the four members of a rink to an international gathering, curling supper or annual meeting, and the lasting friendships formed on overseas tours, which increase in number each year, bring ever nearer to fulfilment the principal aim of the Royal Club – adopted by the International Curling Federation: 'to unite curlers throughout the world into one brotherhood of the rink'.

Index

N.B. The names in illustration captions are not included in the Index.